Dr. Andrew Turnbull

And

The New Smyrna Colony

of Florida

Carita Doggett, A.B., A.M.

With Original Correspondence
from 1768 to 1793

 Light Messages

Dr. Andrew Turnbull
   and the New Smyrna Colony of Florida
Carita Doggett, A.B., A.M.

Original edition 1919
The Drew Press, Florida

Reprinted December 2012
Copyright © 2012 Light Messages Publishing
Durham, North Carolina 27713
www.lightmessages.com

Printed in the United States of America
ISBN: 978-1-61153-026-1

1919

Dedicated to

My Father

whose interest and encouragement

made the work of this book

a pleasure for me.

2012

Dedicated with gratitude to

Irene Beckham

and

Jim McGee

who love, share and preserve

the heritage of New Smyrna.

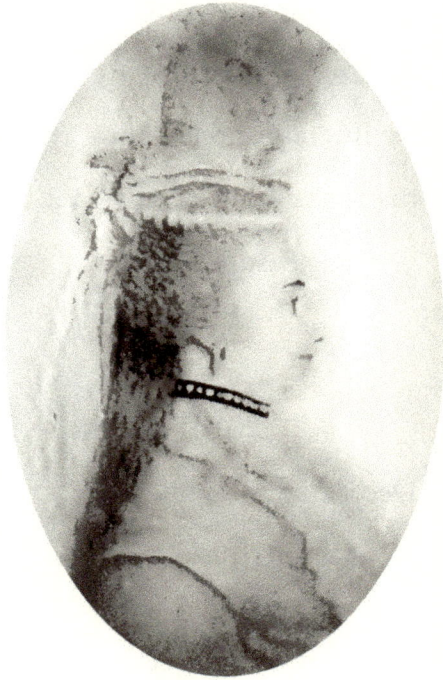

Gracia Dura Bin

The Grecian wife of Dr. Turnbull

Dr. Andrew Turnbull

ABBREVIATIONS IN MONOGRAPHIC REFERENCES

Public Record Office documents in London.

C. O.—Colonial Office.
      (e. g. 5/544=Class 5, Volume 544).

P. C.—Privy Council.

W. O.—War Office.

T.—Treasury.

A. O.—Audit Office.

TABLE OF CONTENTS

EDITOR'S NOTES

The 116 pages of correspondence, added as an appendix to this edition, contain dozens of fascinating letters between Dr. Andrew Turnbull, Governor James Grant, Lord George Grenville, Sir William Duncan, and other interested parties between 1768 and 1793. Most of these letters were not available to Carita Doggett when she published the first edition of this book.

The transcripts of letters and Smyrnéa drawings are published courtesy of Dr. Daniel Schafer and the website *Florida History Online*. Gracious permission was granted by the Laird of Ballindalloch to include the correspondence of General James Grant of Ballindalloch. Mr. Iain Flett kindly granted permission for the inclusion of correspondence of Sir William Duncan on loan to the Dundee City Archives.

Some of the letters have been excerpted to include the more pertinent portions. Illegible words and sections of the original letters have been replaced by ellipses. Words in parentheses are editorial notes added for clarity.

The correspondence of General James Grant, archived for centuries in the tower of his castle in Ballindalloch, Scotland, was brought to light in 1999 when John W. Kluge, Chairman of the U.S. Library of Congress James Madison Council, visited the Laird of Ballindalloch, Clare Macpherson-Grant Russell, and her husband, Oliver Russell. This valuable trove provides a highly personal view of the colonization of Florida and early history of the United States.

Presented in chronological sequence, these letters confirm Carita Doggett's understanding and description of Dr. Andrew Turnbull, his intentions, and his great personal concern for the settlers of Smyrnéa. They greatly enhance this already valuable work as they transport the reader back in time. The dreams, efforts, successes, and calamities of Andrew Turnbull and the Smyrna colonists come to life in this diary-like correspondence which is memorable and frequently very emotional.

New Smyrna, Smyrnéa, or New Smyrnéa? Andrew Turnbull wrote to his partner Sir William Duncan that "Before I arrived in this country the governor had given the name of New Smyrna to our settlement. I have only changed it to Smyrnéa which is bad Greek for New Smyrna." Smyrnéa and New Smyrna sometimes became New Smyrnéa in the included correspondence. Carita Doggett uses the name New Smyrna in this book. New Smyrna is the name of the contemporary town that grew out of the original settlement.

In addition to the works referenced in the bibliography, information about Andrew Turnbull and New Smyrna is available from the New Smyrna Museum of History *www.nsbhistory.org,* the Southeast Volusia Historical Society, 120 Sams Avenue, New Smyrna Beach, Florida 32168, and the Turnbull Clan Association *www.turnbullclan.com.*

PREFACE

Every old inhabitant of Florida knows of Andrew Turnbull. Most tourists on the East Coast have read Susan Turnbull, that romantic and imaginary version of his Minorcan colony, by Archibald Clavering Gunter, and have taken pictures of the old Sugar Mill and "Turnbull's Castle" at New Smyrna. If an old resident is asked about him, he says "Turnbull was a bad sort," in fact Gunter makes a kind of wicked ogre out of him; so that about the great coquina ruins, cleft with palm trees, hovers a sinister mist of traditions.

Reminders of Turnbull are plentiful throughout the State. On the palm covered banks of the North Indian River stands New Smyrna itself, named for Smyrna, Asia Minor, the birthplace of Turnbull's wife. The pretty, modern town is threaded with the main canals of the old colony and water still runs through them in a musical monotone, from Turnbull's great hammock lands to the river. Every year a large winter colony returns to picturesque homes and groves, and the new colonists spend many pleasant hours speculating over the works of their predecessors—the sunken pier, the lovely arches of the old Mission, many stone wells and the heavy foundations of the fort. Then the Turnbull family has continued to be prominent in Florida, and the dark-eyed descendants of those Minorcans who came with him to New Smyrna, a hundred and fifty years ago, now live in St. Augustine and hand down among themselves lurid traditions of the old colony. Nothing dependable from a historical standpoint has ever been attempted in regard to this, the largest colony which ever came to America in a body, but the strange chance of literary fortune preserved and gave prominence to the most garbled account of Turnbull's management there. Despite the fact that his contemporaries, Governor Grant, Chief Justice Drayton, Schoepf, a German traveler, and Mease, a learned Frenchman, testified to his earnest devotion to his colonists, yet it remained for Bernard Romans, a civil engineer with a literary turn, to recall the frightful tales of his Minorcan draughtsman, and to write, for all subsequent historians, the story of Andrew Turnbull. Even his worst enemies did not in his day believe such stories as Romans set forth in his eloquent style. They made extravagant charges against him for political reasons, which were disproved by Turnbull in court, but Romans wrote, years after the events themselves, an account based on what his employee remembered. But he made a good story and Floridians became satisfied that they had harbored a second King Leopold at New Smyrna.

In the meantime, the real account had moved to London and settled in that treasure-house of romantic fact, the British Colonial Office. There it remained secure, like a reasonable man, biding his time, against a day when people would be ready and willing to hear the whole story. And it is so startlingly different from the present idea of Turnbull and his colonists that, it seems to me, both sides, if there remain sides on this question, may be interested to learn of it for themselves. As is often the case in collecting the facts of a dispute, the source of the trouble was a far cry from Turnbull and his colonists; and the trouble itself insignificant, when considered in its proper place in the course of most interesting events.

Only documentary evidence has been relied upon, no statements from secondary sources of information have been accepted without careful verification, and copies of all the original manuscripts have been collected and filed with the Florida Historical Society. These manuscripts are the only copies in this country. A list of these papers has also been appended to this volume, and it will be evident at a glance how full and consecutive this information is. The phraseology and spelling from them have been faithfully copied, wherever quoted, and except for a very few obsolete words and one or two grammatical constructions, it will be readily seen that their authors might well rank as masters of modern English prose.

CHAPTER I
THE OUTLAW PROVINCE

FLORIDA, in the first half of the eighteenth century, was a thorn in the side of the British colonies, for Spain carried on flanking attacks against their commerce and farming from this outlaw stronghold. Carolina planters often lost their slaves across its boundaries and the Spanish governor at St. Augustine refused to antagonize his Indian allies by commanding their return; so many an English slave-hunting expedition, aggravated the quarrel by invading his territory in a search for their property. Pirates of the long, lonely coast line preyed on the tobacco exports and the sorely needed supply ships of England and her colonies, and finally the new Georgia settlement, under Oglethorpe, raised a dispute in 1736, over the Florida boundary line, which brought on twenty-nine years of open warfare between England and Spain.

There followed the ridiculously weak attempts of Georgia to punish Florida, and retaliatory expeditions, by the Spaniards: Oglethorpe camped on Anastasia Island, opposite St. Augustine, and shelled the compact little fortress until his provisions gave out, and a Spanish fleet sailed into St. Simon's and drove the inhabitants inland. But nothing was decided by these excursions. In 1762, however, an astonishing coup by England started the international gamesters to trading. Havana, the pride and center of Spanish America, fell before a British force, and with this rich prize in her hands, England was ready to bargain for peace. This was arranged by the Peace of Paris in 1763, when Spain gave East and West Florida to England in exchange for Havana. At the same time, France yielded Canada to England, thus bringing to the high water mark English power in the New World.

At first sight, East and West Florida seem to us to have been an enormous price to pay for Cuba. East Florida was what we now know as Florida, minus the small section west of the Apalachicola

River, while West Florida included the coast of Alabama, Mississippi and a part of Louisiana. This enormous region was practically undeveloped, however, in spite of one hundred and ninety years of Spanish rule. Three small towns (St. Augustine, Pensacola and Mobile) were the only attempts the Spanish had made at colonizing, and the seven thousand people who were divided among these tiny settlements were of the civil and military class and had received no encouragement from Spain in agricultural ventures, therefore trade with the Indians was their only business.

These Indians of Florida were a special problem in themselves, little understood by the settlers. It must be remembered that they were the bewildering fragments of many races; exiles from Georgia tribes, old nations broken in power by Spanish invasions and wanderers seeking fresh hunting grounds, so that there was no league which had authority among them all, and, therefore, no means of reaching an agreement with them, such as Oglethorpe had made with the Creeks. The English governors were always at a loss to understand why, in spite of treaties and presents to many great chiefs, their settlements were continually plundered and cattle driven off by other Indians.

In spite of these difficulties, England was encouraged to complete her coast possessions by the acquisition of Florida, feeling as she did that she had now proven herself the supreme genius among European powers in colonizing enterprises. From New England to Georgia, prosperous agricultural communities showed the farmer a conqueror, while the French traders and Spanish soldiers were still lost in the immensity of their discoveries. Accordingly, her plan of real estate development was started for Florida in 1763, and books by Bartram, Romans and other writers were the ancestors of that long line of literary praise of Florida which then, just as it does today, dealt less with the actual than with the fancied Florida. In those days, authors were given carte blanche to expatiate on the riches, beauties and luxuries of Florida life, as well as its mild climate, fine soil and valuable products. Parliament added a more substantial persuasion for settlement in 1764, when five hundred pounds a year was set aside as a bounty for the raising of silk, cotton and indigo in East Florida, and extensive land grants were offered for development. For three years that bounty accumulated and Florida's praises continued to be sung without moving the British public to respond.

But there was in London at this time a gentleman of some wealth, who had lived in Asia Minor and other Mediterranean countries, where the climate was similar to Florida's.

This man was Dr. Andrew Turnbull, a Scotchman, whose acquaintance in London included the most influential and wealthy men. He convinced a number of them that a settlement in Florida by people accustomed to a warm climate, and the growing of crops suited to that region, would not only be a good investment, but an enterprise encouraged by the government. Turnbull said he was sure of getting a large number of Greeks from Asia Minor to start a colony, for he had lived there for some years and knew that these people were very restive under the galling yoke of Turkey. He was not only thoroughly acquainted with the Greeks of this region, but about seven years previously he had married the daughter of a Greek merchant of Smyrna, Asia Minor, and he felt confident that he would be favorably received as a leader of such a colony to the new province of Florida. Though at that time a prosperous physician in London, forty-eight years old, he was willing to undertake this tremendous pioneer venture, and to bring his wife and family to Florida. His wife, Maria Gracia, was a no less dauntless spirit than he, and played a courageous part in this undertaking. The little miniature of Mrs. Turnbull shows her dressed in the height of Smyrnian fashion, with a small waist and high coiffure and a carriage erect to the point of hauteur, while the set to her lips shows her a lady of much determination and spirit, a true partner for a pioneer doctor. She faced the dangers of the savage new land resolutely, several times ran the affairs of the settlement when business took her husband to New York or London, and raised her seven children to take a creditable part in the history of Florida and South Carolina. Hers was indeed a life of more variety than was granted to most people of her day—to be reared in Asia Minor, to enjoy the life of London society as a young married woman, to establish her family in a wild land, beset by Indians, and to end her days in Charleston, the most aristocratic city of Colonial times, as a leader there by reason of her cosmopolitan charm and her husband's high position. At the time of the removal to Florida, she was thirty-three years old, at the height of her social career, so that it was a real sacrifice for her to bury herself in the wilderness, and in Turnbull's letters to the Earl of Shelburne, he said that he and his wife often thought with regret of the friends they had left at Bowood and at Shelburne House.[3]

On April 2, 1767, the first partnership agreement concerning the colony was signed by Andrew Turnbull, Sir William Duncan and Sir Richard Temple, Commr. of the Navy.[2] Three adjoining grants of 20,000 acres each had been obtained, one for Duncan, one for Turnbull, one for Temple, the last as trustee in this affair for George Grenville and his heirs. This George Grenville was Prime Minister of England at the time, and felt that he should not act personally in the undertaking. The grants were to be operated for a period of seven years at a joint expense not exceeding 9000 pounds and any subsequent grants to the partners were to be treated in the same way. At the end of this period, equal division was to be made between the partners, a committee of seven disinterested persons determining the division, two chosen by each partner and one by the other six members of the committee. A description of the three equal lots should then be drawn from a box by the partners in turn.[1] This was the original outline of the New Smyrna partnership plan which was destined to be changed twice thereafter.

The first land grant issued to Turnbull on June 18, 1766, allowed him to select his tract of 20,000 acres of unclaimed land in East Florida, and therefore it devolved upon him to go to Florida and look over the country. He arrived there with his family in November, 1767,[4] a month which a native knows is usually mild and clear, after the Equinoctial storms. He had to land at St. Augustine, the capital, and the only city on the East coast, and of course paid his respects at once to Governor Grant, who had already been there three years trying to clean up after the Spaniards. James Grant was a soldier who had played a prominent part in the capture of Havana, and his appointment as Governor of Florida was a direct acknowledgment of his services. St. Augustine had been partially burned and destroyed by the departing Spaniards, even the Spanish governor dismantling his beautiful garden in an outburst of hatred against the temporary English commander, a man of arbitrary methods, who had aroused the bitterest opposition. Grant, however, was as fine an administrator as he was a soldier, and his little capital had grown to three thousand inhabitants by this time.

Turnbull decided to establish his family here until the new colony was well started,[5] so he took one of the typical Spanish houses of the town, with balconies overhanging the narrow streets and a lovely garden behind high stone walls. Turnbull of course noted with pleasure the great variety of fruits and flowers which grew in his inner court. From the piazza, shaded by Tuscan pillars, he could see first the grape arbor before the entrance, and beyond, his garden, as well as many others, contained fig, guava, plantain, pomegranate, lemon, lime, citron, shaddock, bergamot, China and Seville orange trees. The real beauty of Florida is a cultivated beauty which comes out today in the rare court of the Ponce de Leon Hotel at St. Augustine and the gardens at Palm Beach. Wild Florida landscape is unkempt and weird, and Turnbull was glad to see how much could be done with intelligent care. He also enjoyed the climate, which was so temperate that, according to Moorish custom, the houses had been built without fireplaces. There were no windows on the north walls, and when a northeaster blew keen across Matanzas Inlet, a Negro brought an urn of glowing coals and set it in his room.

Governor Grant was noted for his hospitality and a brilliant company often gathered at his table to discuss and to settle peaceably the affairs of the province.[6] Though an autocrat who brooked little opposition to his policies, he was genial, and he took an immediate fancy to Dr. Turnbull, of whom it was said that wherever he went, he carried an atmosphere of gaiety and good humor.[7] And so

Turnbull always found him a wise and liberal assistant throughout the troubles of the colony's first few years. This was the more remarkable because Grant was accounted stingy about government moneys,[8] and because Turnbull favored a more democratic policy of government within the province than Grant allowed.

Many prominent men from England and the colonies had moved to St. Augustine, among them, William Drayton, Chief Justice, and Major Moultrie, afterwards Lieutenant Governor of Florida. The former was to become Turnbull's lifelong friend, and the latter an unrelenting enemy. Other Englishmen who had come to Florida, like himself, to build up the new province, were Dennis Rolle, who had started a unique settlement on the St. Johns River, and Mr. Oswald, the owner of a large sugar plantation on the Halifax river; Sir Charles Burdett, Rev. John Forbes, the admiralty judge; Wm. Stark, the historian; Bernard Romans, civil engineer; William Bartram, naturalist, and Rev. Mr. Frazier. As Turnbull's settlement was by far the most ambitious thing ever attempted in Florida, he must have been the center of attention. Grant saw in him a powerful aid for his governing council, and Turnbull received his appointment to it two months after his return to England. [9] On May 1, 1767, having been appointed Secretary and Clerk of the Council, he felt obliged to resign the office of Clerk of the Crown and Clerk of Common Pleas to which he had been appointed in September[10] while Grant reported to Lord Hillsborough that, in accordance with the King's command[11] every effort would be made to assist Dr. Turnbull. William Gerard de Brahm, the government surveyor, was at once consulted as to the best lands available in East Florida and, with the advice of the other planters, Turnbull decided to visit Mosquito Inlet, the first large harbor south of St. Augustine and distant about seventy-five miles. This region was reported to include some of the most valuable lands in the province, and the year he arrived a colony of ship builders had attempted a settlement there on account of the splendid trees in the vicinity.[12]

He sailed down the coast, past what is now known as Ormond and Daytona Beaches, and entered Mosquito Inlet the morning of the second day. The deep blue waters, set in snowy sand-bars, admitted his ship to the North Indian River, passing by a circular little sheet of water, now known as Turnbull's Bay. On either side the high shell bluffs were crowned with enormous live oaks, and beneath these the ground was clear of underbrush like a park, while beyond could be seen the rich green of a large wild orange grove, famous among the Indians for generations. Magnolias and green bay trees added graceful variety to the scene. This is the description by the famous naturalist, William Bartram, of the site of New Smyrna, which he visited ten years before the settlement was made.[13] Bartram's young son dreamed of this spot for eighteen years after he saw it with his father, and returned to it when he had earned enough money in the Northern colonies to allow him to travel. The beauty and very apparent fertility of the place completely won Turnbull, and he decided to spend his life and risk his fortune in this garden forest. Although a physician, the name "Mosquito Inlet" held no warning for him, because science did not then connect the mosquito with the deadly malarial fevers which, in the next eight years, were to reduce this colony to half its original number. Moreover it was not until summer that he saw his people black with them as they worked at clearing the dense palmetto and vine-tied thickets, and found himself helpless without our modern methods of exterminating these pests, common to the whole Atlantic coast. Life promised much to the pioneer doctor and, in honor of his wife's birthplace, Smyrna, in Asia Minor, and in anticipation of his Greek settlers, he named the future settlement New Smyrna.

Turnbull was so impressed with the agricultural prospects of Florida that before he returned to England he purchased a large cotton plantation at the Mosquitoes and left an overseer in charge, with orders to buy cattle from Georgia and Carolina.[14] By the last of March, 1767, however, he was back in England, and presented his petition to make a settlement in Florida.[15] In his first grant from the crown there had been included twenty thousand acres for himself. Five subsequent grants to Duncan, Grenville and Turnbull, brought their whole tract to 101,400 acres.[16]

Van de Sande Studio, New Smyrna, Fla.

THE GRACEFUL VARIETY OF FOLIAGE ON THE OLD KING'S ROAD, NEW SMYRNA

Lord Grenville, at this time head of the ministry in England, was inclined to favor agricultural enterprises such as this, not only because he was Turnbull's partner, but in order to offset the severity of his measures against smuggling in the colonies. The Lords of Trade granted Turnbull's request for a sloop of war to be used as a transport, and the forty-five hundred pounds of bounty on East Florida products was represented by the young Lord Shelburne, secretary for the colonies, as necessary for starting the settlement. Four hundred pounds was to be used for roads, bridges and ferries, one hundred pounds for a "Parson and Schoolmaster" and three pounds apiece for the cost of transportation of each colonist to the settlement.[17] It is, therefore, evident that the English government was as much interested in this undertaking as any shareholder in the Company. It also continued to give substantial assistance for at least four years thereafter.

General James Grant
Laird of Ballindalloch (1720–1806)
first colonial governor of East Florida 1763-1771

CHAPTER II
THE MAKING OF NEW SMYRNA

ARLY in the spring of 1767, Turnbull set sail in his converted sloop to collect settlers from Greece. This vessel was manned and provisioned by Turnbull himself[18] no small investment for one individual in those days of slow travel, and as he proceeded to gather his colonists, his fleet grew to considerable size. He had difficulty, however, in persuading the Greeks to emigrate because the Turkish Government opposed his scheme.[19] Nevertheless he secured two hundred wild tribesmen from the mountains in the southernmost part of the Peloponnesus, who had always defied Turkish rule and who lived under chiefs in a state of civil war, when they were not fighting the Turks. These recruits did not produce a favorable impression on the Ottoman Empire and when Turnbull sent a ship's crew ashore for water at Modon in the Morea, the commander of the garrison seized them as rebels. This officer was prevailed upon by presents to release them, but everywhere the Turks placed obstacles in the way of the enterprise.[20]

Finally Turnbull decided to go to Leghorn in Southern Italy for recruits, for the Governor there agreed to allow Italians to sign contracts with him, on condition that he take no Genoese silk manufacturers.[21] One hundred and ten Italians joined the expedition, but when the governor saw that he was really about to lose these men, he sent many threatening messages to them. The British consul aided Turnbull in getting away with them, however, and the Italians themselves told Turnbull that the majority of them were unemployed and strangers in the city of Leghorn, and therefore liable to deportation at any time. His agreement with the settlers was, that they were to have their way paid and to be established on the Florida grant. After they had paid off their indebtedness to the Company by from seven to eight years' labor, each was to receive fifty acres of land, with five additional acres for each child in his family.[22] If they were not contented with the land, they were to be allowed to return to their own country in six months.[23]

While Turnbull was having difficulty in persuading settlers to emigrate to Florida, news reached him that crops in the island of Minorca had failed for the third consecutive year and that a large part of the farming population was on the verge of starvation. It seemed to him that these were the people who would join in an agricultural enterprise in a country that promised rich soil and plenty of land. Minorca had been an English possession since 1713, so it would not involve any bargaining with a foreign government or cause his colonists any uneasiness, such as might be occasioned by a change of allegiance. Although there was widespread discontent there, on account of England's policy of restricting the correspondence and activities of the Catholic priests of Minorca, she had promised Spain to allow them the freedom of their faith. She did not keep her treaty promises of freedom of religion in Minorca or Florida as she did in Canada, however. In proof of this, one condition of Turnbull's grants from the crown was that the settlers were all to be Protestants.[24] When Turnbull first received his grant, this did not promise to be a difficulty, for the original plan had been to obtain Greeks, and since the Greek Catholic Church has always been regarded by the Church of England as an affiliation, their church was not antagonistic to the Protestant provision of the grants. But Minorcans, though English subjects, were Roman Catholics, and if they were to be colonists, their religion had to be ignored, as had been done in the other English colonies, Maryland excepted. Still, Turnbull argued, the situation did not promise to be any more acute in one colony of England, such as Minorca or Virginia, than in another, namely Florida. So when he decided to enlist the Minorcans, he allowed them to take a priest and monk with them, with letters and credentials from the Vicar General of Minorca[25]

The island of Minorca lies among a flock of sister islands under the lee of Spain in the Mediterranean. Its inhabitants are of Spanish extraction and appearance, speak a language similar to Spanish, and are devout Catholics. Most of them belong to the farming class, and, usually, they are sober, industrious and law-abiding, as Governor Grant testified when he expressly stated that they refused, to a man, to join the riots of Greeks and Italians which broke out the year the colony was started.[1]

In Minorca, Turnbull's project succeeded like wildfire. Crowds of starving people thronged the decks as soon as his ships dropped anchor in Port Mahon, the capital of Minorca under English rule, and one of the finest harbors in the Mediterranean.[27] They begged him to take three times as many of them as he had planned, because they were in such pitiable condition that their Bishop had even been obliged to dispense them from the Ecclesiastical law of fast and abstinence.[28]

Now, there was another clause of Turnbull's grant which made him eager for as many settlers as possible. It provided that if one-third of his land was not settled in three years, in the proportion of one person to every hundred acres, the whole should be forfeited to the Crown, and that if the remainder was not so settled in ten years, it was likewise to be forfeited.[29] Therefore, he was delighted rather than daunted by the increasing size of his colony, and gave his approval when many of the Italians in the expedition married Minorcan girls, who were thus recruited for the colony.[30] Turnbull had already enough land in the Company's name for six hundred people and was planning for more grants, so he at once proceeded to enlarge his fleet to eight ships. The enormous increase in the expense of the undertaking seemed to him to be worth the risk, since he had complete Government support. Lord Hillsborough, successor to Lord Shelburne in charge of the colonies, was indeed delighted when he heard of the sudden increase in numbers, calling it a "Noble addition" to Florida's settlement.[31] Turnbull, however, had yet to learn that one may have too much, even of such a good thing, as will develop later. By March 10, 1768, a letter from Hillsborough to the Governor of Florida informed him that Turnbull had finally sailed from Minorca.[32]

Thus Turnbull scoured the Mediterranean for recruits, and collected a heterogeneous company—unruly Greek tribesmen of a strange language and different religion from the others, devout Roman Catholic farmers and a small but turbulent band of Italians. Being on the ground, Turnbull saw a great opportunity for England's colonies in these settlers. His vision was very large and he wrote that many thousands of Italians and Greeks could be sent to America if the ships could be obtained to recruit them. Governor Grant, looking upon the practical aspect of this one colony, humorously declared, "I flatter myself I shall be able to keep them (the Indians) quiet—but to prevent the Greeks, Italians and Mahonese[33] from doing mischief to themselves" he considered a harder problem.[34] This farsighted official, on hearing that Minorcans were among the colonists, called the Indians in the vicinity of New Smyrna together, and explained to them, "that the people at the Mosquitoes[35] were not the English but that they were Subjects to the Great King—that they lived upon a little Island in a warm climate—that they had been oppressed by the Spaniards and hated them, and had come here to help their Brothers, the English."[34] In this way, Grant tried to keep the Indians from avenging hundreds of years of Spanish cruelty upon the people who so closely resembled them. He was partially successful, in spite of the fact that the government was slow to build a fort to protect the colony. After he left the country, the Indians were loosed on these unfortunate people by Turnbull's political enemies, so that it is small wonder that they found life unsupportable at Mosquito.

When the colonists at length left Gibraltar and started for the open Atlantic, there were about fifteen hundred souls in all, divided among the eight ships.[36] This was the largest colony at its start that had ever come to the New World.[37] The Virginia colony at Jamestown did not exceed five hundred people at any time until it passed from a proprietary to a royal government; and it took the Massachusetts colony seven years to work up to fifteen hundred people.

In addition to the settlers, the ships carried "cotton gins for the cleaning of cotton and other models of engines of agriculture,"[38] and the carefully packed cuttings for grapes, olives and mulberries. A realization of the magnitude of his undertaking did not daunt Turnbull. He wrote to Lord Shelburne when he sailed: "Though I have heard, My Lord, that America is now separated from your Department, as your Lordship's assistance and encouragement engaged me to enter into the colonizing scheme in a much larger way than I at first intended, I will trouble you now and again with an account of how my little colony goes on."[39]

The British frigate Carysfort agreed to act as convoy for the transports to Gibraltar, to protect them from the Barbary pirates[40] and they intended to start on March 29, 1767, but at the last minute Turnbull found that instead of losing colonists by desertion as he had expected, he had more than he could carry, on account of the eager enlistment of the Minorcans.[41] Luckily he secured a Danish ship to carry his overflow as far as Gibraltar and, since it could not go further, hired two small English vessels for the journey overseas.

At Gibraltar, the Earl of Shelburne's recommendations secured Turnbull every attention, and Commodore Spry ordered the Carysfort to convoy his eight vessels, full of colonists, as far as the Madeiras, because reports had come in of raids by Algerian pirates upon Dutch and French shipping.

The English government rightly considered this a most important and promising enterprise, and for a time at least gave it all the assistance possible. Florida bade fair to catch up with the other colonies in giant strides. To readers today, it will seem incredible that an undertaking of this magnitude should have been launched the very year the Stamp Act was repealed—that wealthy men and statesmen would have invested their own and the Government's money in a colony while open rebellion and clashes with the government officials over the rigid enforcement of smuggling penalties were spreading in every English colony in America. It is indeed a far cry from present day investments, which rise and fall like a barometer in response to the changes in the political atmosphere. English statesmen were very ignorant and indifferent to American public opinion, even upon such a stirring subject as the Stamp Act. "There was not the smallest evidence that either Pitt or Cumberland, or any of the other statesmen who were concerned with the negotiation, at St. Augustine, the other four having fallen a little to the north. "They dropt in slowly," wrote Governor Grant, "but all of them got safe to this Port."[42] The Spanish houses, and general plan of St. Augustine were a pleasing sight to the Latin portion of the immigrants, and they remembered the close walled town throughout their residence in New Smyrna, and, after eight years, returned to it in a body, to live under its friendly shelter. At this time, however, they were dispatched at once by land and water to the Mosquitoes, to prepare for the other settlers who were delayed. As always happens when a large and elaborate plan approaches its culmination, many important phases went wrong. A ship containing five hundred Negroes, who had been purchased and brought direct from Africa to clear the land and do the first rough work of the settlement, was wrecked on the southern coast of Florida, and all hands were lost.[43]

Strenuous measures were necessary to take care of such a great company of people, suddenly set down in a wild country. Governor Grant had four months provisions placed there[44] and some great shacks erected for living quarters[45] but the families were crowded for shelter and sleeping during the first weeks of organization, for, since nearly three times as many people had come as were expected, they were not prepared for them. Hominy was cooked in huge copper kettles in the open, and at meal time a drum summoned the workers from the woods to line up for their share of food. Clothes by the wholesale, of heavy durable material, and mostly of uniform pattern, were distributed, so as to save the colonists what was left of their wardrobes. Most of them were badly off, in the first place, so far as clothes were concerned, and this, therefore, was a much-needed measure. Strange to say, however, all of these ways of caring for the settlers were mentioned as great grievances by their historian,

Romans. This was the accepted way of providing for people in new colonies, the way that the Virginia, Georgia, Plymouth and Carolina colonists had lived for the first years of their pioneer life, but these people are reported to have been disappointed because they encountered these hardships.

Governor Grant gives a more favorable report of them, however. He says that by August 10, 1768, they were all located on plantations, appeared contented and pleased with their prospects and were obedient to their overseers.[46] In the directing of so many people for a division of labor and for information on their needs and progress, overseers were selected, partly from their own number and partly imported from the Northern colonies, the latter because of their knowledge of New World agriculture. Many of the colonists were entirely ignorant of the methods of clearing and planting, all of them had to learn how to raise hemp, cotton and indigo, the articles on which England had placed a bounty. But these English overseers came from plantations where Negroes had been used as laborers and, in addition to being unable to understand the language of their Minorcan, Italian and Greek charges, they made themselves unpopular by their arbitrary manner and impatience at what they claimed was the stupidity and laziness of some of the settlers. Also, the colonists had all come, as generations before and after them, with dreams of ease and plenty to be enjoyed without work in Florida. So it was not long before peremptory commands and the strict discipline necessary to preserve order in the new colony brought about a clash between the unruly element and their directors.

ONE OF THE MANY COQUINA-LINED WELLS AT NEW SMYRNA

Van de Sande Studio, New Smyrna, Fla.

CHAPTER III
THE UPRISING OF 1768[47]

ALL seemed peaceful and busy on August 8, 1768, two months after the last colonist had arrived at New Smyrna, when Turnbull brought some planters from the Carolinas down to see the progress his settlers had made. The distinguished visitors rode over the fields where brush and pine stumps were burning, the fresh-cut outlines of the farms were just showing and the great wharfs and wells were being built of coquina. Turnbull showed them the quarries of this curious rock which is composed of innumerable tiny shells, held together by a natural cement, a rough and durable material which the Spaniards had used to build the fort and sea-wall at St. Augustine. The colonists were much awed by the splendid equipment and retinue with which these visitors traveled, but the visitors were equally impressed by the extent of the undertaking before them. They saw that this was the largest number of people which had ever come to the colonies in one body; that the possibilities of the country were at last to be found in agriculture, instead of myths of gold and silver, and that within his grasp Turnbull held the realization of all the visions of past invaders of this strange land. They declared to their delighted host that this colony bade fair to be "the best in all the British provinces," and added that their own experienced laborers could not have done better than these people in preparing the plantations.

That day the distinguished company rode on its way to St. Augustine, accompanied by Dr. Turnbull, and stopped for the night at Mt. Oswald, the large sugar cane plantation on the Halifax River. The natural surroundings of this country seat are today the wonder and delight of tourists at Daytona and Ormond. But how different was life there then! These planters lived on their huge land grants, surrounded by slaves and in danger of Indians. They could only reach St. Augustine by rough corduroy roads or a sail down the coast, with the possibility of being captured by pirates, and they were now about to be treated to a new realization of the vicissitudes of pioneer life. On the night of the 19th, they sat around the great hall in Mr. Oswald's home, resting from their tour of inspection, until about ten o'clock, when they retired, in order to be ready to start on their way to St. Augustine the next morning. At midnight an express rider dashed up to the quiet house and hammered on the door, calling for Dr. Turnbull. Candles were hurriedly lit by the house servants and the distracted messenger admitted to the doctor's room, where he delivered himself of a tale of black calamity. It seemed that Carlo Forni, one of the Italian overseers, that very morning, about eleven o'clock, had marched into the square, at New Smyrna, at the head of twenty malcontents, and delivered a speech to the settlers, who left their work and crowded around the storehouse to hear him. He declared himself commander-in-chief of the Italians and Greeks, whom he intended to lead to Havana. Spain, he argued, would be glad to protect them from the English, and they would be freed from this life of hard work and stern masters. The sandy, desolate shores of Florida held nothing but sickness and danger for them and he was prepared to deliver them from all their troubles. As he talked, the crowd grew excited. Clotha Corona, one of his Greek followers, broke the door of the storehouse and casks of rum were rolled into the street. At this moment, Cutter, one of the English overseers, arrived on the scene and tried to order the crowd away. He was wounded in the struggle with Forni's men and locked in one of the closets of the storeroom. Excited with this violence and by the rum, which was now circulating freely in the mob, the adherents of Forni rapidly increased until they numbered about three hundred. They seized firearms and ammunition in the storehouse and compelled the Minorcans to submit to their commands, though the latter refused to a man to join the rioting. For this, their dwellings were plundered and their belongings thrown into the road. But other and richer prizes soon diverted the mob. A ship of provisions, lying in the river, was seized, and the work of loading her for the trip to Cuba commenced. Clothes, blankets, linen and fishing tackle were carried down to the shore by the hundreds of armfuls, and the rum and oil casks which could not be loaded were staved in the streets. The number of men actively implicated included nearly all the Greeks and Italians in the colony, and Carlo Forni threatened that anyone who tried to escape and warn the authorities would be put to death. Nevertheless, two faithful Italians slipped into the swamp at dusk and made their way to Turnbull's plantation, four miles from New Smyrna. There was no one but the overseer in charge here and their terrified version of the course of events, as delivered to him, sounded like the end of New Smyrna's young settlement. So he sent an "express" rider through the woods that very evening, and this was the story that had reached the doctor at midnight and dashed his high hopes for his model settlement. As he sat and listened, he saw one hundred and sixty thousand dollars, which included his own fortune, and the money of his powerful friends, sunk in a community of violent and unprincipled men. Two years of hard preparatory work gone, extensive plans half executed, and himself a ruined man. But he roused himself at once, and thanked God that his wife and children were still in St. Augustine, waiting the completion of their new home. He dismissed the messenger for rest and refreshment, and sat down at once to write Governor Grant a full account of what had happened. He asked that help be sent him at once to New Smyrna, where he was returning that very night in the hope of checking the uprising. And, in the small hours of the morning, another express rider started at top speed for St. Augustine, while Turnbull bade goodbye to his friends and former guests, and set his face toward New Smyrna.

He arrived at his plantation some time in the morning- of the 20th, and at once started, with a small company of servants, to rescue his wounded overseer. The marauders were down at the waterfront, loading their spoils, and the terrified Minorcans were hiding in their quarters, so he went down the littered street to the storehouse without interruption. Cutter was soon located and brought out— one of his ears and two fingers had been cut off and continued bleeding and severe handling had reduced him to a serious condition. All other considerations faded before the need for the services of a doctor, and so Turnbull had Cutter carried back to the plantation, where he treated his wounds and cared for him, while waiting for word from the Governor.

The next day passed without events of any moment. Messengers from New Smyrna reported to Turnbull that the mutineers did not seem to be hurrying to leave, that they were feasting and drinking aboard their ship most of the night and had not yet finished loading. Cutter was very ill all day and required constant attention, raving at his imagined assailants. The night came, and with it word that the rebel ship would sail on the morning's tide, so it was an anxious vigil for the doctor. Early in the morning, he rode over to the shore and mournfully watched the sails go up on the crowded vessel, as it moved down the river and out of sight, to anchor at the bar and wait for the eleven o'clock tide. The loss of three hundred able-bodied men out of the colony was a staggering blow, not to mention thousands of dollars worth of supplies and the ship. He turned his horse and rode slowly along the bank toward Mosquito Inlet. Suddenly, within a mile of the bar, he heard a gun fired and his heart leaped with excitement and renewed hope. He dashed along the shore and reached the Inlet in time to see the East Florida, with another vessel behind her, sail down upon the escaping ship, on the very tide which was to have carried her off to Cuba. The rebel's deck was swarming with terrified men who waved white rags and showed that they were ready to surrender. Before the government ships could get to her, however, Turnbull saw about thirty-five men escape in an open boat and row frantically around the wooded shore. A few hours later, he met the officer in charge of the relief expedition at the wharf, and watched with immense relief the unloading of his property by the frightened mutineers, who had been deserted by their leader and his accomplices. They eagerly obeyed the soldiers in charge of them. In talking with the captain, he heard how Grant had received his letter the evening of the day- he had sent it, had loaded his ships all night long and sent them out on the 21st. Two days sail had completed their journey and brought them to New Smyrna in the nick of time. Turnbull felt very happy at this moment; realizing that most of these mutineers were like simple sheep following a few ringleaders as blundering as they were lawless, he recommended that only a few of the most guilty be taken to St. Augustine for trial. Inquiry among the insurgents proved that they were as enraged with their leaders on account of their desertion, as Turnbull was for their lawlessness.

As soon as things were quiet again, and Turnbull was sure that a small guard could maintain order in the colony, the relief expedition sent one ship in search of the ringleaders, whom they expected to catch easily, while the other returned to St. Augustine. A strange chase for the escaped men took place down the long open coast. It was four months before the government ship overtook them on the Florida Keys, and then it is probable that their dreadful hardships had made them anxious to be caught. All through the Fall season of terrible northeast storms, these thirty-five men had traveled in an open boat along the shore, camping and hunting sometimes, not daring to stay long on land for fear of Indians and wild beasts, or long on water because of storms and their pursuers. It is small wonder that their wretched appearance moved the jurors in St. Augustine to pity. Governor Grant himself wrote to the Earl of Hillsborough that he thought the men had been punished enough by their experience, and that justice dealt to two or three flagrant offenders would be sufficient for the whole three hundred. So three were finally convicted of piracy, and one of these pardoned on a curiously cruel condition—that he be the executioner of the other two. (English law was still very severe in those days—there is a petition from the Governor of Massachusetts about this time, asking that the death penalty for forgery be changed). The two men who were executed were Carlo Forni, guilty of leading the insurrection, and the man who was responsible for the death of Cutter, who had since succumbed to his wounds. Three Greeks, convicted of less violent crimes, were pardoned by Grant on the recommendation of Hillsborough. Turnbull estimated his losses, after affairs had settled down, at four or five hundred pounds. In the light of the English law of the day and its heavy penalties, the offenders at New Smyrna were certainly gently dealt with, just as all wise and enlightened authorities usually manage a large number of lawbreakers. The whole three hundred of them were guilty of piracy; but their future good conduct was assured by lenient measures. All previous accounts of this uprising have been based upon Bernard Romans' version, which he included in his "History of Florida," on the authority of his irresponsible youthful draughtsman. All subsequent historians are unanimous in pronouncing Romans' History as lurid and unreliable, yet they took his word for a most barbarous recital of cruelty on Turnbull's part, and none of them consulted the detailed report of this affair by the governor of the province to the British Secretary of State, surely a most sane and authoritative source of information, and the one on which this account is based.[48]

Yet we may surely draw our own conclusions from the course of events themselves. The leaders of the revolt could not have had the welfare of the whole community at heart, for they planned to leave New Smyrna in a ship which had a capacity of not more than one-fifth of the people, and they destroyed the provisions they could not take with them. Also, they were not even capable of effecting their own escape, but spent three days in rioting and drinking—enough time for two government ships to load troops and make the journey from St. Augustine. So this rebellion was nothing more than the haphazard rioting of lawless men who used rum and vain promises to lead their unthinking companions into mischief.

Governor Grant summed up the affair by saying it was to be expected that a large number of people imported from all parts of the world to a new country would have such troubles; and he ended his report by recommending that a fort be built at New Smyrna for the double purpose of protecting the settlers from the Indians and of protecting the other planters from the settlers.[49] Already, he said, the plantations around New Smyrna were the most prosperous in Florida, and deserved the utmost care from the Government. A fort was accordingly started but never finished, though a guard of a sergeant and eight men was stationed there permanently.[50]

CHAPTER IV
ENGLAND LENDS FINANCIAL AID

BY December 1st, Grant wrote the home Government that the Greeks and Italians were quiet, but that scurvy had broken out, as a result of their long sea voyage and the scarcity of fresh foods at that season of the year; so that the settlement had lost about three hundred old people and children from sickness.[51] The remedy of green vegetables and fruits was not far off, however, for, he said, the gardens of that vicinity were about as far advanced as they were in England by the end of April and, with a touch of planter's pride, "I took care to save a considerable quantity (of seeds) for Mr. Turnbull from my own garden, of which a grain does not fail here."

A clear statement of coming financial troubles occurs in this same letter which Grant wrote to the Earl of Hillsborough, the new Secretary for the colonies. "Twenty thousand pounds sterling have already been laid out for the Embarkation, Provisions and Clothing of those people." Certainly this does not sound like an illiberal scale so far. He continued, "So large a Sum is not to be recovered but by perseverance and a further Expense, the settlers may do a little for themselves in the course of the Winter and Spring, but they must be subsisted for many months and clothed at least for two years before Returns can reasonably be expected—though they are supplied with Economy and good management—I am much afraid that the Expense of supporting so large a Settlement will be found too considerable for private pockets.[52] I give Mr. Turnbull every little assistance in my power, and I can safely say that I am as anxious about his success as he can be himself; but unless your Lordship is pleased to take this Greek Settlement under your Protection and include it in the Estimate for 1769, I am apprehensive that Mr. Turnbull will find great difficulty in carrying the projected plan into Execution—it is upon a larger bottom than was concerted with his Friends at home, and has already far exceeded double the Sum which they agreed to advance, for which reason, My Lord,

I am under some uneasiness about the future Conduct of those Gentlemen, they may probably tire of paying the large and frequent Bills, which Mr. Turnbull is under the absolute necessity of drawing upon them—their affairs certainly could not be in better hands, the Doctor is active, intelligent and assiduous—but his Friends, tho' they have the highest opinion of Mr. Turnbull's integrity and Ability may possibly be alarmed at risking such large sums in a New World without a more immediate prospect of Returns for their Money— what I now mention to your Lordship is entirely from my private opinion for I am sure the Doctor is convinced of my Friendship and good wishes—I cannot help considering the dreadful situation which the Doctor and his Greeks would be reduced to, if such a misfortune was to happen, a single Bill being returned, My Lord, would put a total stop to his Credit—in such a case of necessity I must run the risk, draw upon the Treasury for the subsistence of those adventurers and depend upon your Lordship's protection to support me in what I do—tho' this affair, My Lord, has hung heavy upon my mind, since the Landing of so great a number of people at a time, without any previous provision being made for them, and without the consent of the other parties concerned, as the Mahonese crowded in unexpectedly upon Mr. Turnbull."[53]

Turnbull had six thousand pounds to start with, and the British Government had only promised him a bounty on the first five hundred colonists, so that the whole scale of his settlement was according to his expected five hundred people; but, when the hundreds of starving Minorcans had thronged the decks of his transports, and begged to be taken from their famine stricken land, his enthusiasm was aroused by the prospect of such a wonderful colony. It seemed reasonable to him to suppose that if five hundred settlers were eagerly welcomed to Florida, fourteen hundred would be even more acceptable, especially when they were of the much needed farming class. But he was beginning to learn that there were many fatal and inevitable complications awaiting him.

By the 4th of March, 1769, the health of the colonists had been restored and they had cleared seven miles of water front along the Hillsborough, now the North Indian River.[54] Each farm house was set 210 feet from the next along the river, with its allotted acreage running back, and Turnbull, whose Mediterranean travels had lasted over many years, wrote that they reminded him of Egyptian farms along the Nile.[55] Their gardens were well started and the drainage of the rich swamp lands was progressing in a thorough and scientific way. But the bills were pouring in now, and every time Turnbull had to send a ship for provisions and clothing he did not know whether payment on them would be stopped or not. To avoid drawing any more money, he would wait until the last possible moment to replenish his stores. Governor Grant understood his predicament perfectly and knew his reluctance to call upon his friends any further, but he would not allow him to run too great a risk or depend on an exact date for a sailing vessel's arrival. "I have always recommended to him to have Six Months provisions constantly in store. Mr. Turnbull, just as I expected, finds himself, this moment very much pinched for provisions as his Supplies have not arrived exactly to the time and he writes that he has only Indian Corn for a Month at the Mosquitoes. I shall take care to prevent his being distressed, tho' I have no objection to his being a little uneasy," says the Governor humorously, "and therefore without telling him or anybody else, I have sent the "East Florida" to Charleston with directions to load her with Indian Corn, and with private orders to the Captain to proceed directly to New Smyrna, tho' I give out here that the Vessel is going to Savannah for Lumber."[56] So, even if Turnbull had allowed provisions to run low, this able Governor watched the colony too closely to allow it to suffer from hunger. In fact there appears to be ample proof of the care that was centered on these people.

Governor Grant's eloquent plea to Hillsborough of the worthiness of Dr. Turnbull's cause induced the Lords of the Treasury to allow him two thousand pounds for the support of the settlement, when further payments were stopped by the London Company, which, by July 21, 1769, had expended twenty-eight thousand pounds. Grant wrote to Hillsborough again, to tell him that the two thousand pounds would not be sufficient for the support of the colony, and urged that the East Florida bounty of five hundred pounds a year be continued for the benefit of New Smyrna.[57] It is evident that great pressure was brought to bear upon Dr. Turnbull to obtain returns for such an enormous outlay. Grant reported, September 1, 1770, "Dr. Turnbull is diligent and assiduous, he resides constantly with his Greek colonists and does as much as man can do, to repair the first fault of exceeding the number of people to be Imported."[58] The settlers raised a considerable amount of provisions, such as Indian corn, peas, potatoes and greens of all kinds, but the scarcity of money for the further work of the colony is evident from the rest of Grant's letter. "They are destitute of every convenience, they are ill clothed, many of them almost naked—and are obliged to live in small Huts put up in a hurry to shelter them from the Weather upon their first arrival. Dr. Turnbull has neither money nor credit to supply them with clothes and has not the necessary Tools and Materials to build Houses for them, in that distressed situation he can only look up to His Majesty for his most gracious support by ordering the Royal Bounty to be continued to enable him to carry an extensive and useful undertaking into Execution with Success—he presses me to lay his case before Your Lordship and to transmit for Your Lordship's consideration an indent of such things as are absolutely necessary for the existence of the settlement."[59] This indent is interesting because it gives an idea of how extensive financially even a few items for the colony could be. It reads:

"Indent of Clothing, Tools, etc., wanted for the Distressed Greek Settlement at Smyrna, under the direction of Andrew Turnbull, Esq.,

Best blue plains—3000 yards at ¼ s per yard.... 200 pounds
Best white plains—500 yards at ¼ s per yard 33. 6. 8
Check›t Linnens—3000 yards at 1- per yard 150
Strip›t Linnens—2000 yards at 1- per yard 100
Stript Cottons—500 yards at ⅓ d per yard 31. 5
Scots Osnabruggs[60] 4000 yards at 6 d per yard 100
Negro Blankets—600 at 5s each 150
Men's shoes of different sizes .... 600 pr
        at ¾ d per pair 100
Indigo Sickles 60 dozen at 8/6 d per Dozen 25. 10

Broad Hoes, Crowley's of a middling size 60 Dozen
　　　at 20/ per Dozen...60
Building nails the greatest part Six penny......................100

　　　　　　　　　　　　　　　　Lbs 1050. 18

Another shortage of provisions in October, 1770, was caused by Carolina planters who sold their promised cargo to a Spanish vessel, instead of sending it to New Smyrna. A substitute cargo was secured by Grant, however.

While Grant was trying to help him with the Government, Turnbull had made a new arrangement with his partners, to meet the increased scale of his settlement.[61] On October 2, 1769, Duncan and Temple agreed to pay 24,000 pounds on the colony if the shares in the property were divided into fifths, giving them each two-fifths and Turnbull one, in the final dividends. Thus Turnbull lost his one-third share in the company by increasing the expense of the undertaking. He lost land principally, for all further grants he obtained were still to be divided into fifths for the Company. Grenville incidentally advised him to look out for Indian lands, that is, land the Indians were willing to sell. But Turnbull was too busy to do this for several years.

These were some of the difficulties which harassed the administrator at New Smyrna, of which the colonists had no idea. They prospered for the most part in a rough, backwoods way, and their hardships were not to be compared with the sufferings of the earlier colonists of North America. They had a mild climate, soil of wonderful fertility, and a river abounding in fish, oysters and turtles. Game was also plentiful, and while the Indians troubled them, it was as thieves and not as murderers. Still, sickness continued to reduce their numbers and the occasional shortage of clothes, food or tools caused by Turnbull's recalcitrant London partners caused grumblings, which centered on Turnbull himself. He was the only organizer they knew anything about, and him they held responsible for all things, good or bad, which happened to them.

Van de Sande Studio, New Smyrna, Fla.

FOUNDATIONS OF THE FORT WHICH WAS NEVER FINISHED, NEW SMYRNA, FLORIDA

CHAPTER V
GOVERNOR GRANT
LEAVES FLORIDA

I N the brief accounts of this colony-there has been room only for the troubles that assailed it on all sides, so that its five or six years of remarkable progress are passed over with little comment. William Bartram, in his famous "Travels Through the Southern Provinces," commented on the pretty, thriving town on the west bank of the North Indian River; Johann Schoepf, a German traveler, also described its plantations extending for miles along the banks, the palmetto cottages of the settlers forming the picturesque center of each family's allotted acreage. The colony grew the necessities of life first—maize, sugar, cotton and rice, which they shipped from their great coquina wharfs. They also gathered sea weed and burned it for barilla, the ash of which makes sodium carbonate of an impure sort. Indigo, too, proved very successful, and they dug huge vats in the fields for boiling it. At the end of the first year, Turnbull was able to dispose of five thousand bushels of corn, after the supply for the colony had been deducted; while in 1772 the shipment of indigo brought them three thousand pounds[62] a sum which, of course, meant more then than it does now. Mulberry trees for silkworms were planted and grapevines set out. Turnbull also imported cochineal insects for making scarlet dye. These insects may still be seen, clinging in white webs to the cactus plants in the woods about New Smyrna.

With the dawning era of success for the colony, Turnbull became a leader in the new province. He had been made a member of the East Florida Council, May 13, 1767, that is, as soon as it was definitely known that he would live in Florida. Grant had written, October 20, 1768, that the management of New Smyrna consumed so much of Turnbull's time that he was unable to act as Clerk of the East Florida Council and Secretary of the Province, and a Mr. Yeats was temporarily performing these duties for him, but they remained his honorary posts.[63] He was so prominent and had made such a good impression on the home government that the Earl of Hillsborough began to urge his appointment as successor to Governor Grant,[64] when the latter was obliged, on account of failing health, to resign his office, in 1770. This resignation was a very disastrous event for the future of Florida and New Smyrna. Governor Grant, whose tireless care for this province had given it the greatest era of prosperity in its long tragic history, was not only obliged to resign his office, but to leave Florida. By October 19, 1770, he had received his Majesty's license to return to England, but he did not go until the last of March, 1771, because he was needed in the colony. Two important questions occupied him—the selection of his successor, and the continuance of the bounty for the New Smyrna colony—and in both of them Turnbull was concerned. Hillsborough sent him a list of candidates for the governorship for him to pass upon, and he commented as follows:

"Mr. Wooldridge would not do at all. Mr. Jolly—also objected to Mr. Turnbull, the third your Lordship mentions is unexceptionable, but his constant Residence at Smyrna is absolutely and indispensably necessary. Without his presence the business of the Settlement could not go on. He and his Constituents have too much at Stake to neglect the Greek Colony which requires his attention. He is not to be thought of—I only count on him as an honorary Councellor, who I do not expect to see but once a year and that only for a day or two. When he came last from Smyrna, it was to pass some days at my Plantation to see the process of making Indigo, in which great Improvements have been made this year by my Manufactures."[65]

Thus it is evident that Turnbull had to sacrifice everything to his colony—all governmental or professional honors which offered a wide field with few contestants in Florida. As he was one of the three doctors in East Florida he came in for that affection and respect from the people in the province which only a doctor can command. In spite of his remoteness from people he gained renown for his skill in treating the diseases of Southern countries.[66]

Hillsborough was still reluctant to give up his name for the governorship however, and Grant wrote again, "Doctor Turnbull obliged to constant Residence at Smyrna, could not with propriety think of entering into the Administration, if he was to be continued in it— and of course as things are Circumstanced will not interfere with Mr. Moultrie." John Moultrie was the man urged for the position by Grant, for he was one of the largest planters, owned the magnificent estate of Bella Vista, seven miles from St. Augustine, and moreover, "If he does not succeed to the Administration in my absence, we shall certainly lose him," concluded Grant. Hillsborough yielded to the extent of appointing Moultrie Lieutenant-Governor, but the opinion of the people in the province persisted that Turnbull would soon be made Governor.[67]

While Grant prevented the appointment of Turnbull as Governor, he sought to make up for it by his constant concern for the much needed bounty for the next year. "Transmitting my Letter to the Board of Treasury, My Lord, will not procure the Bounty for the Greek Settlement, if my request is not supported by your Lordship's approbation of the Measure, which I think in the end would be attended with much Utility to the Publick—by enabling Dr. Turnbull to carry his extensive Plans into Execution, the Progress of which must be very slow, indeed the Subsistence of his People will be precarious if he is not better established, before the Royal Bounty is withdrawn.[68]

It has been shown what splendid support Grant had given the Turnbull settlement, and how necessary the close cooperation of the Government had been for the bare existence of the colony, and so it can easily be imagined that even a lukewarm attitude by the administration would make matters very difficult at New Smyrna, while any opposition could easily send the costly undertaking into bankruptcy. By this time, George Grenville was dead, Shelburne out of favor and the Home Government much too engrossed in events in the North to listen to Florida's troubles. Early in the year the Boston Massacre had put the colonists into disfavor with the Home Government, and Hillsborough was not inclined to continue his benevolence, even toward New Smyrna. The large sums they had spent in Georgia on colonies had not repaid them for their efforts, and besides, the Government had never felt obligated to care for Turnbull's colony; they had only promised bounty for five hundred colonists; they had afterwards granted the two thousand pounds as a special relief measure, on condition that the Treasury should not be put to any more expense; and now, they flatly refused any more assistance. Grant drew Hillsborough's displeasure upon himself by his insistence on this bounty. "I have already acquainted you that I had communicated to the Lords of the Treasury the Request for a further Allowance for the Support of Dr. Turnbull's colony of Greeks.[69] But he had nothing to add to his former statement. "I cannot take upon me to authorize any further expense to the public on that Account." Henceforth New Smyrna had to shift for itself, and Turnbull to do the best he could to recover from the agricultural efforts of his colonists the great sums sunk in their undertaking.

CHAPTER VI
THE NEW GOVERNOR

IFE at New Smyrna proceeded uneventfully on the surface for a time. Mr. Frazier, the Protestant Minister at New Smyrna, died in 1772, and Moultrie wrote the Earl of Hillsborough that he had arranged for Mr. Forbes, the Minister at St. Augustine, to visit New Smyrna at intervals. Mrs. Turnbull, with her seven children, and her nephew, Andrew, presided in the Turnbull mansion, a large house, built of coquina, which stood about four miles back from the settlement, and there Mr. Forbes was entertained, as were the prominent men who travelled to see the colony by sailing vessel or horseback. Grant had provided for the building of a splendid road to New Smyrna, which Moultrie continued. The roads built during the English occupation of Florida, are still called King's Roads, and show how well they were built, by their splendid lasting qualities. One ran from St. Augustine to New Smyrna, and another to Cowsford, (now Jacksonville) and thence to the St. Mary's River. There were many wealthy planters from the Carolinas and several noblemen from England who were the grantees of large tracts of land, among the latter, Lords Hauks, Egmont, Sir William Duncan and Messrs. Rolls, Oswald, Taylor, Bisset, Potts, Strachey, Tonyn and Turnbull.[70] Large plantations, with beautiful homes and groves were scattered over the vicinity of St. Augustine and New Smyrna and along the St. Johns River. There were now few unclaimed lands around New Smyrna. Turnbull's neighbors, as shown by the old survey maps[71] were Messrs. Wright, Alortz, Samuel Campbell, Robert Paris Taylor, John Grayhurst, James Moultrie, Robert Oswald, Captain Samuel Barrington and Col. Wm. Faucet. Small holdings in the names of W. Waldron, T. Warron and Angus Clark filled in the long line of plantations. Bella Vista, the home of Lieutenant Governor Moultrie, was particularly famous for its beautiful grounds. The social center of all this prosperity was St. Augustine, and the little town was very gay under English administration.

As in all frontier posts, the brilliancy of the Governor's functions was furnished by the military. The officers of Fort George did not look favorably upon Moultrie's appointment, because they thought him lacking in force and decision, and, moreover, they were all staunch friends of Turnbull, whom they felt should have been made Governor. Chief Justice Drayton was another friend who now held aloof from the official Mansion. He belonged to one of South Carolina's most prominent families, his grandfather and uncle both having been Lieutenant Governors there, and though Moultrie also came from South Carolina, the two had long been unfriendly. The attitude of the military was a source of irritation to Moultrie, and Turnbull he regarded with suspicion, but Drayton was the point of contact which set off the long train of explosive disagreements which finally led to New Smyrna's downfall. As has been said, Turnbull and Chief Justice Drayton were firm friends. They had long wished to see the governmental machinery, which England had provided for Florida, put in operation. The original letters patent of the Province had provided for a governor, council and elected assembly, but Grant had refused, throughout his administration, to allow the formation of the assembly. Turnbull had always disagreed with him on this subject, and, when Moultrie succeeded Grant, he and Drayton urged the election of an assembly, in the council meetings.[72] All parties in the council agreed that this was a good measure, since Florida had now enough people to merit a representative form of colonial government, but demonstrations against England in the Northern colonies, especially the clash between the inhabitants of Boston and British troops, in 1770, known as the Boston Massacre, had again alarmed the British ministry, and as there were, even in Florida, two parties on the question of the extent to which representative government should go at this time, much delay in this direction was experienced by the Florida colony. Florida was, in reality, too recently settled by the English and too evidently benefited by British rule to really wish for independence, but the King's party, with Moultrie at its head, advised elections to be held only once in three years, so as to control popular opinion, while Turnbull, Drayton and many other prominent men declared for annual elections. The same question was being agitated in England, from 1770-1771, where the Prime Minister, Chatham, was engaged in collecting opinion on the subject. Chatham favored annual elections, while Burke opposed them as lessening the power and prestige of Parliament.[73] As usual, Turnbull, who kept in touch with English politics, brought the latest question from England to Florida. The dispute on this subject between Drayton and Moultrie grew very heated, and finally extended to other matters, such as administrative and judicial business of the province, until these two gentlemen, "high-minded Carolinians," as Forbes terms them, were involved in an irremediable quarrel, Turnbull standing by the Chief Justice, both from conviction and friendship. The plan for an assembly failed entirely as a result, and Drayton resigned his seat in the council. Soon afterward, Turnbull resigned also; but whether to show his affiliation with Drayton, or because he really was too busy to attend the meetings, Moultrie could not decide.[74] No further difference developed between Turnbull and Moultrie, however, for some years, probably because of the remoteness of New Smyrna from the capital. On February 19, 1773, Moultrie reported a visit which he had made to the Greek Colony, where he evidently found everything entirely satisfactory, for he wrote to the Earl of Dartmouth: "Since I last had the honor of addressing your Lordship, I have visited all the Plantations and Settlements on the Mosquito River, and I am happy to inform you that as well on this visitation as that of St. Johns River, I have reason to be pleased, and that a Spirit of Improvement, of Industry and good humor everywhere prevails among the Settlers; of which they feel the good effects. Their plantations carry the appearance of Improvement; they have plenty around them and are beginning to recover the expenses they have been at on their first setting down in this New Colony."[75] These are strange words for an official who, a little later, was to charge the originator of this settlement with poor management and starving and maltreating his colonists; certainly he must have been blind to have seen on every plantation prosperity and good humor where hideous cruelty and famine were only a short time afterwards represented by him to prevail. In that day as well as now, politics played a large part in coloring the picture of existing conditions. Turnbull was well satisfied with the way the colony was prospering, for he wrote on October 3, 1774, "I have now laid a solid foundation, though it was against the opinion of some men, who prefer a flash of present gain, tho extorted from the laborer and land, to greater advantages in future."[76] These are the words of a patient as well as a wise director. He could not suppress this hard earned sense of gratification, because his big undertaking had brought such slow returns, that most of his friends had doubted his ultimate success and all had urged him to get his money back as quickly as possible.

With success now clearly in view, he made some important improvements which seemed to him necessary for farming in this climate. The parallel between Florida and the southern Mediterranean countries which he knew so well in former years of travel, was always before his mind, and so when a severe drought scorched his crops, he decided to institute the Egyptian method of irrigating the land,[77] which is by a closely woven net-work of canals.[78] This was entirely new to American planters and they looked on the large scale of his irrigation plan with doubtful eyes. It does indeed seem strange that in a land so plentifully watered, such an extensive irrigation scheme as can now be clearly traced in the canal system at New Smyrna should have been thought necessary, and visitors to the old site of New Smyrna have always thought them solely a drainage plan. But Turnbull had seen this method work marvels in the Nile country, and knew of it as a practical agricultural aid, for in 1763, just before he came to Florida, the great canal between Cairo and the Red Sea had been repaired to supply fresh water to the towns on the Suez Canal. At any rate, in this letter Turnbull expressly stated that his canals were originally for the purpose of irrigation and not of drainage[79] though of course they accomplished the double purpose of draining the marshes and watering the high land. In a recent survey of the vicinity of New Smyrna, these canals were pronounced a fine engineering feat and designed in the best possible way to irrigate and drain that country.

CHAPTER VII
SPANISH INTRIGUE

T HERE was no middle class in Florida at this time. Slaves were brought in ship loads direct from Africa, and some of the planters along the St. Johns River owned thousands of them. Thus the colonists at New Smyrna were an isolated class, ignored by their wealthy white neighbors as poor and small farmers, and looked upon by the Negroes as "poor white trash," just as the few poor people of the Carolinas and Virginia were regarded by the slaves, all of which was naturally resented by the Minor-cans. This was the feeling as well, of the indentured colonists in Georgia and Virginia, only not so pronounced, because their nationality was the same as those about them, and in a few years they could not be marked out; while the Minorcans remained a distinct class in Florida for many years. Yet, the Minorcans proved themselves vastly superior to the rest of Turnbull's colonists at New Smyrna in industry and honesty, and, while unpopular alike with Greeks, Italians and English, they kept together, and worked steadily at paying off their debt to the Company. The main complaint which they had to make against their situation, was the number of deaths which had occurred among them up to 1773, for their numbers dwindled in that time from fourteen hundred to six hundred in the nine years that they lived at New Smyrna. But aside from the natural course of events, many things happened to them which molded the opinions of succeeding generations. One of these was a plot of the Spaniards to gain a foothold in Florida once more.

For many years the political correspondence of English governors in America had been full of the activities of France and Spain, who were trying to regain their lost provinces there. This one in the Minorcan colony was a most carefully concealed campaign, and little attention has been paid to the discovery of it, or the effect of it on these inhabitants of Florida, though the entire correspondence of the ambassadors of the King of Spain and the Catholic Bishops interested (as naive an acknowledgment as was ever recorded) has long been in print in this country. These were collected in what are known as the A. M. Brooks papers, from the records in Seville, Spain; and a translation of these documents, published under the title of "Unwritten History of St. Augustine" by Mrs. Avarette. The letters in their proper order, tell the story for themselves.

On October 20, 1769, a Spanish fishing vessel touched at the Mosquitoes on its way south to Havana and, though this was forbidden in these times of mutual suspicion and sudden warfare, Don Campos, the parish priest of the Minorcans, managed secretly to give a letter to the Master of the vessel to be delivered to the Bishop of Cuba. The substance of the letter was that upon sailing from Minorca, Don Campos had received from the Pope authority as parish priest for three years at New Smyrna, and now that this term had expired, he wished an extension of this time for himself and Father Casanovas, the monk who had accompanied him. He also asked for Holy oil and two assistant priests for conducting divine service. The secrecy and apparent difficulty with which the letter was sent created a real stir in Catholic circles. According to subsequent letters, it seems that Don Campos was only a good, laborious priest who had been with the Minorcans three years before they sailed from home, and his secret method of communicating with his Bishop was caused by previous experience with the policy of the English Government in Minorca and Florida, of preventing correspondence between Catholic priests. But the Bishop of Cuba proceeded very cautiously to make sure that the two priests and the Minorcans were indeed Catholics, and then referred the matter to the King of Spain, so that the latter might insist upon England fulfilling her treaty promise to allow freedom of religion to her Catholic subjects, and also that Don Campos and the Minorcans might be inspired by gratitude to his Catholic Majesty for the privileges obtained for them, and be willing agents for the Spanish Government.

A secret correspondence with Havana continued for five years when, in 1774, a vessel which had lurked suspiciously near the colony, was seized by Turnbull's order, and evidence of these activities found in letters in charge of the master of the vessel. Great was the agitation of all the Minorcans! Terror seized those directly implicated, and grief the rest, because now the comforting assurances of their nearest Bishop were interrupted. A priest and several Minorcans were convicted at St. Augustine of high treason and executed, and strange fishing vessels were henceforth forbidden to touch at New Smyrna. These events definitely antagonized the Minorcans, and they continued to hear indirectly from Cuba through the few Spaniards who still remained in Florida, and who had been opposed to English rule from the first, on account of the harsh policy of Major Ogilvie, the military commander of Florida before Grant's arrival. Thus the best element of New Smyrna endured the hardships and suffered the restrictions of living in a new land under foreign masters, but joined at once the political plots of a tireless enemy of England. It is not, therefore, surprising, but nevertheless amusing, to note that the sympathetic and excitable Romans reported the seizure of the fishing vessel as 'a diabolical assault on the kindly tars for giving food to the starving Minorcans!'

A very decided change came over the affairs of administration in Florida after Moultrie's appointment as Lieutenant-Governor. In the smallest matters he showed indecision, appealed for support of his opinions to those about him and bothered Hillsborough with plaintive letters on the disobedience of his subordinates. Governor Grant had not been absent a month from Florida before Moultrie had to deal with Indian troubles at New Smyrna and his sense of insufficiency became evident.

Seventy-two Indians, led by Cowkeeper, a Creek Chief, came to New Smyrna the first part of May, under the impression that it was a settlement of Spaniards and Yemassee Indians, both bitter enemies of the Creeks. They were very sulky and, on meeting a boat's crew at Turnbull's cow pens, beat the Minor-cans severely and terrified the whole community. Turnbull treated the Indians diplomatically, invited the head man to his house and gave them plenty to eat and more to drink, so that they were restored to a good humor, when he explained to them the nationality of the Minorcans, as Grant had done before, and told them that the new Governor at St. Augustine would be glad to see them. The Indians departed peaceably, though Turnbull took the precaution to send Langley Bryant and Black Sandy, a slave, to watch them until they were safely on their way.[80] Turnbull wrote to Moultrie, informing him that the Indian's attack had been a false alarm, and Moultrie reported it thus to Hillsborough. But ten days later Turnbull came to St. Augustine to confer with Moultrie, saying that he was still uneasy about the Indians and had written to his partner, Sir William Duncan, asking him to tell Hillsborough so. Moultrie was much flurried and provoked with Turnbull for not reporting this changed opinion to him before he wrote to England, and persisted in his belief that there was no danger. Elaborate explanations were hurried to England by Moultrie with a copy of Turnbull's first letter, and a reiteration by the Lieutenant Governor that there was not the slightest cause for alarm.[81] Nevertheless, Moultrie called the Council together, and told them that since the Minorcans were disturbed, reinforcements might be sent to New Smyrna. Moultrie said the Council agreed with him that there was no danger, but that he would send a detachment of troops to the colony. It is perfectly apparent now, either there was danger and troops should have gone, or there was not and no troops should have gone! Still, Moultrie wrote to Major MacKenzie, commanding His Majesty's forces in East Florida, requesting him to send twelve men to reinforce the eight soldiers of the 31st Regiment permanently stationed there. MacKenzie's opinion of the Lieutenant Governor may be seen from the contents of his letter:

"St. Augustine,
June 6th, 1771.

Sir:

Dr. Turnbull is a Gentleman that I have the greatest regard and esteem for, and wou'd gladly wish it was in my power to quiet the Apprehensions and fears of his new Settlers by sending a reinforcement of Soldiers to the Musqueto's, as you require with the advice of his Majesty's Council. The detachment of the 31st Reg't already there is very sufficient in my humble opinion, to answer the purpose that they were sent for, that is, to prevent Mutiny and insurrection among the Greek Settlers on that Plantation. If any other Accident shou'd happen to make it seriously necessary to have more Troops sent to the Musquetos, you'll be so good as to make application to General Gage, the Commander in Chief, who no doubt will give me orders relative thereto.

I have the pleasure to be, etc.

(signed) Alec. MacKenzie." [82]

This was most cavalier treatment—it would have taken three months to get orders from General Gage for those twelve men! There ensued more complaints from Moultrie to Hillsborough, and the latter said that Moultrie was within his rights to ask for the soldiers. [83] The treatment which Moultrie received is all the more proof of his weakness when it is known that he was acting permissibly. First, he was annoyed that any report, however small, to the home government of the affair, should differ from his; then he gave his opinion that there was no danger, yet ordered the soldiers sent to New Smyrna, and was snubbed by the officer in command at St. Augustine.

This is but one instance of Moultrie's insecure position while in authority. He had no friends among the military men of St. Augustine, and he seemed to lack the power to make men obey him.

In the meantime, affairs in the Northern colonies had taken on such a serious aspect that the British Government wished for a stronger hand in Florida to steer her clear of the spreading discontent, for Florida people were watching the course of events with eager interest.

The Gaspin, a British revenue vessel, was blown up in Narragansett Bay, in 1772, and the tea ships sailed in 1773 for Charleston, Philadelphia, New York, and Boston. The colonial world held its breath in dread and expectation of their arrival, and a responsive thrill of enthusiasm ran down the coast when Boston dumped the tea into her harbor on December 16th. Now England became finally aware of the unanimous and determined attitude of her colonies, and, with kindred stubbornness, set herself to subdue them to her will.

"It was the changes, vacillation, divisions, and weaknesses of the English ministers, the utter disintegration of English parties, the rapid alterations of severity and indulgence, which had rendered all resistance to authority popular," writes one of the leading English historians of this day.[84]

A campaign of severity was in vogue from now on, and Florida had her share of it. As Turnbull, Drayton and their friends were in official disfavor since the assembly dispute, it was decided to send a man direct from England, with orders to proceed summarily to stamp out the first sign of revolutionary opinions. Colonel Tonyn, a protégé of Lord Marchmont, arrived as Governor, in March, 1774; and his first act was to issue a proclamation inviting loyal Americans to come to Florida and quit the provinces then in revolt. Florida was, by this time, the only loyal province south of Canada, and many Tories responded to his invitation, a circumstance which at once strengthened Tonyn's influence in England.

CHAPTER VIII
TURNBULL AND DRAYTON
VS. TONYN AND MOULTRIE

THE outburst of anger which met the Boston Port Bill, and the calling of the First Colonial Congress at Philadelphia show what strides the Revolution had made by this time. Florida and Georgia were the only colonies which were not represented at the Congress, and England took drastic measures to cut them off from the contagion. Tonyn's orders were to do something and do it quickly. It was up to him to prove to the anxious ministers that he could balk the whirlwind, and he proceeded to issue more proclamations of violent condemnation against the Revolutionists. In reality, Florida was little in sympathy with the movement because her settlers were still few and far between. Therefore, Drayton and Turnbull, with their friends, were inclined to smile at the impetuosity of the new Governor,—the Chief Justice, in particular, incurring the displeasure of the peppery colonel by his "caviling"[85] as Tonyn expressed it.

Moultrie retained his post as Lieutenant Governor, and attached himself to his new superior with ardor. He was still smarting under the slights which the officers of the garrison had dealt him, and he bore no love for Drayton and Turnbull for their part in the elections dispute, so it was natural for him to enlist the sympathies of Tonyn against them.

In November a plan of Drayton's for obtaining lands from the Indians came to light, and appeared to Tonyn a good opportunity to discipline his opponent. Jonathan Bryan, a friend of Drayton's uncle, who was then Governor of South Carolina, had offered him, two years before, a share in Apalachee Old Fields, a large tract of land on the St. Johns River which the Indians, he said, were willing to sell, because they were about to move back to the body of their nation. When Drayton had suggested going to Governor Grant with this measure, Bryan replied that the Governor was a hard bargainer in money matters and he preferred to have some one else use his influence directly in England to have the treaty ratified. Drayton told him that he had no influence there, but his friend, Dr. Turnbull, had, and that as that gentleman was about to sail for England, if Bryan wished to include the Doctor in the plan, he would ask his assistance. Bryan consented, and set about his dealings with the Indians, while Turnbull consulted his lawyers in England, who told him the affair was quite lawful[86] A short time before his death, George Grenville had also told Turnbull to look up such a proposition and Turnbull, with his characteristic enthusiasm, urged this one along. Bryan secured the lease of the land for ninety-nine years, and left it with the Indians to show all their people; but, in 1774, at a meeting with the Governor of Georgia, this pending treaty was discovered and, as it was unknown to the authorities, Bryan, the only person named in the transaction, stood in ill favor with them.[87] Turnbull and Drayton had not yet seen the terms of the treaty or consented to be his partners—they had simply been waiting to see what he had to offer them; but when Tonyn started to prosecute Bryan for trying to make such a treaty, Drayton took up his cause. He urged that a private company had secured lands on the Ohio River in a similar fashion and been authorized to occupy them by the Government, and that since Mr. Grenville, while Prime Minister, had advised such a course, he thought it quite permissible. There was evidently a conflict of legal opinion on this score, however, for a letter of Tonyn's to the Earl of Dartmouth refers to the latter's disapproval of such treaties.[88] That Drayton planned, nevertheless, to oppose Tonyn, is shown by the same letter. "My Lord, I am perfectly informed that Dr. Turnbull, Mr. Penman, with a few more of the Chief Justice's Creatures, are intriguing and endeavoring to raise a Faction from which I expect some hostile proceedings in our next General Sessions in December."[89] In one year, relations be-tween Tonyn and Drayton had certainly become anything but cordial; and the General Sessions in December justified the Governor's expectations. Turnbull said that the Governor insulted the Grand Jury,[90] of which he was a member. That body drew up an address to the Honorable William Drayton, giving their opinion that he was entirely blameless so far as he had been concerned in the Bryan affair.[91] In addition, Drayton wrote a complete and dignified account of his letters and conversations with Bryan and presented it to the Governor. In it he said that the only reason Bryan had approached him was because he wished to get governmental sanction for his treaty and, therefore, he did not see how the matter could be viewed as an attempt to evade the law.[92] He concluded, "From the character which, I flatter myself, I have established with all that know me, for Honour and Veracity; I hope that this Representation of my every Concern in this affair, which I avow before God to be strictly true, will set my Conduct in a favorable Light, and that if it does not totally exculpate me from the imputation of having committed an Error, it will at least relieve me from the Censure of guilt."[93] Tonyn continued to write to Germain, successor to Hillsborough as Secretary of the colonies, that "Dr. Turnbull and Mr. Drayton have associated with Bryan in his scandalous undertaking. That, my Lord, the blame must fall with an oppressive weight upon the Chief Justice"[94]—these extracts of letters have been given to show the impersonal manner of Drayton in contrast to the ever violent and vindictive language of Tonyn. The latter, throughout this correspondence, distinguished himself in the number of personal libels he collected to hurl at his opponents.

The early part of 1776, Tonyn suspended Drayton from his office for his championing of Bryan and wrote to England for sanction of his act.[95] St. Augustine and the plantations hummed with excitement and divided opinion. Drayton came of a prominent South Carolina family, and so the interest was by no means local. Tonyn warned Turnbull that his name had been mentioned in the proceedings, though he had not charged him before the Board,[96] but this did not stop the angry Scotchman in defense of his friend. He felt they were in the right and he was sure of support from his friends in the home Government, so he proceeded with a strong hand. Tonyn had said that he did not believe there were six loyal subjects in the province/1' and to disprove his assertion, Drayton's friends called a meeting of the citizens of Florida, to prepare an address of loyalty to the King, on February 27th, at Wood's Tavern. From the list of distinguished names signed to this paper, there must have been a representative gathering, though Tonyn tried to discredit it by saying that many men of no property signed their names. Turnbull parried by saying that that may have been so, "For it is not always known whether men have Property or not, but Governor Tonyn does not mention what is well known, which is, that many of them singly have more property in the Province than the Governor and Council all put together, the Lieut. Governor excepted."[97] He ended this question sensibly by stating what was true in comparison with the other colonies—"I wish, however, for the Governor's Honor and Credit of the People that he had not said anything about Property, for that of his Province is very little indeed."[98] At any rate, there are seventy-eight names signed to this interesting Address, some of them still well known in Florida, though the majority of these people left when England gave Florida back to Spain. At the bottom, Turnbull signed his name again "on behalf of upwards of two hundred families of Greeks and other Foreigners at the Smyrna settlement. The full list included:

The Humble Address of the Inhabitants of East Florida. The full list included:

A. Turnbull	William Mills
Spencer Man	Joseph Stout
Rob. Bisset	James Brown
James Penman	Fredk. Rolfes
Charles Delap	John Tennant
Will Short	George Grassell
Tho. Mowbray	Wm. Johnson
Tho. Clark	James Henderson
Henry Hares	And. Turnbull, Junr.
Ralph Laidler	Peter Bachop
George Simpson	Joseph Michael
Abraham Cooke	Jacobus Kip
G. Mid Powell	Abr. Marshall
James Tims	Wm. Taylor
John Newcomb	W. Woodvill

Donald McLean
George Lowthrup
George Rolplies
John Doran
Lewis Cuenoud
James Isaac Pouly
Samuel Reworth
Thomas Johnson
John Bunkley
Rob Bunkley
Thomas Tustin
Thomas Williamson
Alex. Bisset
Henry Sowerby
Arch Lundle
Rich Sill
Stephen White
William Reddy
Francis Philip Fatio
James Smith
Lewis Fatio
Rob. Stafford
Joseph Broomhead

Alexr. Daniel
Tho. Smart James Barns
Enoch Barton
Tho. Higgins
John Cookson
James Moncrief
Isaac Rwaz
Wm. Wilson
Patrick Robinson
Frs. Phi. Fatio, Junr.
Wm. Drayton
James Waights
William Sherwood
Alex Grant
Charles Bernard
Wm. Watson
John Mason
John Speir
A. Turnbull for upwards of two hundred Families of Greeks and other Foreigners on the Smyrna Settlement. [99]

Turnbull presided at this meeting and was appointed to carry the address to England, while a committee was selected to present a copy of it to the Governor. At the conclusion of business, most of the men lingered to discuss the topic of the day—Drayton's suspension—and as Turnbull had a copy of the defense of Drayton, he read it aloud, ending by asking those around him if they did not think Drayton had justified himself. [100] Another address of praise of Drayton's judicial character was the result of this talk, [101] and trouble grew apace from all these occurrences.

The next day the committee, consisting of Turnbull, Captain Bisset and other prominent men, [102] waited upon the Governor to present him with a copy of the address. "I, expecting that they were to deliver to me the original," wrote the pompous Tonyn to Germain, "fixed ten a Clock the next day for receiving it. Mr. Turnbull and six other gentlemen waited upon me and delivered the enclosed copy No. 1.

Van de Sande Studio, New Smyrna, Fla.

A GLIMPSE OF ONE OF THE TURNBULL CANALS, NEW SMYRNA, FLORIDA

Upon reading it I observed that I was well pleased to see such a loyal Address; but, I was surprised that there were no names subscribed. Mr. Turnbull told me, he had the original to take home to England with him. Upon which I said "Gentlemen, I cannot conceive, that, an address presented, by a private person, can be so graciously received, as it would be through His Majesty's Representative; that I could not countenance such methods of driving things out of their proper Channel; that I considered this manner of coming to me, with a copy, without names, as an insult to me, and His Majesty's Government of this Province and, that when I received an insult, I always knew how to treat it. Having said this, I immediately retired into another Room."[103] With his letter, Tonyn sent another address to the King, with the names of all his friends on it! On these men and their Negroes, he said, the Government could depend for assistance in case of invasion. "Your Lordship will perceive the contrast between these (latter) subjects and two hundred Roman Catholics fit to bear arms at the Smyrna settlement, where there has been for some time a detachment from this Garrison to keep them in order, in case of an insurrection, and for whom Mr. Turnbull in his letter to me No 5, wants further protection." This referred to the nine soldiers who had remained stationed at New Smyrna since the uprising of 1768,[104] by request from the neighboring planters.[105] Tonyn's opinion of the Minorcans was at a very low ebb at this time because they had refused to join the militia[106] which was then being raised to protect Florida from an invasion by the Revolutionists. The conclusion of this letter is an open plea for Germain's favor. "I would not trouble your Lordship with the minute details of these matters, inconsiderable in themselves, were it not that your Lordship's humanity may lead you, my Lord, to give Mr. Drayton a hearing and perhaps Mr. Turnbull, of whose conduct I shall take notice, and that your Lordship may be guarded against misrepresentation, and falsehood and may see the necessity, of the civil officers, that are within this Province, giving their assistance to Government, 1instead of flying in the Face of it, which has been the case, upon every possible opportunity, by a faction here."

On March 4th, Tonyn wrote to Turnbull, and peremptorily demanded if it were true that he had discussed Mr. Drayton's case at the meeting in Wood's Tavern.[107] Turnbull answered sarcastically, "I am desired to give Information against myself, on a subject, which your Excellency seems to think culpable. If I had done anything which had a tendency that way, it would not be prudent to inform against myself, nor could it be required of me. But as I am conscious of my own innocence, and that what I did, on the occasion you mention, was to assist a most worthy and respectable man under disagreeable Circumstances, I will relate to you, Sir, how that affair happened."[108] His account is the same as has been given, but his letter is a stinging arraignment of Tonyn. "Why am I not permitted to give my opinion in Conversation, when that opinion is founded on Conviction, and from a most intimate knowledge of Mr. Drayton in his publick and private capacities?

"If it is to gratify the Resentment which your Excellency threatened me and others with on the 28th of last Month[109] when at your own request, a committee of seven, myself included, of the oldest and principal inhabitants of this province, waited on your Excellency in a most respectful manner to present to you a Copy" etc.—"Reflect, Sir, that, after that publick threat, all will appear to spring from that motive—I beg leave also to remind your Excellency that I settled here under the Auspices of His present Majesty. I was even made happy by his Most Gracious wishes for my success in an undertaking never before attempted on so large a Scale by any private person, and that His Majesty was pleased to order His Governor of this Province to assist me as much as was in his power." Turnbull particularly drew blood by his slur on Tonyn's friends who were, indeed, not the most aristocratic in the community. "Weigh me, Sir, in the Balance against the Men who are your Informers, and I dare say, Sir, that you will find them men of little Property, Credit or Consequence, I cannot have any Enemies but such as come under this description—The Intentions of such Men are easily discoverable, Sir, by that Just and never failing Criterion, that all good Men endeavor to conciliate differences, but bad Men busy themselves in making and widening Breaches in Friendship and Mutual Confidence[110]

This letter must have given the writer some artistic satisfaction for its eloquence, but it was, certainly, not a soothing message to send an official who was touchy about his dignity. The reply is a perfect blast of fury. "It is not my Intention, and it is contrary to my very nature to encroach upon the Rights of private Judgment, but I will not dispense with the power of calling the Servants of the Crown within this Province to answer and account for their Conduct when I think them blamable. I plainly and fairly acquaint you, that I think your Behavior upon that occasion is of such a Nature that I intend to lay such Circumstances of it, as are come to my knowledge before the Council. I am not to be intimidated from doing what I conceive to be my duty from an apprehension that narrow-minded People may suspect me of Mean Resentments.—Pray, Sir, what threats do you pretend I made use of? I mentioned no Threats, I meant none—I should be sorry to be the means of any Person's ruin. I heartily sympathize with all, in disagreeable Circumstances, even when their misfortunes are premeditatedly of their own acquiring, notwithstanding frequent Reproofs and Warnings of their doing wrong indeed with no Effect. But however disagreeable it may be to me I must do my Duty." The constant source of annoyance to the ceremony-loving Tonyn comes up again in this letter. "If to this Moment I have not shown you marks of Civility and Attention it is owing to yourself, as you have not done me the favour of calling upon me, on the several Times you have been lately in Town.—I cannot omit to thank you for the favorable opinion you entertain of my Judgment in the choice I make of my Acquaintance when I am well convinced that they are of the Stamp you insinuate them to be of, I shall most certainly look out for others."[111]

RUINS OF THE OLD MISSION HOUSE, NEW SMYRNA, FLORIDA

Van de Sande Studio, New Smyrna, Fla.

CHAPTER IX
THE FLIGHT TO ENGLAND

ILLIAM DRAYTON, since his suspension, had been visiting Turnbull, and Tonyn's reply must have caused the friends much amusement, since he had not failed to storm at every sarcastic bit in Turnbull's letter; but it struck a note of warning, for Turnbull was to be suspended, and they had no room to doubt that Tonyn's resentment would not stop there. Through many channels, other warnings came to New Smyrna, and made them realize that they must now take drastic measures to protect themselves from Tonyn's anger. Turnbull said he had "received an Information from undoubted Authority, that Governor Tonyn intended to throw me, with some others, into the Dungeon in the Fort, where we must have perished in the hot Season from the Damp, and a total Exclusion of all circulating Air.—I was informed of this Intention by a gentleman of Truth and Honour, to whom the Governor had trusted this Secret. I have leave to mention his name if necessary; for he acquainted us all with Govr. Tonyn's Designs against us. I was also advised of it in a letter sent by Express to me. This letter is now in my Custody. This Imprisonment was intended because we had said that, in our opinion, Govr. Tonyn had suspended Mr. Drayton to gratify a private Resentment, and not for anything which he had done to deserve such a Punishment."[112] Turnbull, accordingly, planned to go to England with Drayton, secretly, before Tonyn could seize them.

In November, Tonyn had told Turnbull that he had no objection to the latter's going to England, but, considering the letter in which he had said Turnbull was to be charged before the Council, as a notice that he was not to leave Florida, Tonyn did not think he would dare to sail without written permission, especially since once in a tiff over writing the leave, Turnbull had said that during Grant's time such a formality had not been necessary, but that now he wished to comply with every regulation. Another aggravation—but the Governor felt secure in having Turnbull as long as he withheld the leave.

No hint of his preparations for departure reached St. Augustine, until the morning of the day a vessel was to sail, when Tonyn heard a rumor of his intentions. He called the Captain of the vessel and asked him if this were true and the Captain replied "No, not that he knew of, that he (Turnbull) had first taken passage, and then given it up."[113] Finding, however, that Turnbull was in town, the Governor sent the Deputy Clerk of the Council to him to say that if he intended to leave for England that day, the Governor wished to see him. Turnbull said he had been warned that this man was a spy who was to be appointed Secretary in his place, so he did not answer him pleasantly. He sent word to Tonyn "That he was going to see his Son on Board, and that Mr. Penman was going with him."[114] Mr. Penman was later to suffer also for his part in this affair, but, in the meantime, Turnbull and Drayton escaped to England.

On March 30th, Tonyn held a council meeting, submitted an account of all the facts here mentioned and suspended Turnbull as Secretary of the Province and Clerk of the Council. The accusations against him were, First, publicly discussing Drayton's case, Second, Presenting only a copy of the Address to the Governor, and Third, Leaving the Province without notice or permission. Two of the members of the Council who had voted against Drayton's suspension were absent from this meeting and Turnbull said they were probably not notified[115] At any rate, he had one friend there who insisted at every accusation on a minority report of his objections to this suspension. This reads "Mr. Jollie observed that he had been acquainted with Mr. Turnbull for several years, and that he could not believe that Mr. Turnbull could intend to bring the Government of this Province into contempt, and that he did not think his conduct on that occasion had that tendency."[116] "Mr. Jollie is of opinion that Mr. Turnbull ought not to be suspended at this time."[117] Mr. Jollie resigned his seat in the Council and from the Bench as Assistant Judge, as a result of these proceedings.[118]

This was certainly the action of a brave man, as well as a loyal friend, for one does not find people who are participants in an unrighteous cause sacrificing themselves so promptly. Undoubtedly, Mr. Jollie had reason to believe that Governor Tonyn's actions would not be upheld in England. This account of Turnbull's alleged misdeeds is especially interesting, because no word of censure with regard to the management of New Smyrna is to be found there, nor any reference to the Minor-cans. Tonyn had every opportunity to know of conditions at New Smyrna, for Mr. Forbes was still the visiting Minister there, and his own friend and adherent; and, if there had been anything which they, at that time, thought wrong, there is no doubt but that they would have put it down to Turnbull's discredit.

Tonyn was very anxious about what Turnbull and Drayton might say of him in England, however. He began to write Germain that this quarrel was not of his making, but had its roots far back in Grant's administration. "Sensible of the mean artifices and misrepresentations that these two gentlemen have made use of, to operate upon the minds of his Majesty's good Subjects of this Province; and that your Lordship may not imagine that this dissatisfaction has arisen, since I have had the honour of being Governor of this Province, or that it is well grounded, give me leave, My Lord, to mention the source from whence it has sprung."

About the time Governor Grant left this Province, he recommended Mr. Moultrie to be appointed Lieutenant Governor.

Mr. Turnbull expected his Friends in England would have procured him that honour.

"An enmity had subsisted between Mr. Moultrie and Mr. Drayton, Mr. Moultrie's promotion, and a considerable addition of large fortune, by the death of his father-in-law, has added envy to dislike. Mr. Turnbull's disappointment, and the malignant envy of the other, entirely corresponded, and lead them to resign their Seats in Council, and to behold every measure of internal Government in an unfavorable light." Then comes his greatest effort to discredit his enemies. "But not satisfied with that, they carried their sympathy so far as to become Patriots for the cause of America. It is notorious that these Servants of the Crown have reprobated the measures carried on by His Majesty's Ministers; and, that Mr. Turnbull in particular declared in Company, in a debate with Lt. Governor Moultrie, that America was in the right, the King's Ministers in the wrong, that Lord North would answer for the measures with his Head."[119] Such heresies must have made the Secretary for the Colonies smile when he remembered the thundering speeches of Burke in the sacred precincts of Parliament itself against these very measures of Government. Many loyal British subjects said openly that America was right, but did not believe she was wise to separate herself from England. But Tonyn tried to arouse Germain. "If such freedom was taken in Publick Company, where the King's Friends and Servants were present, what must have passed in their private Cabals? It is well known that the rebels have had exceedingly good information concerning the state of this Garrison, and of everything carrying on here."[120] Turnbull would have looked with amused disdain on the outburst in the final paragraph of this letter. "There are many facts which I might mention to your Lordship, that strongly mark their characters; but, none more than, the precipitate, mean secret manner that Mr. Turnbull took in leaving this Province."

On May 10th, Turnbull presented his loyal Address to Germain in London, to be delivered to the King, and asked an audience of the Secretary for the Colonies. The first result of this interview, comes out in a letter of stern reproof, from Germain to Governor Tonyn, on his treatment of William Drayton. "In times like the present it were much to be wished that all His Majesty's faithful subjects would forego every smaller consideration, and apply their Attention to the public Safety and Advantage—I will hope that your own good sense will lead you to set the Example of burying in oblivion every little Injury or Subject of Complaint, which appears to have been more the effect of Pique, or hasty Resentment, than any malevolence to your person, or settled purpose to disturb your Administration.

"In this light the Lords of Trade have considered Mr. Drayton's conduct toward you, and their Lordships have, upon a full Examination of the Charges brought against him, reported to His Majesty their opinion that his Suspension from his office of Chief Justice ought to be removed—and I am commanded by the King to signify to you His Majesty's Pleasure that you do accordingly remove his Suspension and reinstate him in his office of Chief Justice, and that no part of his Salary be withheld on account of his suspension."[121] A curtain must be drawn on the mortification and rage of the Governor who considered his authority so precious that he was even insulted to have an address to the King through any source than his own reports. But another part of Germain's letter gave him the cue to his revenge. It read: "The very great advantage which the public must derive from the valuable Settlement at Smyrna, gives it a Claim to particular Attention; and as, in the absence of Doctor Turnbull, occurrences may arise which will require the Aid and Protection of the Government, I must recommend it to you to be very watchful to prevent any Injury or Detriment happening to the Settlement, and to give every Encouragement in your power to promote its Growth and the Advantage of the Proprietors"[122] Tonyn proceeded to do very queer things for the growth of New Smyrna—things which now make it a vine-choked jungle behind the cheerful little American town bearing its name.

Turnbull carried out the formality of being on leave of absence from Florida, by requesting of Germain, on July 1st, an extension of the time he had mentioned to Tonyn that he would be away. He was busy preparing a memorial for the Lords Commissioners of Trade and Plantations, wherein his charges against Governor Tonyn were fully and formally set forth.[123] Germain's letter of reproof to the Governor did not reach Florida until September, and in the meantime Tonyn showed no open hostility to the settlement. On July 19th he reported that a band of Indians had broken into some of the colonists' homes, stolen clothes and robbed the beehives and cornfields. Tonyn said that he called the Indians together and told them that in his country such crimes were punishable by death, but beyond warning them he took no action.[124]

Turnbull received complaints from his son, that the Governor gave them no protection from these raids and that he had also prevented them being supplied with the staple foods, which they still bought by ship loads.[125] It was for this reason, Turnbull claimed, that the Minorcans refused to join the Battalion of militia which was then being raised.[126] At any rate, whether from their long-standing quarrel with England, their anti-Protestant feeling or their antipathy to the Governor, as Turnbull claimed, Tonyn said, "I fear by what Colonel Bisset mentions, we cannot venture to raise at Doctor Turnbull's Settlement more than one Company."[127] The probabilities are that the long absence of Turnbull, and the hostility of the Governor, had precipitated many troubles. Andrew Turnbull, Jr., his nephew, was not able to control his overseers, who were, undoubtedly, brutal to the people. These farmers had come from an island where there was no great aristocracy to oppress them, and they were independent and often impertinent by their own reports[128] but their punishments must have been out of all proportion to their offenses. Whenever they complained to young Andrew Turnbull, they had to speak through their interpreters, the very men who oppressed them.[129] The lash and irons, so frequently and cruelly used in England and the other colonies,—Virginia, for example—were new to them, and their hatred of their oppressors grew daily. Indian depredations and trouble with food shipments completed their disgust. So when the news of the successful invasion of Florida by the new American Government, hostile to England, reached them, they began to hope that their deliverance was at hand. Andrew Turnbull, Jr., wrote on September 1st, when an American Privateer appeared on the coast, "I cannot say what might be the consequence regarding the white people, as there is a good number of them at present a little discontented, and I am fully persuaded would join the Rebels immediately on their landing at Smyrna."[129] He knew by experience that it was useless to apply directly to Governor Tonyn for help, but wrote to Mr. Gordon and Colonel Bisset, who wrote to Tonyn that "This Information is very alarming, especially with regard to Dr. Turnbull's people, a great number of whom would certainly join them—those that joined them of the Smyrna Settlements, would endeavor to plunder our plantations—I shall set out immediately for Smyrna and will make the best disposition I can for the defense of the Place by arming those we can trust and disarming the suspected."[130]

Then came the letter reinstating Drayton, and the fate of New Smyrna was sealed. Tonyn wrote to Germain, "I have always been active to promote the prosperity of it (New Smyrna) although I have ever doubted of its success. Such, My Lord, has been the state of that Settlement from its Commencement, that it has been always necessary to post a military guard there, to prevent trouble and insurrection"—(those eight soldiers who acted as policemen for that whole section of the country)—"and I am sorry to acquaint your Lordship, that at this Critical Juncture, it is a thorn in our side, as I am just now obliged to reinforce that Guard to preserve internal good order, when the Troops are much wanted to oppose the depredations of the Rebels on our north frontiers."[131]

Meanwhile, Turnbull thought he was settling all his troubles in England. On September 19th,[132] and December 6th[133] he presented two Memorials before the Lords of Trade. The gist of both is the same, except that one is fuller of detail in some charges, one in others. When the first Memorial was presented, Lord Marchmont (Tonyn's sponsor) appeared before the Lords of Trade and had the charges set aside on the grounds that they included crimes other than so-called State Crimes and so did not come under the business of that body. Therefore, Turnbull prepared the second Memorial, confining himself to Tonyn's State Crimes.[134] They include the most serious accusations—everything, in fact, except disloyalty to England. He commenced by saying that Tonyn had refused "to grant lands to many Persons who had Titles to claim the same, particularly to your Memorialist, to William Drayton, James Penman, Donald Maclean and others. And the said Governor has taken upon himself to grant Lands to such as had no claim nor Right thereto, namely to Alexander Gray, Alexander Skinner, James Forbes and others, which may be proved by the Records in the Secretary's Office."[135] Second, that he had "Taken it upon him, to decide Causes cognizable in the Courts of Justice only, and also of examining into private contracts and agreements, particularly in calling for, and examining into the Validity of the Deeds of Agreement between your Memorialist and the People of the Smyrnia Settlement"[136] "Which created such a Diffidence and Apprehension of the Validity of these Deeds of Agreement as disturbed the Peace, Order and Industry of the Smyrnia Settlement so much that its Ruin and Loss of that great Property was with Difficulty prevented by your Memorialist."[137] So, evidently the contracts had been investigated before Turnbull left for England, and had been found valid, for no settlers left New Smyrna until two years after this. But the alarm of the Minorcans here referred to was due to a doubt which Tonyn circulated as to their right to own lands in Florida under the grant which Turnbull held. The old clause requiring" that the settlers be Protestants was unearthed and challenged, and the Minorcans were told that Turnbull intended to cheat them of their allotted land when their term of servitude had expired. It required little effort to spread the inference that since this could be done, it had been planned by Turnbull from the beginning. It was with difficulty that he had explained that by the same clause he could have deprived them three years after they had settled. And the damning fact remained that somebody actually could deprive them of their hard-earned land by officially revealing their religion and producing Turnbull's grant. It mattered little to them that England and not Turnbull was responsible for this policy—they hated England and longed for Spanish rule to bring again their familiar language and the Catholic religion to Florida. Their confidence in Turnbull was destroyed and his name became an anathema to them. This was the situation which Turnbull left behind him in Florida though he did not know that Tonyn would be bold enough to deliberately push on the ruin of New Smyrna in the face of ministerial disapproval. Tonyn was indeed unprincipled in all his methods, for the Memorials continued to say that he had borrowed money from many people in Florida, giving them in exchange, bills pa)'able by men in London, and these men had declared "they had none of Tonyn's money in their hands" so the bills were protested and returned to America through the hands of Mr. John Graham of Georgia and Mr. James Penman of Florida. Turnbull flatly called this swindling, and declared with withering sarcasm that as it had not been tried before in Florida, it must be termed one of Governor Tonyn's innovations![138] In addition to this practice, Tonyn had contrived to get Receipts for public work done and then refused to pay the carpenters and other workmen, so that the chief master builder refused to repair the platform for the guns in Fort George on this account.[139] Tonyn had also bought up staple provisions and put them in the hands of a monopoly to be sold at double price.[140] An accusation against Tonyn which followed this is particularly interesting because a year later Tonyn made the same charges against Turnbull. Turnbull said "That Govr. Tonyn's Cruelties to his Servants and Negroes which he often inflicts with his own Hands, (for he generally is the Executioner himself), is an intolerable Nuisance, and greatly distressing to the Inhabitants of St. Augustine; not only by the Cries of the Sufferers, and a total disregard of all Decency in the Mode of his Punishments, but also by the Severity of them, which he carries to an incredible Height of Inhumanity, and by Cruelties unheard of before in that Province."[141] Turnbull claimed that Drayton had been suspended two days before the trial of Tonyn's coachman for flogging a man to death, because Drayton would have found out that Tonyn was present and party to that crime.[142] What irony of fate it is to know that the writer of these words has, through Tonyn's friends, borne a more terrible name for cruelty than even his shocked description of the Governor's actions portrayed! Finally, by suspending Chief Justice Drayton, and Turnbull, and by accusing the last Grand Jury of being "Drayton's Creatures," he had acted from personal rancor rather than a sense of justice. "Govr. Tonyn's conduct on the whole has been such as has entirely lost him the Confidence of the People. Your Memorialist therefore prays That, for the Honour and Advantage of His Majesty's Service, and for restoring the Peace and Tranquillity of the Province of East Florida, Govr. Tonyn be removed from that Government."[143] Certainly this is a black record, but north of Florida there were thousands of Revolutionists engaged in depriving England herself of an empire, and their crimes seemed to the Lords of Trade more serious than the misdeeds of Tonyn against individuals. Moreover, here was a governor who had stuck to his post when every other Royal governor had been driven from the colonies. Turnbull could not say Tonyn had any sympathy for America's cause—far from it—he had sent Indians, privateers, proclamations, a small reign of terror by land and sea, against the colonials. Therefore, Germain, who presided at these meetings of the Lords of Trade, advised Turnbull not to insist on his complaints being heard at that time, alleging that "It would be a tedious and troublesome Business to Administration, who then had Affairs of great National Importance on their Hands." "You also, engaged, My Lord," wrote Turnbull, recalling this audience, "that Govr. Tonyn would be more cautious in future, which I then doubted, but was answered by your Lordship, that there were such Promises and Vouchers for him, that he would certainly behave better than before."[144] And so, Tonyn did not lose his office, but received another reproof from Germain.[145] and an order, from the Lords of Trade, to "Lose no time in preparing such proofs and depositions as he may think necessary for his own defense, and to give full license for the same purpose to all persons on behalf of the Memorialists."[146] Turnbull waited in London and made his defense before the Lords of Trade to that list of charges for which Tonyn had suspended him on March 30, 1776. As Drayton had already been exonerated from his part in the Bryan affair, and as Turnbull's part was even less than his, it is not necessary to relate his answer to this part of the charge. The next was that Turnbull had made use of his faction to have himself appointed, instead of the Governor, to present a "Loyal Address" to the King. Turnbull denied this, and said that the Agent of the Province had first been considered, instead of the Governor, the latter of whom "The voters objected to, as he had shown himself adverse and hostile to the meeting of the Inhabitants, suspecting that it was intended to draw up Complaints against him."[147] The last charge, Turnbull's leaving the Province without written permit had already been dismissed by Germain who himself granted Turnbull an extension of leave.

Turnbull's business in England was (concluded by April 14, 1777, when Germain wrote the result of the investigations to Governor Tonyn. It is a statesman-like document, and worthy to be quoted for its handling of the whole question.

Whitehall

14th April 1777

Governor Tonyn

Sir,

In my Letter to you of the 2d Instant, I avoided taking notice of your Suspension of Dr. Turnbull from his Office of Secretary, and of the Instances you State of his Misbehavior which induced you to take that Step; for as he had also exhibited a Complaint against you, to the Board of Trade, it necessarily became my Duty to lay the whole Matter before their Lordships, and until they should make their Report to His Majesty, no Opinion could be formed of the propriety of your Conduct.

A Discussion of this nature, especially where the Parties have many & powerful Friends who, on account of their great Property in Florida will naturally interest themselves in the Decision, soon becomes a more serious Business than the original Matter seemed to promise; and in this Case, whatever the final Determination might have been, the Consequences of the Proceeding must unavoidably have proved disagreeable to you.

The Common Rules of Justice would have required that you should have been heard in support of your Charge against Dr. Turnbull, as well as in your Defense against the Accusations brought by him against you, and I could not have advised the King to permit you to leave the Province of East Florida at such a Crisis without sending out a Person to succeed you in the Governm't on whose Ability and Zeal for His Majesty's Service I could have the same Reliance as I have upon yours. To avoid the Necessity of so disagreeable a Step, I thought it best to endeavor to get rid of the whole Matter, and which I was the more desirous of doing, as from what I had seen of it, there did not appear to be any sufficient Ground for a serious Inquiry. I took, therefore, some Pains to convince Dr. Turnbull that it was greatly (to) his Interest, and that of his Connexions, as a Planter, as well as his Duty as a Servant of the Crown to live upon good Terms with the Governor of the Province; that where nothing of Injustice or Violence could be alleged to have happened, offences proceeding from mere Mistakes, or Infirmities that were perhaps constitutional, should be passed over among Men engaged in the common Cause of supporting the Rights of the Crown & promoting the Prosperity of the Province; That, on your part, I had no doubt he would find a Disposition to bury in Oblivion every past Offence

& to show him that Civility & Attention which his great Share in the public Stake so well entitled him to, and that if he conducted himself with the same Propriety towards you, mutual confidence and Friendship must be the happy effect, an Event which must greatly serve to promote the public prosperity, by restoring Harmony among the principal people of the Province. Finding what I had said made all the Impression I could wish, & perceiving him thoroughly disposed to adopt the Mode of Conduct I had recommended, I proposed to him, that ,he should take the first Step towards a Reconciliation, and withdraw his complaint against you; That I would then withhold from the Lords of Trade all Cognizance of your Charges against him, and recommend to you to remove his Suspension, upon Condition of his making a suitable Acknowledgment of the Impropriety of his Conduct in quitting the Province without your Leave in Writing, & giving Assurance of a candid & respectful Behavior towards you in future. This proposal he very readily embraced, and as I cannot doubt his Sincerity, it now only remains with you to accept of the Conditions, and to put an End to an Altercation which must, in the present Circumstances of Affairs be very injurious to the King's Service, and highly detrimental to the Province. To afford a proper Opportunity for so desirable an Issue, I make Dr. Turnbull the Bearer of this Letter; and I shall extend it no further than to add my sincere Wishes that it may be the Occasion of restoring that good Humour & mutual Confidence among the King's Officers, which is at all times necessary, but at present is so essential to the public Safety and Advantage.

I am &c.

Geo. Germain.[148]

CHAPTER X
THE FALL OF NEW SMYRNA

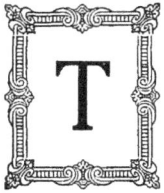

TONYN had known, since Drayton's reinstatement, which way the wind blew; and he had been proceeding industriously to execute justice upon his enemies himself. Tempting offers were made to the Minorcans to join the Militia, freedom from indentures, land in St. Augustine, assurances of protection if they ran away—all were put before them by Mr. Forbes' agents, most conspicuous of whom was Joseph Purcell, the Minorcan interpreter, who later went to work as draughtsman for Romans.

The latter part of March, a few of the settlers came to St. Augustine. The manner of their escape from New Smyrna is picturesquely told by Romans. On the pretense of making a fishing trip to the coast, (Romans must have forgotten that he had said previously the Minorcans were forbidden to fish) a small group of men received leave of absence for several days, and, on reaching the beach, at once set out to walk the eighty miles north to St. Augustine. They were hardy countrymen now, and knew their ground, so they reached St. Augustine safely, and swam Matanzas Inlet with their clothes on their heads. Tonyn simply told Germain that they were persuaded to return, but they must have received some assurances of support for, the 1st of May, ninety men appeared in town, demanding to be released from their indentures, which they declared had expired. They applied to the District Attorney, Mr. Henry Yonge, Jr., who told them they must make their complaints before a Justice of the Peace, which they accordingly did. Eighteen men were chosen to represent the rest who were told by Governor Tonyn to return and secure the crops.[149] Mr. Yonge formally reported these occurrences to the Governor and said: "I observe a number of Cruelties and indeed Murders committed by some of the Doctor's servants (which from his character certainly could never had come to his knowledge). I therefore think it my duty to lay a Copy of the Several

Depositions before your Excellency."[150] How he could have read the depositions, as sworn to by the Minorcans, and thought that Turnbull was ignorant of them is inconceivable. Either his statement is a studied pose, or he did not believe all the accusations made in these documents, for many of them were astonishing charges against Turnbull himself.

Upon first reading these short but dreadful papers, the writer was inclined to try to revise the point of view of this narrative and to show Turnbull as the villain he was painted, but the whole preceding correspondence, mass of documents and public papers were in direct conflict with such a viewpoint and clearly showed such a position historically wrong—they bore nothing but testimonials in Turnbull's favor. Then, on re-reading the Minorcans' statements, and thoroughly analyzing them, a harmonizing solution offered itself, for it was found that all the charges of violent crime were placed against Turnbull's overseers, without implicating Turnbull himself. The misdeeds with which he was personally credited, were fraudulent dealings with his settlers, or small meannesses worthy only of an irresponsible or ignorant underling or servant. The most serious charges made against Turnbull were that he refused to allow the men to leave when their indentured time was up, and even forced two witnesses to sign a forged contract against Lewis Sanche in order to prolong his term.[151]

Sanche was an overseer, but one who was in favor with those of the colony who made complaints. He said that Turnbull had ordered him to beat the people very hard and not to mind killing a man, but that he had refused. Beyond a doubt, if these charges were true, Turnbull was not the good man that he had always been considered, but the hitherto unknown events leading up to these affidavits have been related in much detail because they do not by any means bear out these statements. Turnbull was the friend and partner of a Prime Minister and a Member of the British Cabinet, he was well known to have other powerful friends[152] and to have been the social protege of that estimable man, the Earl of Shelburne.[153] The lifelong friendship of such men as William Drayton, James Penman and

Captain Bisset is testimonial enough that he could not have been such a petty schemer and monster of cruelty as these accusations describe. When it is considered that his reputation rests upon the statement of a Governor who had been for two years his outspoken enemy for other reasons, and the accusations of a few of the poor foreigners, whom no one could blame for wishing to escape servitude, it must be left to the impartial judge to declare whether their stories of Turnbull are true or not. There is no reason to believe that during the latter period of the colony, the Minorcans at times were not ill-treated by the overseers, however. Their stories of the ingenious cruelties of some of their overseers are too fully and heartrendingly told to be denied. They are the voices of the innumerable difficulties of the colony now reaching a climax. The undertaking was too large for a private concern and yet the English government was unwilling to shoulder it in such turbulent times, while the Governor was a political enemy of the proprietor, and reluctant to guard against Indian raids or to urge merchants to deliver shipments of supplies in the face of Revolutionary disturbances. Add to this the religious pressure brought to bear by Spain on the colonists and their natural distaste for a long term of service in a community of freeholders and it is easy to see how men without proper authority or scruples could lead the Minorcans to believe that the future held nothing for them at New Smyrna.

Between May and July, 1777, Tonyn said that many of the settlers were freed by the Courts and the rest set at liberty by Turnbull's attorneys.[154] As a matter of fact, the only ones freed by the Courts were a few who had been contracted for by their parents when under age. The Court of Sessions declared the others still legally bound to serve the proprietors of New Smyrna and ordered them back to the settlement.[155] But Governor Tonyn had by this time firmly implanted in their minds the idea that he would protect them if they repudiated their contracts. When they were confined to prison and a diet of bread and water until they should consent to fulfill their contracts, Tonyn sent them extra provisions and forced Mr. Penman, Turnbull's attorney, to pay for these things.[156] Encouraged by the

Governor's disregard of the Courts, the whole settlement moved bag and baggage to St. Augustine, despite the protests of Turnbull's attorneys. But no provision whatever had been made for housing or feeding these people, and sixty-five of them died (without medical attendance being offered them) after sleeping under the trees and beside old walls in the heavy rains of August and September.[157] There had not been a single death at New Smyrna during the ten months of Turnbull's absence in England, but there were ten deaths a week among these unfortunates after they came to St. Augustine. In December over a hundred women and children were begging around the Governor's house for bread. The men who were still able bodied had taken service on the cruisers or enlisted in the corps of Rangers, and the remainder were left to build miserable hovels for the women and children on the small lots assigned to them north of St. Augustine. They had no money with which to buy supplies to start farming and led a most precarious existence as fishermen along the shore of the Inlet. Tonyn was not seriously concerned about them—they had served his purpose and were left to shift for themselves.

Since Turnbull could not say that Tonyn was disloyal, he did not succeed in having him removed from office, but he returned to America triumphantly bearing his own reinstatement in office.[158] When he landed in New York in November, 1777, he received his first news of the ruin of New Smyrna and an embargo on ships held him there in a state of great uncertainty and distress for some time. Needless to say, his relations with the Governor were anything but cordial when he finally reached Florida. He found his colonists settled in St. Augustine, without provisions, his property damaged by American raiders and Indians, and crops in the worst condition they had been in since the beginning of the colony. He openly accused Tonyn of being the cause of this wholesale destruction. Some idea of the value of the larger part of the equipment at New Smyrna and of the extent of this loss is given in the account of carpentry work completed by 1777 :[159]

	Pounds
Dr. Turnbull's house	270
2 Large store houses	500
1 Smaller store house	100
Windmill	300
Indigo house	100
145 Other houses @ 35 pounds each.	5075
4 Bridges, cedar, @ 30 pounds each	120
22 Double sets of Indigo vats	1100

$$17,565$$
$$\text{or } \$37,390.01 \, \tfrac{1}{4}$$

One of Tonyn›s methods of working among the Minorcans is revealed in a short battle of words over the aforementioned Joseph Purcell, one of Tonyn›s interpreters. Turnbull accused Purcell of serving the ends of his enemies and stirring up revolt at New Smyrna; and Purcell wrote to the Governor to be exonerated, receiving in reply a letter of praise for his upright character and a broadside of condemnation for Turnbull. «You are at liberty to make use of this Letter in your Justification against the Calumnies of the Malicious,» concluded the Governor. Turnbull must have, also, accused Purcell of exaggerating the charges of the colonists, for Tonyn says, in the same letter, «I had no reason to think that in the presence of so many Witnesses, that you did not explain that Language into English without exaggeration.»[160]

Tonyn's description to Germain of his coup de grace at New Smyrna is not without grim humor. "In obedience to your Lordship's commands, I have paid, My Lord, and shall pay, particular attention to the Smyrna Settlement ; but, my Lord, I am convinced that your Lordship does not desire that I should give the least countenance to Injustice, Tyranny and Oppression.[161] He took occasion to complain that Drayton refused to have the Minorcans' case brought before him, directing another Magistrate to preside. Drayton was always careful to avoid the appearance of partisanship while in office. The judge who took his place instructed the colonists to return to New Smyrna and finish their contracts with Turnbull, a decision which would certainly have been challenged as colored by friendship for Turnbull if it had been rendered by Drayton. Tonyn calmly announced the most evident falsehood concerning the financial consequences of his actions at New Smyrna: "Whatever Ideas the gentlemen in England concerned in it (New Smyrna) have of its success, I will venture My Lord, to affirm, and I am confident that the discharging of the white people will be no real loss to them; as the expense of their and their Families' maintenance will ever equal the value of their labor."[162] Germain's opinion of his high handed course may be gathered from his reply to Tonyn.

"Whitehall
19th Feby. 1778

Govr. Tonyn

Sir

The desertion of the Smyrna Settlement by the People is an unfortunate circumstance for the province and must occasion a severe loss to the Proprietors. If it be in your power to lessen that loss, or to give them any assistance in retrieving their Affairs, I must desire you will exert your Endeavors on their behalf.

I am, etc.,
Geo. Germain."[163]

No comment on the black charges heaped against Turnbull is to be found. Tonyn had spent his thunder in England in vain, but he had accomplished his destructive purposes in Florida without official sanction. Turnbull found that the young men of the colony had been sent to help the Indians scalp the American settlers on the Georgia border, a mission which Tonyn declared was favored by England. "If this is the case, I cannot expect any redress," wrote Turnbull in great indignation at this cruelty to defenseless women and children, but he added, "If the Grenvilles join me, I am resolved to pursue this Governor of an American Province to infamy."[164] Messrs. Penman, Drayton and Bisset declared that Tonyn deliberately broke up the settlement to get recruits for his Rangers, since there were more men of fighting age in the colony than in the rest of the Province.[165]

On August 7, 1778, Turnbull wrote a curt note to Tonyn, saying that he intended to live in St. Augustine henceforth, and would act himself as Secretary and Clerk of the Council[166] Tonyn stood his ground—he replied that he could enjoy the salary, but that his conduct, since his return from England, had been so extraordinary that he would not allow him the exercise of his offices.[167] This conduct was admitted and described by Turnbull himself: "The misery and wretchedness in which I found the Smyrnean people provoked me to reproach Governor Tonyn with it in such a tone and terms as I never made use of before to any Gentleman; which contrary to his usual manner, he took very tamely."[168] But Tonyn sent some one else to do his righting for him. "A few days ago," wrote Turnbull, "he sent a big man of his connections to insult me, but he proved so much of a bully that he put up with the reproof of a good cane for his Impertinence." The old Scotchman was not to be tamed, and so Tonyn retaliated by depriving him of his Secretaryship. Though he continued to fight gamely, his ruin and the failure of his long cherished settlement weighed heavily upon Turnbull. "I do not give Tonyn or his mean Prowler Lieut. Gov. Moultrie, the Satisfaction of seeing that their underhand Machinations or avowed oppressions affect me in the least."[169] It was the harshness with which his family was treated in his absence which had wounded Turnbull most of all. Mrs. Turnbull had been kept in a constant state of terror by the governor who refused to send protection to the settlement, but sent such threats, rumors and warnings to induce her to leave her post at New Smyrna, that she kept a small vessel ready to fly at a moment's notice, to the Bahamas. Her health and spirits were for a time seriously impaired, and Turnbull vowed that "The treatment of my family in my absence can never be forgiven. "[170] I really believe," he said in the tone of fond protection which he always used when alluding to his wife, "that he is the only Person, male or female, she ever knew that would have given her such Pain, especially when without a Protector."[171]

A letter to Germain from Tonyn again begs for Turnbull's dismissal, but on the ground of disloyalty to England, very probably because of the latter's outspoken disapproval of the scalping raid into Georgia. Tonyn makes an interesting admission about the Revolution in this letter[172] "They (Turnbull and his friends) are gentlemen, but, my Lord, in all the colonies, Georgia excepted, the principal people have been at the head of this rebellion."[173] This must have been a very reluctant admission on Tonyn's part, for Turnbull's disdain had dug deep into his official pride. Twice he mentioned in letters the fact that, for two years, when Turnbull came to town, he had not paid his respects at the Governor's house, but passed by with his friends in haughty aloofness. The fact that the higher officers at the post in St. Augustine still sided with Turnbull was a similar thorn in the Governor's side, for not only did they treat him cavalierly, but their absence deprived his court of their social prestige. Tonyn accused General Prevost and Lieut. Colonel Fuser of disloyalty and affection for Turnbull's cause, adding to this list Mr. Penman and Mr. Mann.[174] The longer the Governor's list of "traitors" grew, the more creditable they appeared—the soldiers and planters who had made Florida prosperous under Governor Grant.

Both of Turnbull's partners had died, and the period for division of their grants had passed, so their heirs in England, seeing that the colonists were disbanded, now requested a division of the grants according to their agreement. Tonyn, of course, received this information officially, and though Turnbull protested that he was quite willing to divide and had filed his papers and accounts with the Attorney General, the management of the property was taken over by Tonyn. The latter said that Turnbull's conduct during these proceedings was extravagant, and it may well be imagined that the hot-headed old Scotchman, long an autocrat in Florida, fought at bay like a wounded tiger. His family was living in St. Augustine, now, his younger sons at school, his grown son and daughters joining the faction which was rocking the tiny capital with its quarrel. In one of his complaints against this friction, an interesting hint of the extent of his former travels comes out, "It is extraordinary that a man who lived long in Turkey, who wandered among wild Arabs and was even respected in Barbary, cannot live under the

English Governor of an American province."[175] The Minorcans, who lived in the section of the city assigned to them by Tonyn, did not detract from the bitterness of the feeling" on both sides, and their former condition of indenture was represented to them by the champions of the Governor as degrading and cruel. It was, verily, a tempest in a teapot. On June 24, 1778, when about one thousand Americans landed at Amelia Narrows, and started to cut a passage through, there was such dissension between the officers and their men that Colonel Fuser could not muster enough men to oppose the invaders, and had to retire and fortify St. Johns Bluff, near the mouth of the St. Johns River.[176] On August 30th of the same year, the Americans sailed down the coast and carried off thirty Negroes from New Smyrna[177] but soon after this, the brilliant campaign of General Prevost in Georgia, removed the press of the Revolution beyond the Florida boundary.

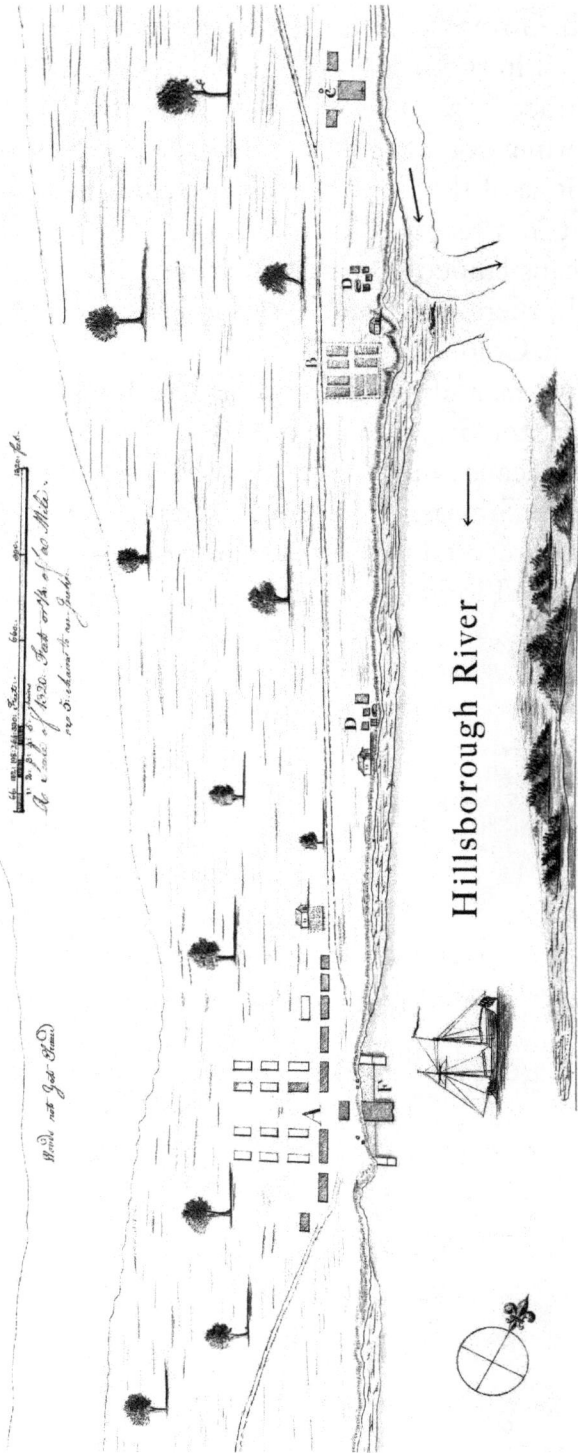

Hillsborough River

CHAPTER XI
THE FIGHT FOR THE PROPERTY

THE suit against Turnbull for division of the New Smyrna property occupied the whole of the year 1779, during which time the estate was in the hands of Moultrie and Tonyn, attorneys for the English partners. [178] It scandalized Turnbull, an ardent student of legal precedent, for Tonyn to act as attorney for his partners, judge in the suit and accuser against him. His letters to Lords Shelburne and Germain fairly bristle with wrath and outraged justice. By this time, however, things had gone so badly with the English cause in America that the harassed ministers paid no attention to him. Things were going very badly for his party in Florida too. Drayton had finally been removed for his refusal to allow the Minorcans' cases to be tried in his court, and was living at Magnolia Gardens, then known as Drayton House, near Charleston. As a final insult, Tonyn declared that he believed Turnbull intended to join Mr. Drayton in Charleston and evade paying an indebtedness charged to him on the Smyrna estate. This was all the more absurd, since Tonyn himself had said that Turnbull's reverses had left him without money, so he had nothing with which to pay anyway.[179] Then an order requiring him to pay four thousand pounds bail was issued against him on February 17, 1780, and on his failure to give it, he was placed in the custody of the Provost Marshal. Turnbull filed his demurrer to this action, in which he declared that, for his own sake, he had no intention of leaving Florida until the estate was divided, and that he had furnished every document and account in his possession to hasten the settlement. [180]

As a matter of fact, Tonyn was using Germain's request, already quoted, that he aid the partners in England in recovering their property, to ruin Turnbull. Tonyn did not at this time even know the names of the heirs of Turnbull's partners and issued his orders against Turnbull, using the name of Earl Temple, who had died previously.

Turnbull did indeed plan to leave Florida as soon as New Smyrna was divided, for he wrote to his old friend the Earl of Shelburne for a letter of introduction to Lord Cornwallis at Charleston.[181] He was still in the custody of the Provost Marshal and the illegality of the measures which had been taken against him by Tonyn was clear and bitter in his mind. His family alone was his consolation. "Mrs. Turnbull presents her Respects to your Lordship. We are happy in seeing that the part of our family which is formed turn out well, two out of three Daughters are married much to our Mind, and the third is promised. My eldest Son, after having had as liberal an Education as I could give him, has most cheerfully taken to farming as an Employment, and for a better Reason, that is, to get a living by it. My three youngest sons are at School here, and promise well. This Detail, my Lord, would be impertinent and troublesome to many, but I am not apprehensive that it will be so to your Lordship."[182]

Two days after this Turnbull wrote another long and masterly account of Tonyn's actions, to Germain, with the advice of his attorney on the many points of law which Tonyn had overridden, but the heirs of his partners, entirely in Tonyn's hands, refused to arbitrate or settle the estate except by a suit in Chancery which Turnbull could not now afford.[183]

Finally through the combined pleas of his attorney, Mr. Penman and his friends in England, he arrived at an understanding with Lady Mary Duncan and the Grenvilles, the heirs of his original partners. Though they owed Turnbull for late disbursements, and though he had secured by his efforts more additional grants of land than they, only a small part of the estate remained for Turnbull.[184] He was not allowed his liberty under any other condition than the surrender of all but a small portion of his share.[185] He accordingly relinquished claim to the other lands and henceforth the properties were owned separately.[186] This was a great relief to Turnbull as he was now free, after being in custody for one year and seven months, but he vowed that as he was the victim of extortion, he would do all in his power to recover his property. He left Florida with his family and Mr. James Penman on May 7th, in a small sailing vessel which he chartered. Another small vessel with all that remained of his personal property was wrecked on the journey north, and so very much reduced in worldly possessions, he landed in Charleston May 13th. Tonyn's malignity never slumbered, however. He had even tried to persuade the captain not to take the Turnbulls and also wrote to Sir Henry Clinton at Charleston, saying he had heard that Mr. Penman was to act as Commissary and that Drayton and Turnbull expected to be employed in the army departments there. Therefore he had taken it upon himself to say that they were men of a desperate faction and ought not to hold office in the government.[187]

As proof of Turnbull's alleged misconduct he declared that when the American army invaded Florida, Turnbull held aloof and did not offer to help make a stand. Turnbull heard of this charge and referred Germain to General Prevost to deny it, since he had traveled one hundred miles to the British camp on the St. John's to offer his services, which were accepted.[188] Thus by actual falsehood, as well as any other means in his power, Tonyn pursued his former Secretary. His influence did not reach Charleston, however, Lord Shelburne wrote to Cornwallis and Sir Guy Carleton in his behalf and Colonels Small and Moncrief and the powerful Drayton family easily convinced the authorities that Turnbull was being made a victim of personal enmity by Tonyn. So, just as Turnbull had vindicated Drayton in Florida, Drayton defended Turnbull in Charleston against their old enemy. The two men remained close friends and Drayton's name appears as executor of Turnbull's will."[189]

Turnbull arrived in Charleston May 13, 1782, and on December 14th of the same year Charleston was evacuated by the British. Turnbull wrote to Shelburne that as Tonyn held the papers he must give the Auditors of the New Smyrna Estate, he felt obliged to stay there and try to get them, rather than return to England without them.[190] In a footnote to a list of claims, with remarks by Mr. Geo. Miller[191] there is an interesting account of what happened to Turnbull under these conditions:

"Immediately after the evacuation of Charleston Dr. Turnbull and Mr. James Penman were required to become citizens, which they refusing to do, and being men of respectable character, the matter was left to the decision of a committee of the Legislature then sitting, who agreed that they should remain as His Majesty's subjects; the only instance, I believe of the kind, that happened between the Evacuation of this Province and the peace, which redounds much to their honour, since it is at once a proof of their sturdy Loyalty and the high respect in which their Characters were held."

Andrew Turnbull, Jr., also was included in the Certificates

"of their being His Majesty's subjects and in no sense Citizens of any of the United States and have produced proof to me that they pay the Alien Duty (i.e. 4% ad valorem on goods imported into the province)."

And so Turnbull stuck to his determination of remaining a British subject in the face of all suspicion. He had said to Germain, "It is probable that Govr. Tonyn flatters himself of being able to drive me, thro' Despair, to such a Step, but he will find himself grossly mistaken, for the Amor Patriae, and of the British Constitution, while it lasts, will always hold me fast as a British Subject, which, however, is not meant to imply, that I am in love with the present Ministers, nor with their Measures,"[192] he concluded dryly.

This loyalty was all the more praiseworthy when it is known that he was still in sore financial straits as a result of Germain's latest policy of simply letting the trouble with Tonyn wait until the greater question of the rebellious colonies was settled.

To relieve some of the burden of his father's large family, Nichol Turnbull had stayed at St. Augustine as Assistant to the Deputy Commissary of Provisions, and though he had a good education took the first work that offered itself, issuing rations to the garrison. The two oldest girls had married but their husbands died at the very beginning of their careers, and one young widow had returned to her father with her two children, while the other had remarried. Three sons still at school and the child of one of Turnbull's friends (who had been persecuted to his death by Tonyn, in the opinion of Turnbull) lived at home, making a family of nine people dependent upon the efforts of the doctor, now in his sixty-second year.

When Turnbull wrote again to Germain, he said he had left Florida and would never return while Tonyn was governor.[193] Germain therefore accepted his resignation and his former Deputy, Mr. Yeats, became Secretary. Mr. Yeats was the husband of Tonyn's niece and therefore very acceptable to the governor.

The state of New Smyrna by 1783 may be judged from the following description attached to one of the grants:

"I was at Smirna last in November 1783. The place was very well situated for trade being so near the Inlet; and the Country round it for planting as the land was of a good quality, the river also abounded in a remarkable degree with various kinds of fish—I had the curiosity when there to count all the houses both in Town and Country and to the best of my recollection there were some few more than one hundred fram'd buildings left standing, or unburnt, including those in the homble—Grenville's part—many of them were inhabited by Refugees at that time."(194)

Governor Tonyn's undisputed authority was short-lived, however. On September 3, 1783, a treaty was promulgated whereby Florida was ceded to Spain and the English were given eighteen months to get out or become Catholics. The heaviness of this calamity to the English inhabitants must be described to be appreciated. For twenty years the English government had induced many wealthy men to aid in the settlement of Florida and in 1778 alone nearly seven thousand loyal planters had been persuaded to leave the rebel colonies[195] so that they were now unable, on account of their open stand against America, to return to the United States. It may be imagined that Governor Tonyn was not popular with these men then. The property of the planters consisted mainly of lands and slaves, and when they were obliged to sell at once to any Spaniard willing or in any way able to buy, the result was ruinous. The British government sent a fleet of transports to Amelia Harbor at the mouth of the St. Mary's river to take the refugees away, and there ensued as melancholy a spectacle as that of the Acadian deportation from Nova Scotia. Families and friends said goodbye forever and left their beautiful Florida homes, some for England, others for Nova Scotia, the Bahamas and Jamaica. The Minorcans gave Tonyn to understand that they intended to leave also, and some actually were sent to Dominica, the Bahamas and Europe.[196] But when Governor de Zespedes came to Florida in June, 1784, he brought a promotion for Pietro Campo, the Minorcan priest, and soon the majority of the Minorcans were firmly ensconced as Spanish subjects. This seemed to be a distinct disappointment to Tonyn, who wrote Lord Sydney that he considered it a violation of the treaty of peace.[197]

Since old settlers who had moved from the colonies to Florida before the Revolution were able to return to the United States without the stigma of being refugee loyalists[198] Turnbull felt himself lucky to be received cordially in Charleston, among this number. He soon made a wide reputation in his profession, becoming one of the first members of the South Carolina Medical Society.[199]

The settling of his affairs at New Smyrna continued to be a mournful burden to him, however. On May 2, 1786, hearing that Parliament had finally decided to reimburse former Florida landowners, he made Mr. James Penman, (then living in London as a merchant) attorney for himself and his children, to present their claims for indemnity for the loss of their lands in the cession of Florida.[200] In December of the same year his partners presented a memorial of their losses also, to which the names of former Florida witnesses were attached. From this List we learn that Tonyn had been made a Major General for his services, and Grant a Lieutenant General,[201] so evidently the ministers were not displeased with the final disposition of affairs in Florida.

On March 14, 1788, Mr. Penman succeeded in getting a small part of Turnbull's claim. He had filed two, one for Turnbull himself, for real property, to the amount of £6462.10. for which he received nothing, the other for himself and children for £15057.10. for which he received £916.13.4.[202] Considering that some erstwhile Florida landowners died in want before help reached them, Turnbull was probably fortunate to have recovered the small amount he did. At any rate, it was a material recognition of his loyalty and good conduct as a British subject, after Tonyn's storms of abuse had subsided.

Both Turnbull and Drayton were active men of affairs up to the time of their deaths. Drayton was appointed Judge of the Admiralty Court of South Carolina in 1789, and died the following year. Turnbull died two years afterwards, March 13, 1792. His will[203] is a remarkable expression of his amiable and generous nature. He provided that his wife who was eleven years younger than himself, should remain as an executrix of his will whether she married again or not, and should inherit two-tenths of his estate without the power to give it away before her death, "because her good nature and love for her children might induce her to part with her share and be in distress." Gracia did not marry again, however. In a corner of the old portion of St. Philip's church yard at Charleston, now seldom unlocked, there is a small headstone, which reads:

"Sacred to the
Memory of
Maria Gracia Turnbull, Relict
and Consort of Dr. Andrew Turnbull.
She departed this life Aug. 2nd,
1798, aged 68 years."

No stone of any kind marks Turnbull's grave, but his obituary stated that he was to be buried there. This quaintly worded document, published in the Charleston Gazette, ends—"his name will long live and his virtues be held in the most pleasing remembrance, when this inconsiderable tribute of respect to his memory will be consigned to oblivion."[204]

The tide of subsequent events made strange mock of this remark. For a time everyone forgot about Florida. Scattered in other lands— back in England, away in Nova Scotia or suffering from the jealous policy of their own people in Jamaica, the English exiles of Florida gave little thought to the bitter feuds which had seemed so engrossing to them for the last few years of English rule there.

A force beyond their control had borne down upon them and swept them off forever from that strenuous, happy life, leaving them no connection with it thenceforth. Spain settled once more upon her scanty Florida nest, pursued her usual unenterprising course, and the splendid plantations, which had been built up with so much blood and toil, sank back into the forest, occasionally plundered by Indians, but more permanently injured by ignorance and neglect. Thirty-seven years afterwards, when Spain ceded Florida to the United States, of the English occupation there remained hardly a scratch upon the unkempt face of the wilderness, and the New Smyrna colony had become little more than a memory.

CORRESPONDENCE
1768-1793

Andrew Turnbull to Governor James Grant
Madeira, April 24, 1768

This goes by Mr. Hugh Orr, Master of the Betsey, a brig. I dispatch him to acquaint your Excellency thus far with six other vessels bound to St. Augustine. I left another ship fifty leagues to the Eastward with orders to make the best of his way to St. Augustine. That ship went very bad and would have detained us had I waited for him.

I have upwards of fourteen hundred men, women, and children in the eight ships, the greatest part of them from the Island of Minorca, British born subjects and a very sober industrious people. The Turkey Co. took measures to prevent my having many Greeks, however, hundreds of families will be brought from that country. This Captain Orr carries the families with the smallest children as his brig has a very good space between decks. I beg your Excellency shall take care to get them housed and situated in St. Augustine till I come.

And if Captain Orr will stay till the arrival of the other ships please to agree with him what he must have for each trip from the ships without the bar to the town to land the passengers and provisions. You will see by his charter exactly what I am to pay him. I aim to pay him one hundred and forty pounds and no more, which you may draw on Sir William Duncan for, if he does not choose to wait for my coming, which I hope will be in a week at farthest after this gets to your hands.

If there are any boats and schooners which can be assisted in landing the people from the large ships, you will please to engage them if possible, but in this and everything in which regards this affair, I beg your Excellency would please to act as may be best in your opinion which I am sure is better than mine. I shall want provisions but my people do not eat much flesh meat, however if ten or a dozen of bullocks can be sent for from the Mosquitoes they may be necessary to supply the people with fresh meat for a few days after their arrival.

I have had no letters from St. Augustine later than this time last year which makes me very anxious for my family. The ship rolls so much that I can write no more. Mr. Fitucci who is the overseer with the people will satisfy you to any other particulars you may want to know. The families are engaged to stay on our grounds ten years after they have paid the expenses of settling in the province, so that it ensures them for thirteen or fourteen years at least. I beg my complements to everybody…

I shall hoist a blue or a white ensign main topgallant masthead and beg the assistance of boats pilots etc. as soon as that signal is discovered. Captain Orr has a promissory note for eighty-four pounds which you will please to give a draft for on Sir William Duncan.

James Grant Papers

******

Earl of Hillsborough to Governor James Grant
Whitehall, May 12, 1768
I had a letter lately from Dr. Turnbull from Gibraltar, by which I find he has upwards of 1000 colonists, Greeks and others. This will be a noble addition to your infant settlement. I shall be glad to hear of their safe arrival.

James Grant Papers

******

Settlers Embarked by Doctor Turnbull for His Majesty's province of East Florida in the Levant, at Leghorn, Minorca and Gibraltar:

American Soldier	145
Betsey	120
Charming Betsey	32
Elisabeth	190
Friendship	198
Henry and Carolina	142
Hope	150
New Fortune	226
Total	1403

James Grant Papers

******

Andrew Turnbull to Sir William Duncan
St. Augustine, June 28, 1768
I arrived in St. Augustine the 26th, where I found three of the smallest of our ships with passengers, and a fourth brought me here and three more parted from me the 23rd of this month about thirty leagues from this port, but the winds continuing against them they are not yet in sight. The People by the two first ships are at work, these by the Wind are on their passage to the plantation and the 4th ships passengers are to march with me by land as soon as I can get them ashore.

The Betsey with 240 people on board being a heavy sailor lost company with us before we made the island of Madeira but as his ship is well formed in everything I am not apprehensive of anything happening. By being so long in passage from Gibraltar to here, I'm not lucky. Other ships have still a longer passage and God knows when they'll get here… In passage, twenty-three died for want of proper care, the person appointed to be the trust being ill… But if Mr. Grenville and you are not inclined to be in disburse so long, I can in that case dispose of part of our People to bring expenses and disbursement down. It won't be difficult as the conditions I have these people in are far more advantageous to the Proprietor than ever agreed on before. Notwithstanding I think it would break the heart of our own plantation, and entirely put a stop to my having any more people as they would look on themselves to be sold as slaves. However as circumstances led me beyond what was intended, I must reduce the numbers if you desire it.

As our colony is much greater than first intended, I propose to add 20,000 acres of land to first three grants, which 20,000 will be taken up in family plots, so that the whole to be divided at expiration and agreement will be 80,000 acres, one tract extending from the banks of Hillsborough River to those of St. Johns River giving each a front on both. I flatter myself of scheming into your hands very noble estates at the end.

Dundee City Archives

******

John Graham to Governor James Grant
Savannah, July 2, 1768
I found two of Dr. Turnbull's vessels had put in here ten days ago and that they had been supplied by my brother with provisions and other necessaries. One of them had sprung a leak and was obliged to be laid ashore, and the wind continuing still as favorable I thought it a good opportunity to send to the Doctor by these vessels the corn and other things that were intended to go in the East Florida, which I have accordingly done. By this the East Florida's voyage… I shall now put on board the corn first intended.

James Grant Papers

******

Andrew Turnbull to Sir William Duncan
St. Augustine, July 15, 1768
I arrived from our settlement on the Hillsborough River. Our people are fixing as fast as possible on the line of our tract which makes the banks of the Hillsborough where we have 8 miles in front. This will be all settled in a few days more with families whose houses are about 70 yards one from another. The lots of land they are to cultivate run back. As the land on the banks is very

proper for the culture of vines, cotton plants and mulberry trees for feeding silk worm, I think it will become not only a very advantageous settlement but well equal in beauty to some of the finest prospects on the Nile and as our great expense is now over I hope in two or three years to fix a second range of families on the meadows nigh the great swamp, about two miles backward from the first line. A ridge of pine lands between the first and second range will be a common to both. The edges of the extensive meadows on the side of the swamp farthest back will be a proper situation for a third range, and the banks of the St. Johns River immediately behind the last swamp, will be very proper situation for a fourth. These four lines may have a thousand farms on them in seven or eight years hence and then it will be one of the best and most advantageous tracts in America.

Expense would be too great except we have the government in maintaining the first importation by allowing us from six pence to nine pence a day a head for three-fourths of the year until their labor furnishes them some pat of their food. As to other importations, it will be easy to maintain them from the present establishments now made which will be a trifle of expense to which I am now obliged to for all our provisions are brought from Carolina and Georgia. As no minister knows the advantages of settling a country in this manner better than Lord Hillsborough I flatter myself that he will take us under his protection and assist us in the spirited manner which he is remarkable for when he sees the true interest of Great Britain is advanced by it. Seven of our ships are arrived. The eighth is a strong good ship with plenty of provisions on board so I'm not worried. As soon as I finish business here, I plan to take up my residence on the plantation and will only be in town when it can't be avoided.

Dundee City Archives

✳✳✳✳✳✳

Andrew Turnbull to Sir William Duncan
St. Augustine, July 17, 1768

I came here lately from our Plantation to settle accounts with the captains who brought our People from Europe, and also to provide many things wanted for our colony. I have begun to fix the families on the banks of the Hillsborough where we have eight miles in front. This will be all settled in farms in a few days. Each family to have about seventy yards in front on the River and to run back to as many acres as the family can cultivate. By this disposition every family or farm house will be about two hundred feet one from another and as lands on river are not only good but fit for vines, cotton plants, and mulberry trees for making silk, I flatter myself that it will not only be very advantageous settlement to the proprietors, but it will also form a fine Nilotic prospect. The Increase of families from these now imported will soon admit of furnishing a second range on the sides of the meadow nigh the swamp, about two miles back from River line. A ridge of Pine Lands may be left as a common between both. The sides of the back swamp about five miles from the river will be a proper place for a third line of farms, and a fourth may be formed on the edges of the rich marshes on St. Johns River. I mean that part of it behind and contiguous to our tracts.

If we can have aid of government in maintaining these people for nine months or one year, I can engage with that help and the sum we agreed on to be laid out, that these four lines shall have above a thousand families or farms on them in seven or eight years, which would make our Tracts become the most valuable ones in America. I only mention the maintaining these first People, for others brought afterwards would cost little, from supplies being easy from the first settlers. Consequently this first expense would be the only one necessary for Peopling this Province. This aid to us becomes the more reasonable as the want of labouring hands to raise provisions obliges us to fetch every thing from Georgia and Carolina, which almost doubles the price by expense of freights and other charges.

In a letter from Mahon I mentioned the expedient of an annual ship to bring people from that island to this place, which would be a great help to peopling this province, and I hope that will be done, if nothing is given to us for the maintenance of the Greeks and others now imported. This however would be expensive to government and in a short time would cost more money than what I think ought to be granted us. I presume, Sir William, that you might mention this to Lord Hillsborough, no minister knows the advantages which arise to a nation from this manner of people better than he does, and I flatter myself that he will assist us in that spirited manner which is remarkable, for in the advancement of the commercial interest of the nation, which is certainly the case at present, this province will soon furnish more valuable articles of commerce and in greater quantities than all the northern colonies together. But if no assistance is given to defray a part of the great expence of this first importation tho' it will damp the peopling of this country, and discourage me from future attempts towards it, I will not however, hinder our present settlement, where our people are at work and in high spirits. Seven of our ships are arrived, the eighth and missing is the largest and stoutest of them all. The East Florida Schooner is now loading provisions for us at Savannah in Georgia, and another large schooner is freighted to bring corn and rice for us from Charlestown in South Carolina.

I have desired Col. Laurens to draw on you, Sir William, for the amount which I flatter myself you will order to be punctually paid. I believe that Gov. Grant laid out more money on cattle and Negroes than I intended. The expence for the cattle is a necessary and advantageous one, but I grudge that of the Negroes, as I see that it does not succeed in the extraordinary measures of it. Besides a Negro plantation is of all things the most unpleasant, and instead of peopling a country, often risks unpeopling it. Governor Grant from spending two years in South Carolina, where they cultivate with Negroes, had prejudices in favour of that way of cultivating. But I think he will soon become a convert to our system from seeing the alertness, and quick manner of working of our people. I said nothing to Gov. Grant about what he had done as he takes great pains to do us service.

I wrote you three or four days ago almost in the same words with the first part of this letter, and I propose also to trouble you with a copy of this, which I will send by another ship. The delays of letters by sea makes it in some measure necessary to send copies.

July 27 addendum to acquaint you that the last ship is arrived with the People in good health and Spirits, tho' they have been now four months onboard without setting a foot on shore. The ship proceeds with them tomorrow to land them at the mouth of Hillsborough River.

Dundee City Archives

✳✳✳✳✳✳

Andrew Turnbull to Sir William Duncan
St. Augustine, August 2, 1768
In your last letter of the 11th March you thought it right that I avail myself of the advantages which come from furnishing People for the provinces in America. I intend it and expect to reduce the expenses we have been at for these first settlers to a moderate price. It is very just that every grantee who brings settlers here through me should contribute a part of the expense we have been

I had resolved on sparing some of the people now with me to Mr. John Murray, about as many as would cost a thousand pounds, having drawn on him for the sum, which was laid out with our money, but on proposing it I found it impossible to be done without raising a discontent from separating them. This made me desist from it and consequently I have kept them all on our account. It is imagined by some people that these foreigners will soon leave us. This is so far from being the case that I believe the greatest part of them will never remove from this spot they now settled on which it shall be my care to make them as comfortable as the circumstances will admit of. Our last ship is departed for the mouth of Hillsborough River to land the people he brought and I hope they are ashore by this time.

I have been detained here, chiefly in settling my accounts with the captains. Some endeavored to give me trouble, but they have lost their labour. I've just received your letter of 6th May and am very happy that you are paying my bills. Any demur that way would have ruined me and our scheme absolutely…

The freight of the ships are the heaviest expense we have got to pay. Providing also for so many people for almost one year will also cost a good deal, but not so much by two-thirds as maintaining the same number of people from Great Britain or Ireland, but this need not be mentioned as I flatter myself that maintaining them for six, nine, or twelve months will be at the expense of government. Governor Grant has wrote to Lord Hillsborough about it... I've now laid in and ordered provisions for at least four months, some or rather the greatest part of which is landed and forwarded to our settlement and some of it not yet ship't at Carolina. I'm now going to our plantation.

Dundee City Archives

******

Andrew Turnbull to Governor James Grant
Orange Grove (Daytona), August 22, 1768

I have the honour to inform you that Mr. Toronty's schooner was retaken here this day after the East Florida had fired one gun at her, and she is now aground in going up to the store to unload. About thirty people on got off. Some of them went of on Sir Charles Burdett's boat, some in Mr. Macdougal's canoe, and others went ashore on the South Beach, without water and bread. The chief mutineers are among the last fugitives, and therefore I intend to offer here twenty dollars a head for every one of them who shall be brought to me, and I beg your Excellency would be pleased to desire Mr. Skinner to put up such an advertisement in St. Augustine, which I think the more necessary as I imagine that most of them will cross the Mosquito Inlet and make for towns.

I have one Carlo Forni by me here. He is accused of being the ringleader in this affair. Mr. Watson, Captain Rogers, Mr. Earl, and the soldiers I brought from Mahon surprised him at the store on Friday night and drove a boat away from thence. This store they kept possession of and by that means got to the south point of the Inlet from whence I ordered some good marksmen to annoy the boats employed in emptying out the schooner which I found them doing yesterday morning early when I went down to the Inlet.

I came up here late this evening to meet Captain Rainsford, and to prevent the party with him going any farther if consistent with his orders, but as he is not yet arrived, I intend to go to the store to dispose of the prisoners, having ordered them to be confined on board the shore vessels till my going to them tomorrow morning. As I was on the beach at the Inlet this morning when the sloop and schooner appeared, I observed the surprise of the mutineers, which were so great that fifteen of them jumped into a boat and went ashore at a point on the south side of the Inlet without arms, provisions or anything other. Certainly nothing was ever more expeditious than this success or more on trial for the schooner was then within a cables length of the Bar. The villains are so much the more culpable, as they have stove all the puncheons of rum some etc, which they could not carry off...

All the wounded are recovering. Cutter almost well. Two of the mutineers were killed on Friday night and Saturday morning.

James Grant Papers

******

Andrew Turnbull to Governor James Grant
Orange Grove (Daytona), August 23, 1768

I trouble your Excellency with this to acquaint you that I thought it best to send the Carlo Forni, I mentioned in my letter of last night, and not to put him among the other prisoners as he was one of the chief mutineers. I ordered him here from Earls apprehending that his adherents and accomplices might attempt his rescue if they had been informed of his being so nigh as Earls, he arrived since yesterday about the time the others were taken prisoners by your sloop and Mr. Drayton's schooner. This Carlo pretends that the fourteen or fifteen Greeks and Italians who made their escape in Sir Charles Burdett's boat were the first promoters of the disturbance and the most active in every part of it. They have not provisions to carry them to the Havannah, so that they will certainly be obliged to put ashore on the coast to the southward.

As to the others who went off in Mr. Macdougals canoe, they cannot be far off; as that boat cannot live in a swell. I hope that the hunters will find them and the others who went away in such a fright that they did not even take a bit of bread with them or anything to subsist on. I hope the reward offered will produce most of them. If possible I'll come to town seven or eight days hence to settle with Mr. Loran and Duncan. I recollect also that the New York man has not been paid for his rum, his never having come nigh me was the reason for my forgetting that piece of business...

James Grant Papers

******

Andrew Turnbull to Governor James Grant
New Smyrna, August 25, 1768

I have the honour to acquaint your Excellency that I am now endeavouring to settle everything as before, by sending the families back to their plantations which they had left to form a body here. On examining some of the chief plotters I find that Carlo Forni has been the sole cause of all this disturbance by flattering some of the most unruly of the Greeks and Italians with hopes of great things at the Havannah. These had several consultations when at work in the woods, but the time of the execution of their scheme was not even concluded on till the morning they mutinied.

Carlo Forni then took on him to command, saying these gentlemen had done him the honour to choose him as their chief. They seem to me to have been about twenty at most at first only, but being masters of all the firearms they obliged all the rest, I mean Italians and Greeks, to join them, ordering their sentries to shoot every man who attempted to go off. They then began a general plunder not only of every thing in the stores, but also of what the Mahonese had of effects here. This booty engaged many others to join in plundering, especially after they had given leave to all to take as much rum as they pleased.

Many, however, made their escape to the woods and from thence to Earls, and many from the schooner. All that tribe of pilferers I think of punishing here. As to the plotting men, I send six of them prisoners with Captain Rainsford to take their tryals, and I hope that some of their bodies will be hung in chains in this river as pyrates.

As to Carlo Forni, he is an execrable villain. When he was taken he came on shore to ravish two young girls. I do not, however, condemn him of any intentions of murder. On the contrary, he seemed always inclined to spare every body; except one of the overseers who he ordered to be murdered, but it was not done by the refusal of the person who was to execute the orders. The loss suffered by this affair by their staving of casks of rum , wine and oil amounts to about a hundred pounds, but that of sloops is more considerable, for there was so much corn and bread with them on board that they threw most of them overboard, when they stuck on the bar on Monday morning. I cannot yet tell how much this loss may amount to but I hope it will be under two hundred pounds, which I hope to get out of the sweat of these pilferers brows before they leave me. I am sorry I cannot come to town to settle with Mr. Toronti, Mr. Gordon and Duncan, as Mr. Cutter is still confined to his bed by a wound in the groin, another in the head behind the ear, and a third which carried away three fingers of his right hand and almost cut off the other. He is now in good spirits and desires his respects to your Excellency.

Two of the mutineers were killed. One in retaking the store and another in pilfering from the Mahonese. Several are wounded but none mortally. The Greek priest was forced onto a boat with some other Greeks with whom the boat sunk and the priest was drowned. Some of the Corsican clan of Greeks were persuaded into the plot by their understanding Italian and were active in the mischief of destroying and plundering, but they were not arrived in this place when this was first thought of.

I have desired Captain Rainsford to leave twenty men, as thirty of the mutineers were lurking about the Inlett. A detachment of six with a corporal may be necessary now and then to bring some of them in. We are nigh to three of them today.

Poor Stork died yesterday morning about three hours before I got here. He seemed to be better when we left him, but they tell me that he fell into convulsions when the mutiny began and lost his senses two days afterwards.

We endeavour to come to Town next week to settle with Mr. Toronz, Mr. Gordon and Duncan. You will see, Sir, that this is wrote in a hurry, which I can not avoid at present…

James Grant Papers

******

Andrew Turnbull to Governor James Grant
New Smyrna, August 29, 1768
Your Excellency's letter came to hand yesterday afternoon. I observe what you are so kind to advise about my staying a few days till everything is settled which I intended to do as you will see by my letter of the 26th which Captain Rainsford carried to town. I thought of being in town next Sunday if possible, to settle with Mr. Torontz, Duncan and others, but I am afraid it will be a day or two later as I intend to stay till Mr. Cutter is able to go about as usual. All his wounds are in a fine way.

I gave you a very long account of this disturbance in my letter to Captain Rainsford, therefore shall not trouble you with anything further at present. Only that twelve of the most capable of the mutineers are to come to stay in Captain Regal's Schooner. The others were punished yesterday morning at the whipping post. They are all now at work and I dare say will behave well for the future.

Though this affair carries a loss with it, yet I think it a kind of lucky accident to the colony for at present it not only clears us of villains but it will keep the others in awe for the future. As to the people who are fled I intend to send some hunters after them. I have already spoke to Tompkins, he promised me three days ago to be here tomorrow. I think of sending London with him and a small party of soldiers. Davis went to St. Johns the day of the mutiny and is not yet returned.

I am much obliged to your Excellency for advertising the premium for catching these fellows. I think that most of them will be starved for want of food, but if any of them attempt to escape by land that reward for catching them will probably have a good effect. I am very sorry for six of my best rowers who the mutineers obliged to embark in Sir Charles's boats as the wind was favorable for three days after that boat went out and the weather moderate, I am afraid these people are far to the southward. But whatever is the fate of these people. I think we had great luck in stopping the schooner which was owing entirely to your Excellency having dispatched the sloop and schooner so soon, for a few hours delay would have lost her. When the two vessels came off the bar, the schooner was then behind it, and would have certainly got out next tide or in six hours after they appeared.

Mr. Cutter desires his respects to your Excellency and is sorry that the cheese he intended for you is diminished to a lump, which, however, he sends forward as it is much better than none, even that lump is something. He sends it by Captain Regal who sails down today or tomorrow with the prisoners and soldiers on board. Mr. Delachery also goes with him…

James Grant Papers

******

Governor James Grant to Sir William Duncan
St. Augustine, August 30, 1768

A vessel sails in the morning for Charlestown, Dr. Turnbull is at New Smyrna and of course can't profit of this opportunity to inform you of the State of his affairs and yours in this country. The Mutiny or Riot which was raised in the settlement by the Italians and Greeks will probably make a noise and get into the newspapers with many additions to what really happened. The affair is crushed and I'm convinced no such attempt will be made in future as they were luckily overpowered the third day notwithstanding the distance, but that you may be particularly informed of every circumstance of the affair which has come to my knowledge, I take the liberty to send you for your information only, a copy of my letter to His Majesty's Secretary of State upon that subject, in which for the future security of your settlers and other inhabitants of that part of the country I propose building a fort and establishing a garrison at Mosquito Inlet. I have pointed out a fund to defray the expense, and as Lord Hillsborough is exceedingly exact as to business I make no doubt of receiving immediate orders and directions upon it, if the plan meets with his Lordship's approbation, which probably will be the case, seems to have attention to the Greek settlement and recommends it to my care, that indeed was not necessary for my Friend the Doctor may always depend upon all the aid and assistance I can give him, and I am vastly happy that I succeeded in bringing him out of distress, in this last unlucky affair, which must have hurt the settlement if the mutineers had succeeded.

When I received the Doctors express with the first account of the riot, I was ill of a fever, but I was so uneasy at the Doctor's situation and so anxious to send him assistance, that I forgot the sickness, moved about for some hours, and employed every boat and every man civil and military who I thought could be of use in getting the two vessels in order and readiness to sail. My anxiety about the poor Doctor, was of more use to me than any medicine he could have given me, for I have been in perfect health ever since, yet take the liberty to trouble you with a new account of a cure for fever as it succeeded better with me than bark.

In the Scuffle at New Smyrna Mr. Cutter, the Doctor's principal manager, was confined as a prisoner and wounded in three places in the Head, the right hand and the groin, the poor man has lost three of his fingers but is in a fair way of

Recovery, he is very clever, very intelligent, and at the same time active, sober and faithful, his Death would have been an irreparable loss to your affairs, for he speaks all languages, and from the account I have of him from Mr. Turnbull, and from the Carolina planters who were for some days on the spot and admired Cutters management. I do not believe another man could be found to conduct such a number of people collected together from so many different countries and nations.

Poor Stork the Florida author went to New Smyrna with Mr. Turnbull, where he was taken ill and was left to come round to this place by sea, he fell into convulsions when the mutiny began, lost his senses two days after and died the 24th instant about three hours before Mr. Turnbull got back to New Smyrna.

I had the honour of receiving your letter of 5th February but I did not think it necessary to trouble you with an answer as I did not have anything in particular to communicate to you, about your East Florida affairs, and as I at that time look't every hour for Dr. Turnbull's arrival.

The Embarkation and Importation of so many people must run high, many incidental charges as I expected which the doctor could not foresee, and of course could not enter into his calculations. 'Tis no doubt an immense undertaking but the Doctor is so assiduous, so active, so attentive and in fact so fit in every respect to conduct the whole that I am very sanguine in my expectations of success from his settlements, but the Inhabitants must be kept in order and prevented from playing tricks in future, and as so large a settlement becomes an object of government you surely should be assisted in subsisting the settlers for a certain time, that is till they can reasonably be supposed to raise provisions for themselves. Such a measure I should imagine might be agreed to, tho' government may not think it advisable to pay for the importation of Inhabitants as such an aid should be apply'd for as you are precluded from any Bounty except for Greeks and they are so few in number that it is not worth taking.

James Grant Papers

******

Andrew Turnbull to Sir William Duncan
St. Augustine, September 10, 1768
The Chief of the riot (Carlo Forni) had engaged about twenty to second him, these seized the arms, and compelled above 200 men, women and children to join them, most of whom escaped from them next day, and returned to the plantations. This Carlo Forni intended to carry them all to the Havannah, where he intended to sell them as servants. This was the reason of his compelling such a number to go with him, which he effected the easier by giving them Rum in great Plenty. The Families, then fixed on their Farms, continued there 'till they heard of my being in the neighborhood; they then assembled and were

preparing to join me in order to attack the Rioters, which in the meantime was done by the two armed vessels the governor sent to our assistance, as he has already acquainted you.

Everything is now quiet, and the Families are hard at work, on their Farms which make a line of eight miles on Hillsborough River, each farm having two hundred feet front on the River, with leave to run back as far as they can cultivate. I have begun a second line with twenty Families farther back in the tracts. All these new settlers are hard at work, and ensure such success to our undertaking by their activity and Intelligence, as will certainly reimburse us of the whole of our Expense, both Capital and Interest, before my contract is finished.

All other expenses were put a stop to as soon as I arrived here. But in this I cannot stop. I must either supply them or starve them… as next year must be entirely employed in raising provisions for the year, and that following it… What may be wanted more ought indeed to be reimbursed by me, as I have not yet supplied my share having laid out of my own money no more than £3,400, as you see by the enclosed note drawn out hastily from the general accounts…

If a memorial in my name is necessary, please order it. I mention in my name along, because I imagine you would not choose to appear in it, it may seem to the world that I contracted with you to just such a number of People on your lands here at so much a head. This would make this aid have the appearance of being given to me alone, tho' it must be added to the mass of Expenses, and would be a great help to us. Our Olive Trees are sprouting out very well but most of the vines perished by the long voyage. But this is already partly supplied by the cuttings of the Madeira and other vines. Vineyards will render ten pounds an acre at least in this country.

Dundee City Archives

* * * * * *

Andrew Turnbull to Sir William Duncan
St. Augustine, September 12, 1768
I have letters from Smyrna, all are well and housing themselves for the winter in the best manner they can. I am very impatient to be among them again, but am detained supplying them with many things…

Dr. Stork had been ailing for some time when he desired to go to Smyrna with me. The fatigue of the journey made him worse, notwithstanding he would not return, but went on with me. He complained of lowness of spirits, had a small but quick pulse, and complained of a dull heavy pain under his right ribs. He said his liver was affected, and despaired of recovery, four days after his getting to Smyrna, he fell into convulsive quakings and spasms, and died three days after. I buried him there as decently as I could. I believe his affairs were not in good order which probably affected him. He died the 30th of August.

I intend to write to the Society to acquaint them on which terms I can bring settlers into this Province from the Southern parts of Europe. I intend this as an assistance to our affairs for I will not take the trouble except I can have from ten to fifteen in every hundred for our plantations. Income without expenses, this may help to make our way cheap at last. Tho' very dear at present. I do not however tell them that I propose this advantage which is little enough considering the trouble, fatigue and expense we have been at in settling this affair.

Dundee City Archives

******

Andrew Turnbull to Sir William Duncan
St. Augustine, September 21, 1768

The colonists are getting on well and I am much employed in supplying their many wants… The continual attention necessary for this and for the unavoidable necessity of providing for them daily hinders me from feeling, except at times, the apprehensions which hang over me, of your not accepting my bills. You must see the necessity of going on. Else all lost. People would not only dispense but starve for want of provisions and neglect…

When I arrived here the governor told me that he trembled for me when he considered the difficulty and expense of maintaining such a number of people in a province where everything must be broght from abroad, his apprehensions eased on my laying before him my mode of victualing, and the precautions I had taken not to be distressed for want.

Before I arrived in this country the governor had given the name of New Smyrna to our settlement. I have only changed it to Smyrnéa which is bad Greek for New Smyrna. This is only of one particular spot; I'll name the rest afterwards.

Dundee City Archives

******

Andrew Turnbull to Sir William Duncan
St. Augustine, September 22, 1768

The number of People we brought into the province being more than double the Inhabitants of this place and of the settlers in the province obliges me, at much expense and small trouble, to supply our provisions from the northern colonies, at extraordinary expense and inconvenience. This won't be felt by future settlers. Government should help maintain for at least six or nine months.

Great advantage for the colony could result from introducing settlers from Southern Europe because it would bring along different modes of culture into the province, many of which seem superior to which is generally practiced in America; and we have now a prospect before us of bringing many valuable articles of commerce to market, as cheap if not cheaper than the French and Spaniards. I mean indigo, cotton and wines. Of these, however, and other prospects which now open to me, I shall not say much more for the future until the bringing of them to market carry a confirmation of what I now flatter myself of.

Dundee City Archives

******

Andrew Turnbull to Governor James Grant
Smyrnéa, October 11, 1768
I have the honour to acquaint your Excellency that the Black Captain Cesar of the Batchelor schooner brought in here last Thursday seventeen of the runaways with Sir Charles's boat. I have taken out nine of them and send the other eight to town to take their tryal, as these eight were rather more culpable than those in Town except Carlo Forni.

James Grant Papers

******

Governor James Grant to the Earl of Hillsborough
St. Augustine, October 30, 1768
The principal Italian and Greek mutineers who I mentioned in my Letter no. 9 to have made their escape in boats have since been retaken at the Florida Keys in their way to the Havanah. There are now above twenty of them in goal, 'tis hard to fix upon the most guilty but circumstances will no doubt appear at the tryal, to determine which of them should suffer as examples to the rest, two or three will be sufficient for they'l hardly make such another attempt as not one of them has escaped.

Colonial Office Papers

******

Andrew Turnbull to Sir William Duncan
St. Augustine, October 22, 1768
Our People tried to get everything out of her, he wrote, and they found the flour not much damaged, bread all lost, and I was in great want of bread.

On my arrival at Smyrnéa 18 days ago I found our People sickly and many much disgusted from that sickness having carried off some of the oldest People and several children. This was caused by a sudden and violent storm of wind followed by incessant rain for three days. The Blast of wind uncovered some part of most of the Houses and Hutts, by which the families were exposed to wet and dangers which brought on a violent bloody flux, and carried off such as were afflicted with the scurvy, which manifested itself on many of them sometime after their arrival. An Hospital of 80 foot long was immediately built and I left them all recovering, I mean the sick, the others seeing that the Disorder proceeded from the weather, and that it was accidental recovered their Spirits and activity. Many of them now eat french Beans, pease and other vegetables of their own planting. The quick vegetation of this climate encourages them much.

Our Olive trees had new shoots of fifteen inches long in two months from their being put into the ground, this is reckoned extraordinary by the Olive men. I have also sown much seed for mulberry trees and am preparing land for our first vineyard, but as they do not give immediate profit I intend to plant provisions and cotton only next year, and shall not think of many articles of produce until the vineyards come up. The planting of cotton will be one of the most advantageous articles of cultivation.

Almost all of the Rioters who ran away for fear of punishment are now come in or brought in. Five or six of the most guilty are to take their tryals the next assizes, the other less guilty are at work and promise better behavior, their sufferings in the woods for want of food will I think deter them from future attempts to get off and the more as they found it unprofitable to get away. The many swamps and large rivers in this country make it improbable to strangers, and to those not familiar with proper conveniences for such traveling.

Despite the violent rains, most of new planters make great crops of provisions, and the Indigo and Rice made this year is very good... In looking over our Tracts the last time I was at Smyrnéa, I examined 5000 acres of marsh land which lies before our Tracts. This will be worth five pounds an acre yearly the second year after it is dyked and ditch'd in. This spot is the most valuable part of Hillsborough River.

The rains have been so violent at St. Augustine that none of the Houses held it out. This caused more sickness and fevers here than ever was known before. Now the Sky is clear and every disorder is going off.

Dundee City Archives

✲✲✲✲✲✲

Andrew Turnbull to Governor James Grant
From Smart's Mill, November 10, 1768
I am sorry that Mr. Humphry's takes the alarm so easily; I can hardly think the people can be so mad as to think of running themselves into certain danger, and as to Priest and the other dear suspects, I immagine that things are exaggerated by the Tall Tale Performers. I am much obliged to Your Excellency, however, for sending another sergeant with some healthy men. It may be necessary to keep up some force there, till I can get them supplied more regularly than I have

yet been able to do. I fancy that the want of flour has appeared hard to them. I depart tomorrow morning at day break and will endeavour to get among them as soon as possible, and shall certainly stay some time as you advise…

James Grant Papers

******

Andrew Turnbull to Governor James Grant
Smyrnéa, November 15, 1768

I have the pleasure to acquaint your Excellency that the late apprehensions here were caused by murmurings which might have been of troublesome, rather than serious consequences had they gone further without being taken notice of. The confinement of the two chief chatterers has struck a panick in the rest, and there is not so much as a whisper of discontent. I have put some of the stoutest hands to make a road of six or eight feet wide in the front of the farms that the overseers may visit the workers with more convenience, and other than has been practicable yet.

A scurvy which brought on gangrene mostly in the mouth, is almost the only disorder among us at present. The weather is fine and without a drop of rain since the 18th of last month.

I am sorry the Black Captain does not appear. Mr. Wilson promised to drive him out of that port, if he is still there I should be obliged to Mr. Skinner if he wold put Mr. Wilson in mind of his promise. The sergeant was soon sensible of his error and now accounts himself at one for former faults. He keeps his command in good order, and lends me provisions, however, as he seems to have a spirit of avarice, I hope the other sergeant will still be obliged to concur, if not departed from this place.

Mr. Macdougal, Penman and everybody on the River area are well, a Talk which met Captain Bisset have acquainted that his cotton look't very fine. Mr. Cutter and Humphreys present their respects to your Excellency. They are to be in St. Augustine about the middle of December. I don't know whether I shall come to town before that or not, as I intend to be here before they go to town.

James Grant Papers

******

Andrew Turnbull to Governor James Grant
Smyrnéa, November 21, 1768

I have the honour to inform you that Captain Taylor with command arrived here last Wednesday. Penman, Bissett and Macdougal were here yesterday to take away what they had on board the Diamond. They are well.

CORRESPONDENCE

We are all covered in white this morning with hoar frost, the thermometer was half a degree below the freezing point at sunrise, and ice as thick as a crown. We wanted a bracer, but this is a shocker. I can hardly hold the pen to write this, for our House is very summer…

James Grant Papers

******

Governor James Grant to the Earl of Hillsborough
St. Augustine, December 1, 1768

The Greeks and Italians are quiet, but they have been sickly, a seasoning no doubt was to be expected upon their landing, but it has been attended with worse consequences than I looked for. They have lost above three hundred, chiefly old people and children. Mr. Turnbull writes me that they now begin to recover fast, and that the only disorder remaining among them is a scurvy which brings on gangrenes mostly in the mouth. When their gardens are got into order, 'tis to be hoped vegetables will effectually remove the bad effects of a long and tedious voyage from the Mediterranean, the remedy is not distant as our gardens at present are much in the same situation with those in England about the end of April. At New Smyrna they should rather be farther advanced, and as seeds from England and the other parts of America are not to be depended on, I took care to save a considerable quantity for Mr. Turnbull from my own garden, of which a grain does not fail here, and of course he runs no risk of being disappointed in point of vegetables.

Twenty thousand pounds sterling at least, my Lord, have already been laid out for the embarkation of provisions and clothing of these people, so large a sum is not to be recovered but by perseverance, and a farther expense. The settlers may do a little for themselves in the course of the winter and spring, but they must be assisted for many months and clothed at least for two years before returns can reasonably be expected. Tho' they are supplied with economy and good management there is no trifling article of expence, where twelve hundred people are concerned, even salt and Indian corn exclusive of every other species of provision run high. 'Tis true they have fish the year round, oysters and shell fish in plenty during the winter months, but not withstanding those helps, till they can raise the necessaries of life for themselves, I am much afraid that the expence of supporting so large a settlement, will be found too considerable for private pockets.

I give Mr. Turnbull every little assistance in my power, and I can safely say that I am as anxious about his success as he can be himself; but unless your Lordship is pleased to take the Greek settlement under your protection and include it in the estimate for 1769, I am apprehensive that Mr. Turnbull will find great difficulty in carrying the projected plan into execution. It is upon a larger bottom than was concerted with his friends at home, and has already far exceeded double the sum which they agreed to advance, for which reason, my Lord, I am under some uneasiness about the future conduct of those gentlemen. They may probably tire of paying the large and frequent bills, which Mr. Turnbull is under an absolute necessity of drawing upon them. Their affairs certainly could not be in better hands, the Doctor is active, intelligent, and assiduous, but his friends tho' they have the highest opinion of Mr. Turnbull's integrity and ability, may possibly be alarmed at risking such large sums in a New World without a more immediate prospect of returns for their money.

What I now mention to your Lordship is entirely from private opinion for tho' I am sure the Doctor is convinced of my friendship and good wishes, he has never expressed a doubt to me of his correspondents going on, and therefore I believe he does not doubt of it. But in my situation, my Lord, I cannot avoid having many serious thoughts about a settlement which is of such consequence to this infant colony and tho' I have no reason to suspect that Mr. Turnbull's bills will meet with dishonour, I cannot help considering the dreadful situation which the Doctor and his Greeks would be reduced to if such a misfortune was to happen. A single bill being returned, My Lord, would put a total stop to his credit, and the people in that case must unavoidably perish for want, if I do not support them.

Your Lordship knows that I have no publick money, and indeed if I had a fund in my hands, I have no power to apply it for their situation. But it would be impossible to think of their starving. In such a case of necessity I must run the risk, draw upon the Treasury for the subsistence of these adventurers, and depend upon Your Lordship's protection to support me in what I do. Altho' this affair, My Lord, has hung heavy upon my mind since the landing of so great a number of people at a time, without any previous provisioning made for them, and without the consent of the other parties concerned, as the Mahonese crowded in unexpectedly upon Mr. Turnbull, I was unwilling to express the most distant doubt of his credit or success. But mentioning the circumstances to your Lordship in the manner I have done cannot hurt Mr. Turnbulls affairs…

Colonial Office Papers

＊＊＊＊＊＊

Andrew Turnbull to Sir William Duncan
St. Augustine, December 3, 1768
Our People are now recovered from an Indisposition which has been general in Carolina, Georgia, and this province. It seems to me to proceed from the astounding quantity of rain which fell this autumn, and was computed here to be at least twenty times more than last year. It carried off some of our very old People and a few of the youngest children, although it was not so violent among

us as in this place, and it was more so still in Georgia. I left everybody at work in clearing to plant in the Spring. We shall think of nothing this year but provisions and a few cottons, in the mean time our vines and olives will be coming on.

The People they are all now cheerful and contented; most of them declare that they will never leave their present settlements, and I am positive that if they are properly managed not one in ten will ever remove their present situation, both for advantage and convenience and pleasure being very engaging: every man has a large oyster bank before his door, on the side of a River alive with Fish and he finds that his land throws up an increase of every thing he puts into it. It shall be my care to make them sensible of every advantage and to profit from them... People have not only laid the foundation of peopling the province, but also for supplying other newcomers...

Dundee City Archives

******

Governor James Grant to Andrew Turnbull
St. Augustine, December 10, 1768
Bills are come back protested upon Bernard, which I have long expected, as I was absolutely certain that he he had no power to draw upon Mr. Lillingston. Joe Gray, who is deep in the scrape, has laid hold of the Negroes which Bernard hired to you, they tell me that you have advanced £25 Sterling to Bernard upon that account. If so, I am sorry for it, for you certainly will lose every shilling of the money, and if you have bought the Negroe wench from him, depend upon it she will be claimed and seized by Lord Moira's agent when he arrives, for Stanhope O'Shannon has no right to dispose of her to Bernard, and he has as little right to sell her to you, and I have just been saying to Major Moultrie who called in to tell me that Mrs. Turnbull had some thoughts of sending an Express to acquaint you that Joe Gray had laid hold of the Negroes hired to you, that you might come to town in order to recover the £25 Sterling from Bernard, which I have said would be unnecessary trouble for if you was upon the spot Bernard could not pay you a penny.

Mrs. Turnbull, Mrs. Dames, Moultrie, Box, and Catherwood dine with me tomorrow. I shall have conversation with the Greek about Bernard, she will not approve of the loss of the £25 and will say the Doctor make very bad bargain.

James Grant Papers

******

Earl of Hillsborough to Governor James Grant
Whitehall, December 10, 1768
I have received and laid before the King your dispatches by the Grenville packet numbered from 8 to 13. It has given His Majesty great concern to find that

the settlement carrying on under the direction of Doctor Turnbull, which His Majesty considers as an undertaking of great public utility and advantage, has met with obstruction and the proprietor sustained so considerable a loss from the mutineers behavior of a part of those rnialnists which had been collected at so large an expense and that they should have made so ungrateful a return for the kindness and tenderness with which they appear to have been treated. The assistance you afforded Dr. Turnbull was very reasonable and you conduct upon this occasion has met with His Majesty's approbation.

I entirely agree with the Board of Trade in the opinion they gave in 1766 of the utility of a fort at the Mosquito Inlet, and am sorry that there were any motives to deter you from carrying their Directions into execution, but as it seems highly necessary from the present state of the settlement in that neighborhood that this business should be no longer delayed I will make immediate inquiry into the agents hands and hope by the next opportunity to be able to send you His Majesty's order for carrying on this necessary work.

I am very sorry that the claimants under the pretended Spanish purchases have thought fit to decline the mode of bringing their claims to an issue, which is pointed out in His Majesty's order in council of the 3rd of December 1766 which order appears to have been calculated to give every facility to a fair trial of the right, that could in reason or justice have been desired.

It will be my duty to lay your letter upon this subject and also the paper transmitted with it, before His Majesty in council, in order that such further steps may be taken as shall be thought expedient to get rid of claims so discouraging to the settlement of East Florida, which His Majesty is well pleased to find has notwithstanding made so great a progress.

James Grant Papers

******

Andrew Turnbull to Governor James Grant
Smyrnéa, December 26, 1768
John Davis not coming to drive up the cattle as he promised, puts me to great inconvenience. I do not know what to do with that fellow. but in the meantime I have desired Mr. Humphrey to send me black Sandy, to enquire of the Indians hunting in the neighborhood of the Cowpens, for the cattle. I am afraid these Hunters mistake a steer now and then for a deer. But it will be no wonder as they see them dispersed and many of them without being marked.

My people are now almost all well, and work cheerfully. Mr. Penman's people tell me his great drain is now in the swamp, and that it is two feet deeper than the level of the water.

CORRESPONDENCE

Note enclosed for Captain Tucker:

If you can bring me a cargo of corn to this place, I engage by this to pay you four shillings more Carolina currency for it than the Charlestown price at the time of loading. With this condition however, that you take in eighty barrels of flour for me, at the usual freight from Carolina to this province. That flour is to be ship't by Colonel Laurens at Charlestown, and to be delivered here with the corn.

James Grant Papers

******

Andrew Turnbull to Sir William Duncan
Smyrnéa, January 8, 1769

Our people can not subsist here as yet, nor can anything be removed from hence, but by Sea, and at a great expense, therefore they must perish. As to me, I feel nothing for myself, for I could live, and even amuse myself among Wild Arabs, Savages or Hotentots, if I was drove to such Retreats. It is for these People and for the total loss of all that has been laid out… that I am concerned for.

To abandon these People destitute of their daily supply, without which they can not subsist. They now go on cheerfully, being convinced of the fertility of the soil of their Lands… This dread of starving being only in my Breast has no effect on our affairs. I keep everything going on with Spirit and am resolved to continue until I am forced to stop.

Dundee City Archives

******

Andrew Turnbull to the Earl of Hillsborough
Smyrnéa, January 7, 1769

This colony needs people or it fails, Turnbull stated. Roads were also needed, but people were of major importance.

The Banks of this River, which a few months ago were only marked by the different basking places of tygers, wolves, snakes, and alligators, are now covered with an industrious and cheerful People, for not only the vines and olives trees they have planted come on faster than in Europe, but every seed and plant yet tried come up and thrive.

Dundee City Archives

Governor James Grant to the Earl of Hillsborough
St. Augustine, January 14, 1769

… Carlo Forni, the Ring Leader of the Mosquetto Riot, and Guiseppi Massadoli, alias Bresiano, who wounded Mr. Cutter, Doctor Turnbull's principal manager, have been condemned and suffered as examples to others. I have reprieved and set at liberty Clatha Corrona, George Stephanopoli and Elia Medici until His Majesty's pleasure is known. Several others were tryed and acquit for want of proper evidence, which in fact was not material as two examples were quite sufficient.

Doctor Turnbull has been for some time past with his settlers, they are all in good humor, get into health, and he writes me that they go to work chearfully. If they can only raise provisions for themselves next year, my Lord, everything will be well. Produce must follow, and if Mr. Turnbull can once begin to send Rice, Indigo, Cotton, Silk, Wine or Sugar to market he and his friends may be reimbursed the expence they have been at, which runs very high indeed…

Colonial Office Papers

******

Andrew Turnbull to Sir William Duncan
Smyrnea, January 24, 1769
I have the honour to inform you of the spirit of our affairs here. My former letters were so full of apprehensions that they must have been troublesome to you, but as my fears were grounded on what you wrote me that apologies for them tho' these still hang over me, they have not abated the spirit of our affairs here.

We have not only cleared a great deal of land but have carried on other things in the meantime. The want of conveniences for unloading our provisions pointed out to us the necessity of a wharfe. This we have provided for by building a very solid stone one forty five feet breadth, and carried one hundred feet into the River. It is said to be the best in America, and I find the advantage of it already both in time and labour as we can load or unload at all times of the tide. The want of such a convenience at St. Augustine was not only a great expence to me lately from the loss of time, but also a continual Risk of staving casks, and wetting dry provisions, for there is not a wharf there at which it is possible to load or unload but two hours in twenty-four, when it is high water. The wharfage for goods brought into this part of the country will soon amount to something, for its being the most convenient place in the Southern parts of this Province for shipping, all the produce of south and north Hillsborough with that of Halifax must come here. But without a view to this, we could not have gone on without it.

Another necessary work was a Road to all the Farms, not only for the convenience of the settlers, but also that we might daily and hourly visit them all. The Road I have made for this purpose is broad enough for carriages and is carried along the front of the two tracts which is nigh eight miles. This enables us to see our workers at all hours.

As to buildings all we have as yet is a store of forty five feet long, an Hospital of eighty, and a house thirty six feet long, in which I live with the Clerks. I do not mention ovens, smiths, forges, etc. The mending of Tools, and making what cannot be found for present use employs four Smiths of whom we have very good ones, as well as every other trade necessary in a new colony which enables us to carry on everything as easily, and with as much regularity as if we had been settled for twenty years. I have everything almost ready for two magazines of eighty foot each, and 6 houses of forty foot long each all of which I hope to have up this summer.

As to our farmers, they are comfortably lodged in small houses with palmetto leaves, which makes a good kind of thatch, but I intend to lodge them in very neat houses as soon as possible to engage them to remain with us always, which they are inclined to do at present. I'll endeavor to keep them in that way of thinking.

Our chief employment at the present is cutting the woods on the lands we intend to plant this spring, and we begin to burn the cut down timber the first part of next month and then we prepare the ground for planting. All the land we now clear to be laid out in vineyards, though most of it must be in provisions for two or three years, till I can colect vines enough to plant it all. That range of vineyards to the north of the town will be about five miles in length, that to the south almost three miles. I intend also to begin the planting of olive trees to shade them in the eastern taste. We have many other little things in hands too tedious and trifling to mention.

Marriages go on fast among us, and I observe that most of the women grow bigg apace. The bad weather we met with on this coast before our arrival made many of our pregnant women miscarry. That loss is now in a fair way of being made good…

I think I mentioned in a former letter that I had taken measures to have some Indigo makers from New Orleans and the Mississippi. The Indigo made there is much better than that of Carolina. This proceeds from the Carolina People not being familiar with the proper manner of making it. They have no standard rules but go by guess work in a very uncertain and slovenly manner.

Dundee City Archives

******

Andrew Turnbull to Sir William Duncan
Smyrnéa, February 18, 1769
The need to purchase provisions in September is the main reason for the current extraordinary expenses. It was necessary to purchase all our provisions for the coming summer until a new crop will be in store in May at furthest.

As to my family, they have lived rather penuriously, this was partly of necessity as I was out of the Province, and from a Resolution which I have carried into practice which is that my salary and perquisites as Secretary of East Florida shall maintain my house in Town. As the perquisites increase I shall be able to do more, that is the reason that I have not asked the governor nor any of my friends here to take a dinner with me or drink a glass of wine at my House, which is the custom here…

Dundee City Archives

******

Andrew Turnbull to Sir William Duncan
Smyrnéa, February 19, 1769
Seasoning to the climate has been severe on our old People and young children. The fatigue of a long voyage had weakened them too much, that they cold not stand the shock of such an uncommon bad season as that of last autumn… It gave me pain, and I endeavoured to save them but could not. We have lost about 300 of them, the rest are now in health and spirits.

Two of the chiefs of the August mutiny at Smyrnea were executed here last month, others were reprieved under the gallows, all the fugitives who ran away at that time are brought in to a man, eight of the last arrived here from Providence a month ago, they all seem to be willing to atone for past misconduct. They shall pay every half penny of the Damage sustained in that affair before they get out of my hands.

Dundee City Archives

******

Governor James Grant to the Earl of Hillsborough
St. Augustine, March 4, 1769
… Doctor Turnbull's settlers get into Health, he writes me that they have cleared seven miles in front upon the river, that they have got gardens and work chearfully, but I shall never be easy in my mind about that settlement 'till they raise subsistence for themselves. Mr. Turnbull, to avoid drawing bills upon his constituents in London, runs to near bottom in point of provisions. I have always recommended to him to have six months provisions constantly in store, and have often told him that if he at any time had less than four he might from the disappointment of a vessel run the risk of starving the settlement by not following my advice, and by persisting in too nice computations, which won't do when a thousand people living in a wilderness may be deprived of subsistence by an error in calculation.

Mr. Turnbull, just as I expected, finds himself at the moment very much pinched for provisions, as his supplies have not arrived exactly to the time, and he writes me that he has only Indian corn for a month at the Mosquettos. I shall take care to prevent his being distressed, tho' I have no objection to his being a little uneasy, and therefore without telling him or anybody else, I have sent the East

Florida to Charles Town with directions to my correspondent to load her with Indian corn, and with private orders to the captain to proceed directly from Charles Town to New Smyrna, tho' I give out here that the vessel is going to Savannah for lumber and other things which are wanted.

Colonial Office Papers

******

Andrew Turnbull to Governor James Grant
Smyrnéa, March 5, 1770

I had the honor of your letter last Friday by Moncrief. His going away immediately for fear losing the tide did not give me time to answer it by him.

Debrahm's refusing his Betsy is of a piece with every thing he does and I think consistent with his character, which is mean, proud, dirty and disobliging.

I have calculated the expense of having provisions brought by land and find that it will run high. A horse cannot carry more than three or four bushels of corn. Each horse will cost two dollars a trip besides as much for a man to drive every two or three. I shall want forty loads of corn or flour a week which would cost a hundred dollars at least besides the expenses of carrying it to Smarts, and taking it away from Major Moultries. I am much obliged to you Sir for the offer of your flat to carry it to Smarts, but as the pilot boat will carry one hundred and fifty bushels of corn or flour in proportion, I beg the favor of her if she can be spared.

I would have sent Humphreys to town for the business of loading her if he had been well. He has had a return of his fever and is now in bed with it. This also prevents my coming to town and obliges me to trouble Major Moultrie to dispatch her. I have wrote to him that I would have ten barrels of pork put on board of her and to fill up with corn but if none is to be had, to fill up with flour. It will be as much as I can do to hold out three weeks longer. I have therefore desired the major to dispatch that supply as soon as possible. But if a larger vessel with a thousand or more bushels of corn should come in and if the corn can be purchased on condition of delivering it here, or of another vessel can be hired to bring it here, I have desired the Major to proffer a supply this way to that by the pilot boat.

As to writing to Charlestown or Savannah, my wants do not admit of the tardy way of doing business. In these places I must endeavor to make a shift till either the Georgia vessel, Ryal, or Buckle brings me a supply. The provisions I have in town will be sufficient for me till the latter end of May. The six hundred bushels of corn and peas which I am to have by the Georgia vessel would enable me to hold out a month longer. I look on their vessel as the most certain for I have a letter from John Graham in which he says that he will dispatch her in the beginning of February.

Woodside came to anchor on Thursday last to the northward of this bar, but so far from the land that he was not seen by the two men who were looking out for him. He came closer to the bar next day, was seen, and the pilot sent on board, but a northeaster threatened and he having only a very small rope with a grappling to ride by for he lost the only anchor he had at St. Augustine, got under sail and wrote me that having sprung a leak the night before, if the wind came northerly he would run for the Keys and as soon as he found black Caesar he would send the cargo by him to this place. Such a broken reed to trust to, that I do not depend on what I had on board. The five barrels of pork I was to spare to the soldiers is gone with the rest and the sergeant tells me that they have only one week's provisions. He sends a soldier to town to devise a supply. This letter goes by him. I am with the greatest respect…

James Grant Papers

******

Andrew Turnbull to Governor James Grant
Smyrnéa, March 18, 1769

I have the honor of your letter by the pilot boat and am much obliged to you for her. She, with the Georgia vessel came to anchor off the bar on Tuesday morning. The sloop came in the next day, but the schooner did not get in till yesterday afternoon. The westerly winds had almost filled up our inlets and as our best pilot here was sick, we durst not venture her in 'till some of the cargo was unloaded. Our wants also demanded an immediate supply, consequently no time was lost in taking out part of the cargo with our two large boats, but as this way of unloading her was slow I desired Jemmy Smith to go out to unload some of the corn with the pilot boat. He went out on Thursday morning and came in that afternoon with above two hundred bushels besides some barrels. He objected against this ship as your orders to him were to return to St. Augustine as soon as possible, however he went on my telling him that I would take the blame of it, & did not hesitate, Sir, to take that liberty with you being persuaded that the friendly assistance you mean to us all here is not confused in such circumstances.

If the pilot boat can be spared once more, it would be doing me a singular service to bring me seed potatoes. I laid by a quantity of those I had by Buckle but they sprouted before the time of planting came. I ordered one hundred and fifty bushels by the Georgia schooner and have twenty only on board her. Mr. Graham had engaged for that quantity but when they came to be loaded they were so bad that they could not take them. I expected red peas from him also but he sent me none, though there was room in the schooner for more than she brought from Georgia. He has not observed neither what I wrote him about the flour. Much business often hinders a merchant from doing things well when they are attended with a certain detail. My commissions being trifling probably came in the way when things of greater consequence requiring all his attention Perhaps there may also be a Yankee agitation which infects everybody in America. The merchants do not seem to me to do business with that attention which the orders given require. Perhaps I may be wrong and blame without reason. I send a copy of the letter I wrote him with his answer that you may judge whether he has fallen under the censure here mentioned or not. It is, however, of no consequence as to the other article except the potatoes. It was strange that only twenty bushels of seed potatoes could be found. I can now hold out two months longer. The loan paid me enables me to do this, and I can borrow as much as will serve me one month more. I have a letter from Ryal, he said he would be with me before this time, but had been delayed by Mr. Stephen Drayton's being at Charlestown.

By what I have wrote about John Graham I would not be understood that I mean to blame him so much as to excuse myself for giving you the trouble of lending the Pilot Boat to bring me seed potatoes... I had provided some, these were hurt by the frost. This loss I flattered my self would have been replaced by the hundred and fifty bushels from Georgia, but this resource also failing me I have no other choice but that of having some from St. Augustine, for twenty bushels of seed (potatoes)... would hardly be a mouthful for us. I intend to be in town about the latter end of the week. My stay will be short. I have little business there but much here in this season... The pilot boat could take in one load of wood only. I have put four small turtles on board of her for your Excellency. I am sorry I had no larger for these four were all I had.

James Grant Papers

******

Andrew Turnbull to Sir William Duncan
Smyrnéa, March 22, 1769
All of our People are in good health and spirits and have planted 1,000 grape vine cuttings, in addition to their other work.

Dundee City Archives

******

Andrew Turnbull to Sir William Duncan
St. Augustine, March 28, 1769
Our People are busy and eager and working at raising crops. In addition to that, their chief other work of late has been planting vines - 21,700 many already bearing grapes. Our Farmers find that the soil is excellent for vines... coming on very fast.

Dundee City Archives

Andrew Turnbull to Sir William Duncan
Smyrnéa, May 10, 1769

Everything comes on well. Our vines have shoots this spring of above 12 foot long already, and other growths are in proportion. 4,000 vines generally planted on one acre and one man looks after five acres, Turnbull reported, whereas 1,000 vines makes a pipe of wine at least, although I think ours will do more. Within three to five years vines give good wine grapes.

Dundee City Archives

******

Andrew Turnbull to George Grenville
St. Augustine, May 30, 1769

I readily agree with you in opinion that it is just and equitable that the division of lands cultivated and uncultivated, of Families, and of all other improvements whatever should be made after the term of our contract is elapsed in proportion to the Funds furnished by each of us, and I likewise agree that the revenue arising from the labor of our settlers during the time of our contract should be divided in like manner annually in proportion to the capital sums advanced by the three parties concerned.

Dundee City Archives

******

Andrew Turnbull to Governor James Grant
St. Augustine, May 30, 1769

I can engage to make them anything I please, and I would make them Turks tomorrow if I thought it would make them better planters for it, but this I do not intend nor to turn apostle nor act a Luther to reform them, Tho' I will answer that this will be very soon a Protestant settlement if a Clergyman is sent among them. A hundred pounds was set aside by the Board of Trade for a Greek Priest for our settlement, I brought a Priest with me but he was drowned by accident. That amount, yearly, would be a sufficient salary for a clergyman for Smirnea. But I should be sorry if a person I did not point out was named for it. An awful person might do much mischief...

James Grant Papers

******

Governor James Grant to William Knox
St. Augustine, June 26, 1769

Gentlemen at home, are heartily tired of large and frequent draughts coming upon them, which are unavoidable, and the poor Doctor from the letters he receives becomes uneasy about the fate of his bills. But in fact 'tis no wonder if his copartners are sick of the business as they have already expended £28,000. The little mite thrown in by the government should be laid to as much advantage as possible for the good of the settlers. Provisions shall be bought at a proper season of the year, and at the cheapest possible, which has not hitherto been the case, for my friend the Doctor to save his correspondents runs frequently too near, and is then obliged to pay what was asked, which in fact increased the evil he was most anxiously endeavoring to avoid.

The original error and the cause of his distress was running rashly into numbers at Minorca, and as the embarkation, feeding and future support of fourteen hundred evidently exceeded three times the funds he was allowed by agreement to carry on his plan of settlement, if Lord Hillsborough had not taken up the affair heartily upon receiving my letter, and if Mr. Bradshaw had not thought of an expedient without making this money a charge in the estimate, we should have got nothing. Of course the settlement could not have carried on, and God only knows what would have become of the Mahonese. We could not have fed them and they must have fed upon us. I talk upon the supposition that the partners in London would have stop't payment, which I think must have happened, and will I dare say still happen if government is not induced to continue the same Bounty at least for two years more…

James Grant Papers

******

Governor James Grant to Andrew Turnbull
St. Augustine, June 28, 1769

My letter of the 1st of December to the Earl of Hillsborough upon the subject of your settlement has produced an order to me to supply your colonists to the extent of two thousand Pounds Sterling, specifying service, and drawing bills accompanied with proper vouchers to the account, upon the Treasury. This subsidy is not sufficient and yet it was obtained in consequence of my representation, though the Duke of Grafton and Lord North opposed the measure, to avoid precedents of a like nature. Mr. Bradshaw thought of a method without including it in the estimate.

I had a letter from Sir William Duncan, which is kind with regard to you, but he is tired of the bills, tho' he says he'l endeavor to go on till your proposals arrive, but he informs me that he must do it alone as his copartner will advance no more 'till affairs between you are put upon another footing. I rather hope that your last bills will be paid.

If you will send me a list of provisions which will be wanted for your settlers, I shall order them to be contracted for, and sent when the proper season comes, I mean Rice and Flour, Pork and Rum, Corn and Peas 'tis hoped you'l have enough of.

James Grant Papers

THE NEW SMYRNA COLONY OF FLORIDA

Governor James Grant to the Earl of Hillsborough
St. Augustine, July 21, 1769

The £2000 allowed by His Majesty for the support of the settlement under Mr. Turnbull's direction comes very seasonally for the relief and subsistence of these adventurers. The money shall be lain out in the manner which is thought best adapted to the circumstances and necessities of the colonists, and when I draw for the amount or any part of the fund upon the Treasury, the accounts and proper vouchers shall be laid before your Lordship.

This undertaking has already cost Mr. Turnbull and his associates about £28,000. He was hurried into numbers at Minorca and had no idea of the expence and difficulties he was running himself into. His friends in London had only agreed to pay six thousand pounds and had no intention of laying out such large sums as have since been expended. They are, at this hour my Lord, £24,000 in advance if the Doctor's bills are paid, of which I have some doubt, as I have been informed that the gentlemen in London are most heartily tired of paying such large and frequent bills, which Mr. Turnbull now embarkt cannot avoid drawing. If those gentlemen should stop as I have long expected, the bounty which has been allowed will not be sufficient to maintain and clothe these colonists till they can raise provisions and other produce for their own support.

I therefore think it my duty to inform your Lordship that if Mr. Turnbull's correspondents stop payment the settlement must absolutely perish for want, if His Majesty is not most graciously pleased to continue the bounty, and even that will but just barely supply them with salt and Indian corn. If Mr. Turnbull's bills should return protested I will pay no money upon that account, the whole of the bounty shall be laid out to supply the present necessities of the colonists, for I apprehend I have nothing to do with any debt contracted prior to the order with which your Lordship has honored me.

I send your Lordship the names of the three persons reprieved, 'till His Majesty's pleasure is known, with an account of the crimes for which they were condemned. I was at a mistake and apprehended, my Lord, that His Majesty's approbation of the reprieve was sufficient, without a full pardon, according to the practice of armies abroad, and therefore omitted mentioning the crimes to your Lordship.

List of the names of the three Greeks reprieved by Governor Grant till His Majesty's pleasure is known.

George Stephanopoli–found guilty of felony for forcibly taking and carrying away a boat belonging to Sir Charles Burdett, Baronet.

Clatha Corona–found guilty of felony, for breaking open the warehouse of Doctor Turnbull and stealing from thence linnen, blankets, flour, etc

CORRESPONDENCE

Elia Medici–found guilty of felony, for killing a cow, the property of Doctor Turnbull.

Colonial Office Papers

******

Andrew Turnbull to Sir William Duncan
St. Augustine, August 2, 1769

I have 500 acres of land planted with provisions of different sorts, the drouthy months of June and July have hurt the last planting, but as we now have rains I hope that part of the crop will soon come on again.

Dundee City Archives

******

Sir William Duncan to Andrew Turnbull
London, August 4, 1769

I have received all your letters to the 27th of May, with the bills you have advised us of along with them; I can not help observing that the letters we receive from you are seldom above two months in coming, often under it. You have acknowledged the receipt of the letters we wrote to you the second of December, but none since that time though I wrote to you the beginning of January, of March, and middle of April. We have accepted all your bills to the 27th of May and I will continue to accept them for the £300 you have advised us of, more you cannot want as before that time you must have been informed of the £2000 the government has given us, either by the letters I wrote to you or Governor Grant a great many months ago; or even by the letter sent by the Board of Trade which went in April. In order to save our colony and hinder your bills from being protested, I have exceedingly distressed both Lady Mary and me and ruined all our Schemes of Amusement; and I give you fair warning that I will not accept one bill more after the £300, happen what will. I think I have already advanced 13 or 1400 more than our partner; wherefore if you should want more money at any time for the future, which I scarcely think is possible, you must write to our friend beforehand and persuade him to pay up his share, till that is done I repeat it again, I will not advance one shilling more.

The best method to reconcile both him and myself with the disagreeable situation you have brought us to, if you have not time to send us over accounts how such great sums are expended; at least let us know exactly what you have done for them. Send us over plans of the lands that are cultivated and what productions of all kinds you expect from them. Send us over exact lists of the number of inhabitants both white and black, cattle of all sorts, and what perhaps may have more effect, prevail on Governor Grant to send me over his real opinion of the situation of our affairs in East Florida. You ought not to be surprised to find we

116

are hurt. We have advanced £16,000 more than we had agreed to, and indeed more than in common prudence we ought to have done.

You, my Dear Sir, have your enemies, we all have, and though I have too good an opinion of your good heart and even of your good sense, to give credit to any insinuations in your prejudice whatever; yet the situation between our friend and me is very delicate. You know it was I that recommended you to him, wherefore for God sake make things as clear as you can to him, when he sees your care and diligence, If our settlements thrive, your fortune then becomes our affair as well as it is your own.

I have sent you the part of his last letter related to you enclosed. You will judge from that what you ought to do. I had a bill drawn on me for above £100 by one Toriano in Minorca, so you will be so good as to settle that affair with him, as I could by no means accept it.

Lady Mary and I join in our best compliments to you and Mrs. Turnbull…

Dundee City Archives

******

George Grenville to Sir William Duncan
Wotton, July 20, 1769

I was very sorry to find by your letter of the 17th which I received last night, that Dr. Turnbull has drawn fresh bills upon you for so large a sum as £1031.17, and still sorrier to see that by his letter of the 17th of May he lays in a claim for another draft of about 300 beside some trifling sums to balance his assets with the storekeepers in St. Augustine and for what running expenses he may be at which can neither be foreseen nor avoided so that I see no end to these drafts nor does Dr. Turnbull, yet we seem to be convinced of the absolute necessity there is to put an immediate stop to them.

I cannot help observing that all of the last drafts, great as they have been, are almost entirely for provisions. We were repeatedly assured that after the first crop the settlers wold raise provisions fully sufficient, at least for their own support. They've now been there above a year and in the course of this summer will be able to have raised two crops since their arrival, notwithstanding which I find that they are in a great degree to be supported at our expense till next year and then perhaps to the year after. What is Dr. Turnbull's agreement with the settlers themselves upon this article?

I am sorry to see so much of his attention given to the article of wine which as sanguine as he is, he does not hope to bring to perfection under three or four years, and which has never yet succeeded in any part of America. I heartily wish that instead of this he had at first turned his thoughts entirely to cotton and indigo and etc. which would have been of immediate profit and have defrayed some part at least of the enormous expense he has been at. He might afterwards have tried this project of wine at a less hazard.

I have already paid since our joint letter to him of the 2nd of December, which he acknowledges the receipt of, £1000: the same sum paid by you makes £3200: add to this the £2000 granted by Parliament, the £1200 you have already advanced to him, £1031:17 now drawn for & £300 of which he has given you notice of, and the sums advanced to him in this year exclusive of any sums furnished by himself and by the labor of the people, will amount already to near £8000. This I leave to your consideration who are equally interested in it with myself. You know my repeated declarations that I would upon no account go any farther after the last sums which I advanced and if I would, I really cannot do it at present without great inconvenience to myself.

The consequences of Dr. Turnbull's imprudence in drawing in this manner after the frequent notices given to him will I am sensible be very dangerous to the settlement and possibly fatal to it, but I cannot prevent it if there is no other way of raising the £1031.17 which he now draws for and of £300 which we must expect by his next letter, except by my advancing those sums. The only consideration which could prevail upon me to advance one shilling more than I have done is Dr. Turnbull's consent in his last letter that another agreement should be made between us, by which each partner may reap advantages in proportions to the sums he advances which he admits is highly reasonable and just and says is what he always intended and is willing to give every security in his power to insure those advantages in proportion to our risks and advances.

This is certainly fair in him and after his consent to it in this letter I apprehend that he would be bound to carry that agreement into execution. In return for this behavior, which is fair and candid in him, I should be very sorry to put him under the distress or disgrace of having these bills returned to him, if I could possibly help it, for which purpose therefore I will go as far as I really can do and will advance £650, that is to say half the sum now drawn for, and of the £300 draft expected from him, if you can strain a point for saving him from this dishonor, by raising the £650 which is the other half of these drafts. This is all that is in my power to do and if after the £1200 which you have already advanced you cannot consent to this, the bills must be protested unless Dr. Turnbull's own correspondents in the city will advance the money to prevent it. Whatever is done I think you must write to him immediately to represent the great difficulties which he has already brought both upon himself and us and to put an absolute stop to any other drafts upon us upon any accounts whatever for the future. He will then have the rest on the scrap of paper inclosed.

Dundee City Archives

Andrew Turnbull to Governor James Grant
Smyrnéa, August 31, 1769

As my family will live here, I have desired that some household furniture should be sent by the pilot sloop if you give leave for it, and if there is any room after taking all the provisions for the party here, and the other things wanted on the river.

Notwithstanding all the power of drought, and Egyptian swarms of worms, we shall have some thousands of bushels of peas and corn, if no other plague attacks us. I have planted about twenty-five acres of indigo for seed, it is all come up. Our sesamun also looks well.

Mrs. Turnbull presents her complements to your Excellency. She has had one severe fit of a seasoning fever, but it is now quite recovered, she thinks that the fatigue of the journey from town was the cause of it, which will probably make her apprehensive of taking another jaunt.

Rolle says that Ross would have made fifty pounds of Indigo an acre, the first cutting, if he had had his vatts ready. Much of the leaf was fallen before he began. Bisset had thirty bushels of corn per acre. Macdougal's corn looked as well as his, I should immagine that he will have as much. Penman will have some good rice, but his first planted will not yield above half a crop. Perhaps the later rains will give him a life in the second crop. He is resolved on indigo next year. Mr. Humphreys is going to London by his father's desire, he is to take a look at St. Johns River before he goes. He inclines to come out again, which I shall be glad of…

James Grant Papers

******

Governor James Grant to Andrew Turnbull
St. Augustine, September 1, 1769

I am glad to hear that Mrs. Turnbull has got the better of the indisposition with which she was vexed upon her arrival at Mosquitoes. I beg leave to assure her of my best respects. I wish she may like the place.

Mr. Fraser, the clergyman destined for St. Marks, arrived here a few days ago on board Capt. Fuller. Mrs. Fraser increased the family at sea. I have not seen her, but she is well spoke of and will be a good addition to your society. I shall send Mr. Fraser to New Smyrna as soon as he can conveniently leave this place, but I must beg your assistance to help him to a house when he goes there to prepare for Mrs. Fraser's protection.

There are eighty settlers on board Fuller for the village of Rolle, but the Esq.

and the Capt. differed, and the Member of Parliament (Rolle) was left behind to complain and protest. He will probably follow in another vessel with more adventurers.

James Grant Papers

******

Andrew Turnbull to Governor James Grant
Smyrnéa, September 9, 1769

The news of the cargo of corn being in such forwardness gave me great satisfaction. You have my hearty thanks, Sir, for the great trouble you take in conducting these affairs, which to me is of such consequence...

We keep a good lookout for the schooner. Barber brought in at eleven feet on the barr at half flood. The pilot here never misses it... I will get a house ready for the clergyman as soon as possible. I should be glad if he staid in town a couple of months till the house is ready. My own house is not yet finished, however, Mrs. Fraser... she shall not wait long without doors.

James Grant Papers

******

Andrew Turnbull to Governor James Grant
Smyrnéa, October 7, 1769

I was sorry to hear from Mr. Humphreys that Mr. Bowman had reported some things about our people being starved of hunger here, which is wide of the truth. Before I came here last Mr. Humphreys had advised that the people work't hard and were healthier than formerly and therefore thought that a small augmentation of their provisions was necessary. This augmentation consisted chiefly in rice and flour which I was obliged to diminish when I came here last as our rice and flour would soon have been at an end, but I allowed them in proportions of Indian meal and peas. The quantity of provisions which was ordered for each person per week was three quarts of corn, three quarts of peas, a quart of corn meal and a pint of fine flour made into bread or biskit, a quarter of a pound of rice, a pound of salt beef and some rum, besides green peas and pumpkins when the overseers think it necessary to give them.

What they have weekly from the store, I reckon equal to nine quarts of Indian corn, besides green peas and pumpkins from the fields and cabbages from their own little gardens. That is the allowance which has been continued to them ever since I came down last. What they had before was equal to it. The quantities mentioned above is for the families of men, women and children, which makes the share for grown people greater, as few children eat above a half of what is allowed. The pound of beef a week may seem little, notwithstanding they divide it into five parts for five days of the week. They are not fond of meat, but as a relisher within soups and pottage. They were served half a pound of meat a week in the passage from Mahon to St. Augustine, even that they did not eat sometimes. The single working men have a larger allowance, than that mentioned, especially in meat.

Captain Bisset rode throughout our plantation with me last week. He told me he was glad to see our people look so healthy and well, I am sensible, Sir, that you do not give credit to idle reports, however I thought it necessary to trouble you with this, that you may judge whether there is a foundation for such a report or not. I observed Mr. Bowman had some very large arguments in a most barbarous hard talking French, with a very worthless fellow, who I had often chastened for his laziness and groveling. I immagine it was from him that he had this extraordinary information. I did not interrupt his talk for I could hardly hear his French, tho' we saw he could speak easier than in English, and that he thought quicker and had more ideas in French than in his own language. This speech of his afforded some diversion for Bisset and me. I thought him a little weak brained.

I have received letters from Mr. Duncan lately, but Nixon wrote me that my letter with the proposals not being got to hand has made them think that I have got on their saddle horse, and am riding out of their reach. They talk of procuring orders from the Lord Chancellor and I don't know what more. I have wrote them. I have told them there will be no occasion for such orders, and that if they are resolved to employ the means of Law, they will find that the Laws of England are in full force in this Province, and vigorously put in execution. They are also very anxious about accounts not being sent on time. I have told them more than once that that department was under the care of Mr. Cutter, whose long sickness and death afterwards had distressed me in that point, but that I would get them in order as soon as I possibly could. The letter with proposals was sent to Georgia by Mr. Murray, as there was no opportunity for Charleston direct. Mr. Graham wrote me that he forwarded that packet to Colonel (Laurens) whom was desired to forward the originals and copies by the first ships for England. These are not arrived, and this delay is put down to the account of bad intentions in me, tho' chiefly owing to the long passage of this letter by Johnston. This is not using me well, and as they are not diffident of me, I will endeavour to bring about a separation of goods and chattels. We shall never be friends again. Diffadent like jealousy is hardly ever eased. I immagine that somebody has been intimating some suspicions of my intending to wrong them, which is wide of my intentions.

I have always owned myself in the wrong for bringing so many people into the Province, but, tho' this was more from accident than intention, I resolved to devote my whole time, intentions, and endeavours to make up for that error, and I even flatter myself of beginning to reimburse them next year. But while I am doing my utmost on this, they are thinking that I have intentions of keeping everything to myself, which is just the reverse of my plan. They talk't to Nixon of very violent proceedings if the proposals did not arrive before, tho' they could not be in England before the latter end of August or beginning of September…

October 9th. As the corn vessel from Charlestown does not appear I am more and more apprehensive that some accident has happened to her, and therefore beg your Excellency would please to order the December ship with corn may be hastened. Our own corn and peas will hold out two months more. Our consumption is nigh four hundred bushels of corn per month, and rather more of red and green peas. The rice being almost gone obliges me to give more corn and peas than formerly, as I have already mentioned in this letter.

I wish to have new corn, for the old we had lately was so emptied by the weevils that it was a mere shell and it did not give so much meal as the new corn does, by thirty percent. I flatter myself that new corn may be shipped in November. I have flour enough for all my people for one month at least, without making use of other corn or peas. This in case of necessity, might carry me on to the middle of January, but I shall be sorry to use it all at once, not only as it is a very expensive food, but it would be inconvenient for me to provide more. I have gathered in some fine corn but the worms have destroyed at least nine ears out of ten. My peas got a knock from the last bad weather. Notwithstanding I have a prospect of about a thousand bushels more which I reckon on, and the provisions of peas for two months.

James Grant Papers

✳✳✳✳✳✳

Governor James Grant to Andrew Turnbull
St. Augustine, October 12, 1769
I have had the pleasure to receive your letters up to the 7th current from Smyrnea and am glad to hear that Mrs. Turnbull is well pleased with her house and the prospect of a good garden…

My good Doctor don't be hurt by what Mr. Nixon writes you. Your friends in England have advanced you a great deal of money, nearly twelve thousand pounds apiece, 'tis natural for them to be anxious about so large a capital, which from your being hurried into numbers at Mahon, has been laid out without their concurrence. Far from having a diffidence of you, they have had more confidence than most men have in the money way. You must not differ with them, you are too far embark't. I mean well in what I say, they are strangers to me. I have no connection with them, my concern is and always has been for you.

The division of goods and chattels does not admit of a thought and the interposition of the Lord Chancellor could be of no utility to them, and they will easily be convinced that is not the case. They may in time have returns from the settlement if it continues under your management, but certainly the plan for future emoluments vanishes the moment you quit the direction. Of course the risk of your friends is considerable as the whole depends upon the life of a single man. We are all mortal my Dear Doctor, and if an accident happened to you there would be an end of the business, nobody would undertake or could conduct it. And there is nothing to sell. Your settlers in a body are of value, but separate them and in place of finding people to buy them you could not find people to take them off your hands, and if your friends should think of proceeding to extremities, which I am convinced will not happen.

I shall hear from the Secretary of State upon the subject, and my answer to him and to them will just be or nearly what I have now said.

James Grant Papers

******

Andrew Turnbull to Governor James Grant
Smyrnéa, October 27, 1769
In looking over the list of things ship't in the Cannon schooner, I observed that there are four whip saws which immagined would be a sufficient number for me with the four I have, but on summing up the number of feet of boards and scantlings which I intend to have for vatts, I found that I must have fifteen or sixteen saws continually at work. Fewer saws would do if my people were broken in to sawing. As they are not, I cannot expect that they will be able to do more than one-half the work of old sawyers for the first three or four months. Two of the saws I have now are almost wore out so that with sixteen more I shall not have too many, as two or three of them will be always under the file to be sharpened. If you think, Sir, that the account of tools will mount too high, the first article of falling axes in Mr. Gordon's account may be left out in another order.

I have planted fifty acres of Indigo… Bisset's Indigo begins to set out lately and he is going to do a few vatts from it this year…

James Grant Papers

******

Earl of Hillsborough to Governor James Grant
Whitehall, November 4, 1769
The crimes of George Stephanopoli, Clothia Corona, and Elia Medici having been convicted were such as were left to your own power under the authority of your commission to have pardoned them; but as you have not thought fit to do so,

CORRESPONDENCE

I am now to signify to you that His Majesty considers these persons as fit objects of mercy and that it is his pleasure that you should grant them a free pardon.

James Grant Papers

******

Andrew Turnbull to Sir William Duncan
Smyrnéa, November 9, 1769

In the meantime I go on Indigo. On January 1st I will put fifty men to building of indigo vats and have twelve sets of vats at least at work in June next when the first cutting of the weed will occur, sooner if carry over planting makes it through the Florida winter. At each processing station several separate vats would be located, including a steeper, a beater, and a lime vatt, and one for drying the indigo mud. Steepers and beaters were generally sixteen foot square each, the others were smaller, but the total project would require a large amount of timber and labor.

I asked Mr. Humphreys to show you a sketch of our lands and to give an account. More accurate plans will be sent to you later, after I engage a surveyor. Also, I plan to do an exact account of the number of our People for you, and inventory the cattle as well.

You mentioned Silk in your letter. I agree it can make money. Mulberry trees are propagated by cuttings of branches, like willows. An experimental acre of cotton had been planted at the cowpen, apparently because the price being paid for cotton was high at the time. In addition, some acres of Sesamun are planted and succeed, it yields oil, when fresh, is as sweet and wholesome as Florence oil, it will be of great use to our People. I have tried guinea corn and find it gives the greatest increase of any grain I know. It is foody and strengthening and it makes a good mixture with Indian corn.

Enclosure: Bills from Fraser and Richardson, St. Augustine, November 6, 1769, for 700 pair of shoes for your people, at a price of £95.5.4 1/2, and another bill for £92.5.4 1/2 for shoes previously ordered.

Dundee City Archives

******

Andrew Turnbull to Governor James Grant
Smyrnéa, November 10, 1769

I have the honour to acquaint your Excellency that the Cannon, Captain Smyth, arrived here on Tuesday last. His cargo in good condition, is out except some trifles. I shall dispatch a plan on Monday… with the receipts agreed upon for the cargo. This goes by way of a Boy of Cracker Johnstons who is now selling out…

I intend to begin as soon as possible to prepare for vatts, and shall think it well worth while to come to town, next first cutting in the Spring, to take some lessons from you about Indigo making.

Mrs. Turnbull presents her respects to you, Sir, and will be glad of more seeds. A villainous worm has eat all the cabbages and many other things.

James Grant Papers

******

Andrew Turnbull to Governor James Grant
Smyrnéa, November 13, 1769

As to what Mr. Gordon said about the barr, I am so far following his advice that I am getting two Beacons ready for it, also so you can get to them on foot. I'll acquaint Mr. Gordon with it. Captain Smyth of the schooner did not see the efforts the pilot made to get out, he endeavoured first to go out by a force of oars, finding that would not be, he made sails, but the gale of wind so strong he split his sails and was obliged to anchor. Smyth of the Cannon immagined the pilot was as far out as the barr, and said that if the oars had been held up as a signal he would have come in. This the pilot intended to have done, but he never was within a half-mile of the barr. Many hours labour did not gain him one hundred yards.

I have received a letter from Mr. Duncan of the 4th of August. One of my letters which acquaints him with my readiness to enter into a new agreement, has got to his hands. This seems to have given them a different (view) from what they had when Nixon wrote…

Mrs. Turnbull presents her humble respects to your Excellency. One turnip is the only thing I have yet seen from her garden. There is an appearance of something, but how it will turn out is very uncertain…

I was up at Bissets last week, he hopes to make six or seven vatts. He is ditching his land to drain it, he begins to look for land. He thinks I have some of the right sort, but perhaps not as white as that in the Environs of St. Augustine.

James Grant Papers

******

Andrew Turnbull to Sir William Duncan
Smyrnéa, November 13, 1769

In the future I plan to do business through Mr. Robert Payne, who was sent to St. Augustine as a merchant by Mr. Thomas Nixon. He will supply cheaper than others. Produce will exceed expenses and our incomes will increase every year. The bounty from Lord Hillsborough will be only for provisions purchased until we can raise our own food. Governor Grant arranged this and will hold us to the letter of the order.

Oswald, Taylor, and Elliott all will tell you that even plantations with young Negroes will not raise their own food at first. Their estates started up before ours did, and with Negroes bought at £40 Sterling each on average, yet none raised a sufficiency of food.

Potatoes are indeed a great food for here. If Negroes specially chosen can't raise own food at first, then you can't expect families–with one in three at least not fit to work, and many with one-half children, some more, to be self-sufficient. Still, we hope to raise what we need and to also raise extra to sell.

Dundee City Archives

******

Governor James Grant to Andrew Turnbull
St. Augustine, November 15, 1769
The Pilot Boat sails in the morning with six months provisions for your detachment which is to be relieved… I have sent a little to everybody–saws and bottled liquor for you, with three bottles of garden seeds for Mrs. Turnbull. As soon as the little vessel arrives, send to Carey for turtle for in this cold people are glad to eat them…

I am glad you have heard from Sir William Duncan. Things turn out from that quarter just as I expected, they are embarked and must have patience, and you'l do your best to make them returns, but they must give you time. I have wrote to Mr. Bradshaw that a second year's allowance is absolutely necessary to prevent your people from starving and eating up their neighbours. I have told him that I have applied to Lord Hillsborough and that my application will undoubtedly be laid before the Treasury, and I have mentioned Sir William Duncan's mentioning to me how much you were all obliged to him last year for forming a plan of supply. If we can carry this point I think Doctor you'l get the settlement upon a good footing without further support from your friends, who I think have behaved handsomely. You must not think of their late fears. People will be anxious about property.

My respects to Mrs. Turnbull. I have stopped Parson Fraser from going bodily to Smyrnea, don't encourage him to take such a step for he pleads authority from you. He must live in a separate house, when that is ready tell me and I'll send him, but you must not let a man, his wife and children into your house.

James Grant Papers

Andrew Turnbull to Governor James Grant
Smyrnéa, November 18, 1769

I enclose here the letters I mentioned in my last. The paragraph in question is from a letter I wrote at this place in answer to that in which they desired me to send a proposal for a new agreement. I also acquainted them in that letter that I was going to town to draw up proposals, and that I would forward them to their hands by the first opportunity. The bills mentioned are for Ryals and Buckles cargo. Sir William in one of his letters some time ago seemed to think it needless and partly blamed me for sending to New Orleans for Indigo makers. He now hopes I have dismissed them, none would be engaged, which I am glad of, for now I think them needless.

He desires a plan of the lands. Mr. Humphreys carries one with him, and other information. I wrote them about the cattle and shall give them every other satisfaction possible as soon as I can. You also see, Sir, that they would be glad to have some account of this settlement and affairs from your perspective. Your not having been here may be an objection. Penman has been here lately and Bisset frequently. They may be able to give you some information, however, I shall not mention it to them.

I do not know where Mr. Grenville got his information about using of provisions after the first year. I never said it, tho' Stork affirmed it a thousand times to Sir William, nor can I conceive how he has been led into belief that we are to have two crops this summer. He also seems to think that I give too much attention to vines. The twenty-one thousand I planted do not cover five acres of land, five thousand is the usual number to an acre. This vine land bears more proportion to what I have already planted with Indigo much less than to what I intend to plant next year. I ordered a barrel of Indigo seed from Charlestown… last February. It came to me in May and it is not only planted but almost as much more which Mr. Macdougal lent me, so that I can before hand with that advice in that you see, Sir, that they think that the £2000 bounty comes to be in my hands. If Sir William had asked Pownal about it, he must have told how it was ordered to be disposed of. I have wrote them more than once, that as you had solicited as a provision support for the settlement, you kept that in view, and the more so as the Secretary of State's were pointed as to its being laid out in that way, and that it was mostly to be employed in purchasing provisions, a small part only nails and cloathing. In the whole, however, they seem to come around again, Sir William says that I have enemies, whether this is an excuse for what he desired Nixon to write to me or is really so, I do not know, nor is it any great matter, and therefore I have mentioned nothing of Nixon's letter.

Sir William says that if we succeed my foresight shall be their care. I have no ambition that they can serve me in. I am only ambitions at present to reimburse them the sums they have laid out, which probably will require some years. I then shall think of retiring and not go out into the world again.

Though I am desired to prevail on your Excellency to give them an account of our affairs, I certainly would not have mentioned it could it have been avoided giving you unnecessary trouble. They have been giving credit to some insinuations against me, and would be glad to see it contradicted under your hand. If the spite of such a fool as the malevolent Rolle has been suggesting anything against me they ought to have wrote me about it. I would have answered every article of it without troubling your Excellency about it.

Mrs. Turnbull presents her respects to you, Sir. She begins to think about the Indigo schemes engage you so much this winter that we shall not have the honor of seeing you this year. We must flatter ourselves of it next winter. It has been cold here this week but it has not hurt the Indigo. It is with the greatest respect that I am…

James Grant Papers

******

Andrew Turnbull to Governor James Grant
Smyrnéa, November 20, 1769
I have the honour of your, Excellency's letter of the 15th Instant. The pilot boat and Warner's schooner came in here on Saturday. I sent a boat up for turtle, he lost all of his at the time I lost mine. He has caught five since which he has delivered this evening to Wallace. I have received all the saws and liquor bottles by the pilot sloop. Mrs. Turnbull presents her respects to you, Sir, and returns your thanks for the oranges and seeds. With your help her garden gets on. We have salad and greens from it in small quantities.

I am obliged to you for stopping the Parson, I will follow your advice and will lodge him in a separate house. I had heard enough of the family before to have induced me to this. I think he is lucky in not coming at present. He would have risked a dangerous fever. The party of soldiers here have been attacked, to a man, by a violent fever. Three of them died, and the rest escaped with difficulty. Clerk's family have been all ill also, one seems to be dying. For some months past, in the time of that sickness, I had not one in a hundred of my people sick, and have only lost one man for a month past, he died of consumption of a long standing. For this and other reasons January will be a better month for Mr. Fraser. As for pressing him to come soon, so far from it that I have been fighting off thro' Mr. Forbes, which he will tell you. Fraser has been plaguing me with letters, I have always begged him not to put himself to the least inconvenience but to take his own time. This was always in answer to his apology for not coming down which he was a fool for making to me, because he is to be here, he thinks himself, I believe, entirely under my direction, if you don't put him right as to that I shall acquaint him that I am only one of his parishioners, and not the person from whom he is to receive instructions or orders.

Jemmy Wallace is one of the best Indigo Crackers I have met with, he has certainly studied under an able master. He carrys some of your Indigo in his pocket, which he seems to accidently think of, he takes it out, breaks it with his nail in altar to the sunshine, then puts it under his nose with an air of certain applause. I declared that it was very fine. He swears you have much, a great deal better. He is very happy having found a piece of bad Indigo here, and is in such a hurry to get away, that I suspect he is impatient to exhibit this bit of bad Musketo Indigo in Town. I keep a little of yours to welcome Bissett with, and for John Ross to smell at, he knows from the stink when the vatt is sufficiently beat. We are in hopes of employing two or three more of the senses as auxiliaries in this operation. I immagine we are at least this, of the nose, before the northern (settleers) of the Province. We refine much here, but we make little Indigo.

I acquainted Smyth of the Cannon with what your Excellency wrote to me. He says that the officers of the custom house at Charlestown assured him that a certificate of his having landed his cargo was sufficient...

Bissett is here. He thinks your Indigo is very fine. He is looking at it every minute and declares the colour is charming. He seems to be more in love with it than with Mrs. Gordon.

James Grant Papers

******

Andrew Turnbull to Governor James Grant
Smyrnéa, November 24, 1769
Your boat being still here, I trouble you with this, to mention what I wrote before to your Excellency about desiring a third or a half of our corn provision in peas. I meant this a convenience then to assist in making your cargo for a vessel, if corn was scarce I know becomes a necessity to have part, if possible, in peas. My People have been on two thirds corn and one peas for some days past. This greater quantity of corn than peas does not agree with them so well as nigh an equal mixture, which has been their diet for about four months, except the last month when peas were more scarce than corn. This mixture agreed well with them, and they liked it. Now the quantity of Indian meal being one half more, it gripes and purges them. They are all so sensible of this inconvenience that they beg of me to augment the proportion of peas, and to take it off in Indian meal. For this I should be glad if your Excellency ordered at least a third peas if in time for the next cargo, and also in the last cargo of corn we are to have. I hope this will facilitate the loading of the schooners, for it is reported here that

the crop of peas have been good in Carolina and Georgia. I believe the red pea is generally in abundance, for my agreement with Buckle last May was to have red peas at two shillings currency per bushel cheaper than corn, and black eyed peas at the same price of corn. Either of them go as far with me as corn without the trouble and waste of grinding.

I forgot to mention to your Excellency that I am almost always obliged to put my sick on a rice diet. Tho' we have very few ailing, yet there are continually some, which makes a daily consumption of rice. I have but two barrels left, therefore wold be glad of between twenty and thirty barrels, if it can be done. The small rice which is sold at half price might also be purchased, if corn is dear, it would help out in victualing, but I apprehend that rice will rise as corn is dear. All this I submit, however, to your better judgment and am sorry to be so troublesome, but your Excellency will easily perceive that the unforseen circumstances mentioned have obliged me to alter my opinion in those parts of provisions.

I have desired Mr. Gordon to provide thirty bushels of Indigo seed for me, and as I have only got twenty bushels from Mr. Fairlamb. I intend to desire Mr. Gordon to send me fifty in all, for fear of being obliged to a second planting which may perhaps be the case in a dry season. I have desired him to charge the cost of the Indigo seed to my account.

James Grant Papers

******

Andrew Turnbull to Governor James Grant
Smyrnéa, November 30, 1769
The pilot boat is still detained here by Southeast winds. I sent the launch up to help them out today, but the wind and sea being against him he was obliged to return. We have had very blowing weather with much rain. Wallace has been on the barr to sound it. He found between five and six feet of water at the lowest ebb, in the hollow of a very high sea then running. There are always ten feet at least when nigh high water notwithstanding. I think the bar was better last year. Ross was here two days ago. He continues making Indigo and I think the best that he has yet made. He steeps now thirty-six hours. I put some of yours into his hands, he thinks it equal to his best of late, he has not much.

I forgot to mention to your Excellency that when I was preparing to make some Barilla, I discovered that I have not got as much of this plant within eight miles of me as will make twenty barrels of Barilla. What DeBrahm calls a Barilla marsh of 5000 acres at least, happens to be about eight or nine hundred acres of marsh grass, not a sprig of Barilla in it.

Mrs. Turnbull presents her respects to your Excellency and returns you thanks for your oranges. I troubled you with a letter by Captain Wallace that I am apprehensive you will think a long argument.

James Grant Papers

******

Governor James Grant to Andrew Turnbull
St. Augustine, December 14, 1769

I should have great pleasure in complying with any request of yours, but I cannot take the pen in my hand to give to Sir William Duncan an account or opinion of his affairs in this Province which are under your immediate care and management. You reside on the spot, direct the works which are carried on. The people are constantly under your eye, and as you speak their language and are acquainted with every individual, you can now judge with some degree of precision of what may reasonably be expected from their future labor. Of course information from you to Sir William Duncan must be better found and will be more satisfactory than anything which I could pretend to say upon the subject.

Sir William is probably alarmed and uneasy at the large sums of money which have already been expended by you in forming the Smyrnea settlements, you should not be surprised at that, for tho' your friends place great confidence in you, 'tis natural for men to be anxious about property laid out in a remote uncultivated world, but the money is gone, and 'tis too late for them to chuse or expect you give up the whole of your time to the business and will no doubt use your utmost endeavors to make proportional returns for the money which has been advanced, and your constituents must live in hopes and wait in patience for the event. Easing them of any further charge for the supply of provisions will relieve them in some degree from their apprehensions, and if you can continue to make a tolerable remittance of Indigo next year, it will be an encouragement and inducement to assist you in prosecuting your future plans of cultivation.

'Tis not pleasing to interfere in explaining the transactions of one friend to another. I have great respect for Sir William Duncan and great regard for my friends at Smyrnea, but if I was to write as you say he desired all I could say would be that anxiety, application and attention have not been wanting on your part, but that you was hurried into numbers at Minorca by your zeal for colonizing and by peoples crowding unexpectedly in upon you, that the experience of the embarkations from Mahon and Gibralter was greater than you had formed an idea of and that the subsisting such a number of people after they landed in Florida has been attended with more expense and difficulty than you foresaw or expected. To which I should add that the worst is over, that your settlers have got into health, and that Major Moultrie, Bisset, Penman and the other Mosquito planters all agree that your people of late have done wonders.

As I make no difficulty in telling you my sentiments freely, and as I flatter myself that you are convinced of my sincere good wishes for your success, I must take the liberty to advise you to state things just as they are to Sir William Duncan: the plan at first starting was too extensive to be carried on in a wilderness, and the funds agreed upon by the parties were not adequate to such an undertaking, but you acted to the best of your opinion and 'tis to no purpose to consider whether the steps were proper or prudent. The money is gone. The measure has been carried into execution. You may, and I dare say will get on, but 'tis impossible to retreat. The settlers united in a body are like a great family under your care and may raise considerable estates to you and your friends, but separately those settlers have no intrinsic value. You can neither transfer them or carry them to market, nobody would either employ or buy them. This circumstance may not be pleasing to your constituents, tho' 'tis attended with great advantage and security to their property, for by this means you may keep them as long as your please. They cannot leave you as the indented Palatines do their masters all over America. And they have got so much into your debt, that I consider their servitude according to their term of agreement to be unlimited.

It was lucky that a bounty was obtained from His Majesty for the support of your colony for this fear that additional charge for provisions would have been discouraging, but if government had not given the money your constituents must have paid the money, or have given up every thing which has already been advanced, for as your provision crop failed, if the two thousand had not been thrown in your people must have starved, and as corn is so uncommonly dear in Carolina and Georgia, that money will barely carry you on to next crop. You know I have made a second application to Lord Hillsborough who is well disposed to assist the province, and your settlement in particular, but your friends should wait of His Lordship, and they should at the same time solicit the bounty at the Treasury.

James Grant Papers

******

Governor James Grant to Andrew Turnbull
St. Augustine, December 16, 1769
You'l easily see from the style of my letter of the 14th that I mean you to make what use of it you please, you may transmit the original to Sir William Duncan if you think proper The contents are as far as I can judge a true state of the situation of your affairs, and if they see them in the light I do it will save you the trouble of many explanations. Your people as I have said when united may raise risks to you and your partners, tho' separately they have no intrinsic value, of course in a great measure the whole depends upon you, who from inclination and in justice to your friends will do everything in your power to forward the plan, but they on the other hand must live in hopes, wait with patience, and look

to you for the issue, and 'tis right for them and you that the thing should be so understood, for as matters stand inquiries made from reports and information given by a Rolle or any other idle travelers can answer no end, but to distress and make you uneasy, perhaps hurt your health and of consequence obstruct the business. Think of your provisions in the first place, that is certainly the great object. Indigo and other items of produce must follow.

I have ordered Capt. Wallace to take Smyrnea in this way to Charles Town. He carries eighty barrels of flour, some bottled liquor, a cask of shoes, Mrs. Turnbull's clothes, and other articles for your settlements. But I could not admit the hogsheads of vinegar which Gaspar would have been glad to put on board, as I was obliged to help all the other Mosquito crackers. Fairlamb is in need of many things, he had nothing to drink but water when Penman passed, that's a poor account of the living at Mount Oswald. But I have desired Alert to put port wine and porter on board. Bisset, Makdougal and Ross will fare the better for this trip of the East Florida, she may in this way be of some use to my friends, but she is an unprofitable thorn to me, after Laurence Dundas had not made better contracts with the Treasury. He would have been sorely hurt by his late loss of seventy thousand pounds Sterling in the East Florida stock. MacLean's differences amounted to £79,000 which he declared he could not pay and waddled out of the mess. Poor Colonel Clark paid all his differences with all his fortune and is gone abroad. Barre is not mentioned to me, and 'tis to be covered by MacLean.

Doran arrived a few days ago after a passage of twelve days from Ch. Town. I received a letter from him by Mr. Gordon of the 27th November acquainting me that he had agreed to pay a hundred pounds sterling for the Wanché schooner which carried three hundred barrels of rice, she was to proceed to Savannah, take in a load of corn for you and should sail by Mr. Gordon's account about this time with three thousand bushels of corn for Smyrnea. You'l be kind enough to order a good look out to be kept for her and send all your craft to help her, for the misfortunes of the Cannon have raised freights amazingly. There is another cargo to be in readiness at Savannah, which will nearly amount upon the whole to the bounty. By Mr. Gordon's agreement the Wanché is to return to Savannah to take in the second loading for the same freight of a hundred sterling if you chuse it, or to proceed upon another voyage to a different part of the world, your determination will depend upon the state of your storehouses and the state of your provisions. If the Wanché should arrive before the East Florida leaves you, write to Mr. Gordon by Wallace what you fix upon for the Wanché; if she does not arrive before Wallace sails acquaint me by express what you wish to have done. The master of the Wanché has orders to follow your directions.

I have agreed with a Rhode Island man to deliver eight hundred bushels of corn and peas to Fairlamb at the Mosquitoes for three shillings a bushel. I wish your supplies from Carolina and Georgia may come as cheap. I doubt it much, but there is no help for it, we must take it as the market runs. I wrote to Mr. Gordon by the post express to send you some small rice and a portion of peas if they could be had.

Buckle was applied to and would not go under a hundred. The Wanché carries fifty barrels of rice more than Barton, which was the reason for the preference exclusive of that of Buckles raising the price of freight.

Bisset arrived in perfect health and quite a young man. He never heard of five blankets. Makdougal got wet and is ailing. Indigo has been examined and talked of; Ross mentioned as a model of perfection in his works of December, more northern planters say little but do not give up the point. Wallace may still have a piece in his pocket for the use of his friends in Carolina we venture at times to talk to the Major, and do not always consider him as an oracle. Young Levett in his report mentioned his having seen the ruins of Major Moultrie's vatts. I say some part of them must have been standing like those of Palmers. The Major has been explaining it to Sutherland since dinner.

James Grant Papers

******

Andrew Turnbull to Governor James Grant
Smyrnéa, December 23, 1769
One of Mr. Penman's people tells me that a Negro sets out from the Orange Grove for Town tomorrow morning. He only goes to acquaint your Excellency that the East Florida came to an anchor off this barr on Wednesday morning early. The launches went off and brought off some of the cargo, but the wind being westerly she did not get in till four in the afternoon. Everything was out at Noon today, and as he is in a hurry to get away I have set two or three masons to raise some stones for him for ballast. He will be ready tomorrow, and if the wind comes around will go away immediately. Everything came well and safe. My twenty-five barrels of flour is a comfortable circumstance. I am much obliged to you, Sir, for it, and for the many other things for me by the East Florida.

Mrs. Turnbull desires her respects to you and returns many thanks for the seeds and etc. With such lifts as you give our garden it will get on. I keep a good lookout for the Wanché and shall observe what you write about her and the provisions.

James Grant Papers

******

Andrew Turnbull to Governor James Grant
Smyrnéa, 1769
This will be delivered to you by Captain Barber. You will please to satisfy him as far as forty pounds Sterling for two voyages of his schooner, the Industry. I have

desired Mr. Humphreys to make out the receipts in the manner you direct, a boy on horseback will bring them here, that I may certify or sign them. I wish with all my heart that I could avoid giving your Excellency much trouble in this affair.

Mrs. Turnbull presents her respects to you, Sir, and all my family as well. We have had terrible weather here. The tides were a foot higher than our wharf. They did not affect me; but I am sorry to hear that they have hurt the Major (Moultrie)…

James Grant Papers

******

Andrew Turnbull to Sir William Duncan
Smyrnéa, February 13, 1770
We continued decreasing in numbers until two months ago, we now increase. Our births are double our burials.

Dundee City Archives

******

Andrew Turnbull to Governor James Grant
Smyrnéa, February 15, 1770
Your Excellency's letter of the 11th came to hand today at noon. I thank you Sir, for desiring John Gordon to throw in the whole of the provisions as soon as possible. I am sorry there are no peas to be purchased. I have reason, however, to be thankful that I have plenty of corn. I wish you had supplied yourself from the live oak, it does not, as you will see by the account, cost three shillings per bushel. As to the pork, indigo seed, pumps, etc., I will send bills for them. I wrote for six pump borers or rather six sets of pump borers from England in August. I have no answer of that letter therefore I durst not risk my crop of Indigo on that uncertainty.

As the insurers do not make good the damage, except there is a total loss, I think it indeed is needless expense and am glad your Excellency ordered that to be saved. If the vessels come within our reach we will make a shift to get them into port. I have already lent a little corn to Ross's people to prevent their being starved, and shall supply him with more till he gets his five hundred bushels.

I am apprehensive I shall not be able to come up to the quantity of Indigo you estimate. I will, however, struggle hard for it… I am much better… myself recovered, and as to weather, we have had a most plentiful rain that set the indigo a going. Notwithstanding I am still afraid of putting corn and indigo seed into the ground yet. I believe I shall defer planting of either till the beginning of next month.

Mrs. Turnbull presents her respect to you Sir. Her garden got a knock by the January frosts, but is coming on again. She brought some fine jonquils and other flowers from it yesterday. In the eating way greens and broth with a little salad was all that her effort could exhibit...

James Grant Papers

******

Andrew Turnbull to Governor James Grant
Smyrnéa, March 5, 1770
I had the honour of your letter last Friday by Moncrief, but going away immediately for far of losing the tide did not give me time to answer it by him.

DeBrahm's refusing of his Betsey is of a piece with everything he does, and I think consistent with his character, which is mean, proud, dirty, and disobliging.

I have calculated the cost of having provisions brought by land, and find that it will run high, a horse can not carry more than three or four bushels of corn, each horse will cost two dollars a tripp, besides as much for a man to drive every two or three. I shall want forty load of corn or flour a week, which would cost a hundred dollars at least, besides the expences of carrying it to Smart's, and taking it away from Major Moultries. I am much obliged to you for the offer of your flatt to carry it to Smarts, but as the pilot boat will carry one hundred and fifty bushels of corn or flour in proportion, I beg the favor of her, if she can be spared. I would have sent Humphreys to town for the business of loading her, if he had been well. He has had a return of his fever and is now in bed with it. This also prevents my coming to town, and obliges me to trouble Major Moultrie to dispatch her. I have wrote him that I would have four barrels of pork put on board of her, and to fill up with corn, but if none is to be had, to fill up with flour. It will be as much as I can do to hold out three weeks longer. I have therefore desired the Major to dispatch that supply as soon as possible. But if a larger vessel with a thousand or more bushels of corn should come in, and if the corn can be purchased on condition of delivering it here, or if another vessel can be hired to bring it here, I have desired the major to gather a supply this way...

James Grant Papers

******

Andrew Turnbull to Sir William Duncan and to George Grenville
Smyrnea, March 6, 1770
I am now getting rid of another very troublesome old fellow, I mean one Earl, who I left here when I went to England to manage our Negroes, erect buildings, and prepare every thing for my arriving here. He not only neglected everything but has been a burden to us ever since. His contract with us is out the 22nd of this month. As soon as I get our Negroes and other things out of his hands, I will transmit you very exact lists of the numbers of our People and cattle. This Earl is the last American I will ever employ. Even the best of the American-born are

136

in general of little and narrow minds, limit'd in their views and understandings; and as obstinate as self conceit and ignorance can make them. The common People are an idle, lazy, talking crew, neglecting every thing to set down with anybody who will hear them bragg of their great doings as planters. I have suffered much from two of them, I mean this Earl, and the man who had the care of the black cattle, but I am not the only one, everybody who has employed them have been sufferers. I would not give one of our People for a dozen of them.

Dundee City Archives

******

Andrew Turnbull to Governor James Grant
Smyrnéa, March 12, 1770
I have no other apology for troubling your Excellency with the enclosed for Mr. Gordon, than that of its enclosing bills for the amount of pork, indigo seed, cart wheels, pumps, & etc. I was afraid of its miscarrying through other hands.

I have received the deeds from England. I have signed them and send them to town to go by Mr. Oswald's vessel if she is not gone. The letters which accompanied them from both my partners were friendly and compliment.

All the corn I plant this month is in the ground and almost all of it appears. I am planting Indigo very busily. Penman, Bisset and Mack are all employed at the same work. I shall have boards and scantling here this week for six sets of vats. I intend to go no farther than ten or twelve at most this year.

About two hundred and sixty pounds worth of things are at St. Augustine from London for me among which are indigo, sickles, checks, oznaburggs and other necessary things, which I should be sorry to lose. Therefore I beg the favor of the pilot boat if she can be spared. I would rather be at any expense for her than trust them to Warner's cockleshell, besides I have no opinion of the man. But if she cannot be spared I have ordered Payne to send her down or another larger vessel if he can get one and to put her up on freight. I have almost a cargo myself.

Mrs. Turnbull presents her respects to your Excellency. Gardening is the hobby still. You have lent her a lift to mount that horse. She brought a turnip from the garden the other day for a crock. It measured nineteen inches round, but Bisset told her he had seen one at Mt. Oswald double that size. That was a lowering talk…

James Grant Papers

******

Andrew Turnbull to Governor James Grant
Smyrnéa, March 19, 1770
I am honored with your letter of the fifteenth of this month. The East Florida made a tedious voyage indeed. It is well she is in your hands, she would ruin

a poor man. I am sorry Payne neglected sending me the things from London. I intend to give him a standing order to forward everything for me in future, by the first opportunity which offers after the goods are in his hands. If he is puzzled I shall direct him to trouble you for advice. If Porter comes back and calls at St. Augustine he will bring all he can. The New York man will be a resource if the other should fail. Gaspard is much mistaken about the indigo. I imagined he means planting.

The indigo put into the ground last year in August is now from six inches to a foot high. I mean the new shoots from the old root. Some of the last planted begins to peep out of the ground, but this is very little. The rest I am afraid is dying in the ground. The drought of last week obliged me to leave off planting. I have seed in about two hundred acres, with every fourth row of corn. This reduces the indigo to one hundred and fifty acres. I want moister weather to plant the rest. Penman writes me that he will have sixty acres planted this week. Bisset works day and night. Mak goes on with spirit also. But Ross has been making more leeway by a marriage between his overseer and the coarsest piece of woman I ever saw. Bishop Bisset performed the ceremony, found himself drowsy or something else before night, went to bed, and slept till next morning. The old gentleman likes to take a siesta in an afternoon but this was lethargy. I am afraid that neither Ross nor I will be able to come up to your calculate. He has already laid a foundation of failure by his stay in town. Mine will be certain and determined if the drought continues. I heard nothing of the North Carolina vessel which is to take in red bay. I thank you, Sir, for the chronicles. The letter you sent is an extraordinary one. If his threats are not treason they are very nigh it.

La Jardiniere du Vilage presents her respects to your Excellency. She has hundreds of young sweet orange trees just come out from the seed of the oranges you sent her. I think she rather gets on in that way. She beat the highlander hollow in a wager about green peas. They have wagered their melon grounds against one another…

James Grant Papers

******

Andrew Turnbull to Sir William Duncan
Smyrnéa, April 18, 1770

Inclosed I send you the number of our People with their ages. Our arrival here in the worst and wettest season ever seen in this Country bore very heavy on us. But even this bad season would not probably have proved so mortal, if a previous poor living in the countries where these People came from had not impoverished their Blood. The long voyage added to that bad state, and reduced them so low that they could not stand the shock of such a great change, as that from a dry Mediterranean air to a very moist one. The air of this Country is generally dry and wholesome, but unluckily for us, it was quite the contrary for many months after our arrival. Our loss, which is about half, fell most on the very young and the oldest People. I would have sent you a list of them long ago, but waited till the health of those behind was so much confirmed, as to ensure an increase rather than a decrease in future. This is now the case, and I am very certain of making fine Estates even with these left. When our Debts are paid and every account balanced, it will be easy for me to increase our numbers without stirring from this place, and without such Expenses and Risks as were incurred by our first Tryal. I mean that if it is found expedient, and for our Interest such a step may be taken, I shall not, however, do any thing either in this, or in things of much less moment, without the full consent and approbation of the gentlemen concerned with me in this settlement.

The ages and number of People belonging to the Settlement of Smyrnea in East Florida this 18th of March 1770.

Under one year old	12
From one year to four years old	25
From 4 to 8	47
From 8 to 12	63
From 12 to 16	133
From 16 to 30	361
From 30 to 40	47
From 40 to 50 and upwards	14
In all	702
Males	406
Females	296
Total	702

Andrew Turnbull

Dundee City Archives

******

Andrew Turnbull to Governor James Grant
Smyrnéa, April 19, 1770
Since my return here I have planted all the indigo land which I thought wanted it. The rainy Sunday at St. Augustine scarce produced a shower here. I am not, however, in doubt about a crop. Penman's indigo in his marsh land is very green, healthy, and strong. I hope it will succeed well with him. In the mean time an old uncle at Shrewsbury has left him about two thousand five hundred pounds, most of it in East India Annuities. Bisset and Mack are driving on the Indigo planting. I do not know what John Ross is about. I dare say he is very busy.

I am almost in distress for my checks and oznaburggs. Most of my people are without a shirt to their backs. If Platt is not arrived at St. Augustine I have ordered Gasper to come here and to leave the shipping of the things to Payne who I have desired also to ship some from the house in town for use here. I cannot spare anybody to make us chairs and tables till our indigo vats are up. If I had even a spoon maker I would employ him in making buckets and ladles for beating and stirring the indigo. As we have not enough of chairs for our family here, I send for these from town. I dare say, Sir, you understood the English of this, a word from you to Platt or to any other person who may be sent would make us sit easier.

Mrs. Turnbull desires her respects to your Excellency and talks of adding sulfur to her garden, but all these idle operations were suspended by the grand object, indigo. It may be done in a time of some leisure…

James Grant Papers

******

Andrew Turnbull to Governor James Grant
Smyrnéa, May 6, 1770
Mr. Penman, who is just now arrived here, acquaints me that you Excellency has prevailed on Captain Dundass to call here with some things for us. I send Gasper to ship the packages from England on board of his schooner and the cumbersome furniture on board of Platt. I should be glad for Mrs. Turnbull's burcan purchased of Captain Dundass also. I have some papers of consequence in it which were packed among her things instead of being put among mine.

Our land is very white here and the greatest part of our Indigo seed laying idle in the ground for want of rain; notwithstanding we are preparing our vats. We began to set up Wednesday overnight, and have now three sets up. We aim at fourteen to be all up in July but if this weather continues we shall not work four. Mrs. Turnbull desires her best respects to you.

James Grant Papers

******

Andrew Turnbull to Governor James Grant
Smyrnéa, May 31, 1770
I have been plagued with Body Plat. He wanted more freight for Mr. Fraser's family and furniture than you wrote me, pretending that he did not make any agreement. I insisted on not giving him any more than the eight Guineas for the whole as you desired. He says he will send an account to Dr. Cunningham for the freight of the soldiers provisions, which he says were not mentioned.

His corn was delivered in good condition. Ross left bills with me for his 200 bushels. Mr. Fairlamb settled with Plat himself at Mount Oswald. His hogg's lard is yellow, nasty, and bad, nor is it melted down, but salted as it comes from the hogg, which is not properly hoggs lard, but leaf fat. All these objections hindered me from taking it which he did not insist on as he found it worse than he expected. Penman wanted some, but on opening all the barrels, could not find one fit for use, Mr. Fairlamb got the only one tolerable. We parted good friends this morning as the pilotage in and out of this place is not to cost him anything. The truth is I was glad to get rid of him, for he is tedious, teasing and suspicious in business.

We have a bad prospect of indigo. We had an hours rain when Captain Dundass was here and some very slight showers three days afterwards, all which did not go an inch deep into the ground. We have not had one drop since. My first planted indigo is gone except a stalk here and there. I planted the whole land a second time, that came up as well, but is now disappearing, and I think one week more without rain will burn us up. Bisset has about seven acres of forty. Mack and Ross not more in proportion to what they have planted. Bisset desponds, Ross swears that there is white dry salt in the middle of his field. Mack is plagued with purslane and I am blind with looking for indigo in dry white sand. Rain would ease us all. Penman's low ground holds out well. I intended to have indigo out long ago, but on finding my first and second planting like to fail, I left my earliest weed go to seed, for I am resolved on planting a third time, if the first and second do not come on. I shall begin to cut a second last year's field on Monday. Our heats have been excessive and even wither and wilt the corn at midday.

I hear the English papers are at Penman's. We are obliged to your Excellency for them. I am glad that Major Mackenzie and four companies of the 31st are returned. I have no letters from England. I wish to hear something about the bounty, and beg the favor of an express if it is granted. I shall be glad to pay the expense. I am not afraid, however, of having provisions this year, notwithstanding should be glad of the bounty that would give plenty. My crop will not afford more than sustenance. I am preparing one hundred acres more of land for indigo, no hopes of having a third of a crop from the four hundred. I have not a prospect of having one hundred acres at present. These hundred acres of new land may be thrown into guinea corn and peas if the bounty is not obtained. If it is I'll plant it with indigo. Mr. Drayton has offered me some indigo seed. I have accepted his offer and will send for it when I want it…

James Grant Papers

******

Andrew Turnbull to Governor James Grant
Smyrnéa, June 15, 1770
Platt went to sea the first of this month, as our bar has more water on it now than for some time past. He did not touch coming in nor in going out. He desired

me to speak to the settlers on this river to order a cargo of provisions by him this winter. He says he will bring Indian corn, flour, pork, rum cheaper than anybody. I have promised to write to him if a quantity to make up a cargo is wanted. It would be convenient for us if we could induce vessels to come here direct. Pork, flour, and rum will always be wanted. Though I did not take his leaf fat instead of lard we parted good friends. I did not charge him pilotage and gave him some cuttings of red bay. I have won his heart. He talked of bringing carpenters with him next voyage to cut ship lumber. He was very solicitous with me to pay twenty shillings which he said you owed him for lumber and having made a mistake in the account he gave into your hands. I need not tell you, Sir, that I did not pay him that twenty shillings. He was angry because I would not pay him a separate freight for the soldiers provisions and demanded them to reship and sell them at vendue. This was dropped on my telling him that he must fight the soldiers for them. He owned that you told him he was to have eight guineas for what was on board to which he said he neither objected to nor agreed to. I was plagued with such argumentation as this, till he saw that I would not pay him one farthing more than the eight guineas which he received, and afterwards made out an account for the freight of the provisions sent…

I wish to hear from John Gordon, I have had no letters from him since Tucker went away. I wrote by him to send another cargo before the end of this month and not later. I can hold out longer, but should be glad that it is in forwardness. Penman sent me the papers. We are all obliged to you for them.

We had a smart shower of rain the fifth of this month. It rained all the sixth and showered on the seventh eighth and ninth. We have had none since. Much of the indigo on this land was burnt up before these rains came, and much of what had been planted above three months appeared. We still wish for a little rain to help the indigo to strike a root. I observe that it is easily burnt up before it gets its root out of the reach of the drought. I have much as yet in this ticklish state. I have made some indigo but it is not dry yet. Bisset, Ross, and Mackdougal were here last Saturday, all pleased with the weather. One weeks drought more would have set me to hoeing and planting again. Our corn promises well. I am with the greatest respect…

James Grant Papers

* * * * * *

Andrew Turnbull to Governor James Grant
Smyrnéa, June 23, 1770
I troubled you with a letter last week by a man of Penman's. We had then a bad prospect of indigo. It is better since the rains of this week. I have been at Mr. Oswald to see some of the indigo vats beat. If I knew when you begin to cut I would attend your vats a couple of days, but am afraid I shall be hindered by being obliged to look after my own.

I keep a sharp look out for a corn vessel from John Gordon. A lame Indian called Alakalataki has stole three of my best cart horses. I sent two hunters after him, but they could not come up with him. He stole two from me before, but I got them again before he hid them and recovered one of Penman's which he stole three months before. What shall I do with this thieving fellow. If I catch him I had resolved to send him to you. He is a noted horse stealer, and the other Indians say one of the greatest villains among them.

Ross has begun to cut his last years indigo. Bisset begins ten days hence, Penman about the same time, Mack and I not this fortnight yet...

James Grant Papers

******

Andrew Turnbull to Sir William Duncan
St. Augustine, July 14, 1770

The mosquitoes and sand fleas trouble and tease them so much when at work, that they not only hinder the labour from going on, but fret and vex them into disquietude and uneasiness, to remedy this I give each of them a frock buttoned at the neck and wrists with a pair of long trousers that cover the body and are loose, cool, and easy to work in. I can only give them 2 frocks and 2 pair trousers each, one to wash while the other is in use. Since nineteen yards of cloth was required to make clothing for one person, it was necessary to buy more cloth.

I came to see the governor's overseer make Indigo. I staid two days at his plantation much pleased with his method. He planned to depart for Smyrnéa that day and to be there tomorrow if the horses can hold out.

Dundee City Archives

******

Andrew Turnbull to Governor James Grant
Smyrnéa, July 28, 1770

Enclosed is a letter from Mr. Bradshaw, it came in that of mine from Sir William Duncan, recommended to your care. Sir William desires me to thank you, Sir, and says he has applied to the treasury. His words are 'I beg you will present our best compliments and thanks to governor Grant, and let him know in the best manner you can how sensible we are of his protection and assistance to our settlement. I have not neglected to solicit the Treasury in our behalf and have sent enclosed a second letter to Governor Grant from Mr. Bradshaw, which you will be so good as to deliver.' Both Sir William and Mr. Grenville seem to be satisfied now. The latter is desirous of having more land in this province. They have sent me out two King's orders for five and ten thousand acre tracts, and desire me to purchase another five thousand or more. I think Mr. G intends making other settlements soon. If Cumming's two fives are to be disposed of, I will endeavor to purchase them. Or if the grants do not pass the offices… I beg the favor of having the preference… I find I am to direct the settling of them it will be difficult to do it if they are at a greater distance.

I have desired Mr. Penman to give you a bit of the best indigo which I have made. I cannot produce flora quality, I fall through the true blue into a purple. I wish to be with Mr. Skinner to ask him how I am to avoid that Episcopal color. My indigo weed in general is so thin and so backward that I shall not come to half of your calculate. Ross makes worse indigo than last year. He has two or three wrong notions from the Indigotier which run away with him. Bisset has made some very good. He is apprehensive of the heat and badness of the roads but does not go to town as he intended. He grows old.

I have been obliged to gather some corn not quite ripe and to dry it in the sun. I fancy John Gordon has forgot us, his not sending a vessel distresses us. Now I am past the worst of it, for my corn is coming on fast.

Mrs. Turnbull desires her compliments to your Excellency. She succeeds in the watermelons, but not so well in the other kind. Her garden has a shabby withered look at present. In short she has not one thing to brag or crack of, but the watermelons, of which she cuts twenty in a day sometimes.

This cursed purple or violet in the indigo I make stares one in the face every minute, and obliges me to mention it again. Mr. Skinner would much oblige me in telling me how I am to keep it out of my vats. The samples I brought of his makes it look like bad slate…

James Grant Papers

******

Andrew Turnbull to Governor James Grant
Smyrnéa, August 8, 1770
Stewart arrived here yesterday with your favor of the 1st of this month. Enclosed is a list of the clothing, tools & etc. which I shall want this winter. The amount is as you desired. You will please alter or cancel in that list what you think proper. I leave the mode of Mr. Nixons acting in this affair entirely to your direction to him. I shall write to Sir William what you say also about his mode of help on this business. I hope this scheme of an indent which you have thought of will succeed.

I am going on in indigo making and get more into the good purple of Flora, but sometimes fall into copper, but of the best kind. I endeavor to get at the flora… many experiments, but can ascertain nothing with precision as yet. As I see the over year's gives considerably more than that of this year, I am planting and supplying to establish four hundred acres for next year and intend in the spring to add vats to make twenty four sets in all. I have cut last year's indigo twice and shall cut it a third time in the beginning of next month. I hope to have five cuttings from it unluckily I have little of it. The indigo of this year's planting is so thin that it gives few vats. I see it will be better the next cutting though drought of the months of April and May burnt up nine tenths of it and if we had not had rain in the beginning of June, not a stalk would have escaped.

Ross has got out of his prejudices now makes good indigo. Bisset was ill of a fever last week. I went to his place last Sunday and brought him away bodily with me. He is now recovering. Mackdougal will not make much indigo this year, not from any fault of his for he has taken much pains. I have not been at Penman's lately. Mrs. Turnbull desires her respects to your Excellency...

James Grant Papers

* * * * * *

Andrew Turnbull to Governor James Grant
Smyrnéa, August 17, 1770
A large sloop appeared off this bar last Saturday, and has kept hovering in sight ever since, till yesterday. I had a boat with seven hands at the bar with orders if he came within three or four miles to go on board of him, but he always kept at such a distance as made it dangerous to venture a boat so far out. We made fires by night and signals by day, but he never came nigh enough to see what he was. If it was a vessel bound for this place the Master did not do well in not coming nigher. When we lost sight of him last he stood to the northward. If he puts into St. Augustine and is bound to this place, I doubt not of his being sent here immediately. I have been in some distress for corn. I fed the people with flour and rice as long as they lasted. I am now reduced to all corn, which I am obliged to gather before if is ripe and hard. I began at first with one meal a day of it, having flour bread for the morning and evening. Even this small quantity of corn food brought on disorders of the bowels and swellings. I have lost two men by these disorders, but flatter myself of not losing any more. I built a kiln twenty feet in diameter, which dries one hundred bushels at a time. This kiln drying makes the corn easier to grind and makes it wholesome. So far I have got partly over the inconvenience of soft corn, but am badly off for flour and rice. I have not any rice and but very little flour, consequently I am at a loss for a proper diet for my sick, which is the reason of my troubling you, Sir, with this, to beg that part of last years bounty, if not too late, may be changed from corn into flour and rice, five or six barrels of the latter, and between twenty and thirty of the former would be sufficient for the present. If this cannot be done, you will oblige me much in ordering John Gordon to send these quantities here by the first opportunity. I will send him bills for the amount as soon as I know

how much it is. The hopes of having their supply as part of provisions from the bounty is the reason of my not sending bills with this for it. I am loathe to draw if I can avoid it.

Holroyd who brought corn to Mr. Fairlamb last year is to bring me two pair of millstones to St. Augustine in September. If he has provisions on board he will find a market in this river for twenty or thirty barrels of flour, a dozen puncheons of northward rum, and some corn. Everybody wants one or other of these articles. I think Mr. Fairlamb will want some hundreds of bushels of corn.

I continue making indigo. The four overseers tell me that I have not made one bad vat except two which were beat during a storm of wind and rain on the sixth of June. Ross made a four ounce vat

that day. He is now making excellent indigo and seems… into a good way. Bisset is still here, not yet recovered, but better. We are not much troubled with ague nor any kind of fever this year. If it had not been for my want of dry corn, I should have had a very healthy set of people during this season. These who keep their health work well, however, and I intend to have seventeen sets of vats a going in October. It is not from the quantity of weed that I am obliged to have so many, but from the distance from the field to the vat. What I planted in March will not be fit to cut for the first time till October. I am now supplying and planting to establish four hundred acres complete for next year. Tho' the dry spring has thrown me so far back I can see by what I have done in the making of indigo, that the land will give more weed and cuttings when planted over year, than could be expected. If the latter part of the year is favorable, I shall cut some of last years weed five times. I am sorry, sir, to give you all this trouble for our provisions, and can only plead necessity. I am with the greatest respect…

James Grant Papers

******

Andrew Turnbull to Governor James Grant
Smyrnéa, August 31, 1770, In the evening.
Tucker appeared off here at noon. He is now unloading. He brings one thousand six hundred and seventy three and one-half bushels of corn in bulk, barrels of the same, and fifty two bushels of peas. He also brought half the salt ordered not having room for any more. The rest will be sent by the first opportunity. Mr. Gordon has forwarded some pump borers to me from London with some other trifles. Corn is so much demanded for the Spaniards at La Vera Cruz that it was with much difficulty he found a cargo. The packet which I send with this came by Tucker. John Gordon desires me to forward a packet for you, but Tucker tells me that is gone by Doran or is to go by him…

James Grant Papers

THE NEW SMYRNA COLONY OF FLORIDA

John Gordon to Governor James Grant
Charlestown, September 1, 1770

I wrote to your Excellency a few lines by Mackenfuss acknowledging the weight of your several favors of the 9th, 14th July and 3rd August, with sundry packing letters for Great Britain. The originals are on their passage to Falmouth and the duplicates, and letters for Pensacola, wait the first convenience for their several destinations.

The disappointments and bad success I have met with these three months past have made me so unhappy that I have been almost distracted. The thoughts of Doctor Turnbull's people being in want of provisions until I had a prospect of relieving them now is really intolerable. In Georgia where I had placed my chief dependence, an act of their assembly overset my hopes. I had agents all over this province to no purpose until the crop in the ground was out of the reach of accident. At last I thought myself secure of 3500 bushels in store at Georgetown as I had made an actual purchase of it and had it from under the hands of two substantial men whose words I will no more value, that it would be ready for Captain Tucker whenever he could arrive, but a Spaniard from Campeche shipped in and offered few pence more and Tucker returned here with only 800 bushels on board. My situation was then easier conceived than described and I must drop the subject to preserve my temper.

I am much obliged to your Excellency for settling the difference between Carolina and Burlington pork with the Deputy commissary of stores and provisions. He may now keep Mr. Murphy's except which he promised to deliver to the person I should send the provisions or the £38.7.6 Sterling by. We have had no opportunity but the express to St. Augustine for a long time past except a small vessel of Mr. DeBrahm's that the Reverend William Henderson acquainted me had orders not to carry a letter for any person by her. We had advice that Augustine was almost filled up and the long stay of Doran and Bachop seemed to confirm it. I am rejoiced to hear of the kind of prospects of your East Florida planters and that even your Excellency's own expectations will be succeeded in spite of the traitor Johnson, that fellow should be transported to Carolina. As to my friend Lorry, I suppose he has corn food by. Ross undertakes to convince your Excellency that there is more difficulty in building a whole set of indigo vats than the East Florida planters are aware of and I wish that matter had been seen through sooner for it must hurt the elderly Captain much to see such quantities of fine weed lost for want of steepers.

By all accounts Mr. Fairlamb is the most attentive planter in your province. I have not heard anything of Ross, Penman, Bisset & etc. that way, except that Mr. Ross had lost his crop entirely, which I am sorry for. I ordered some guinea grass seed to be sown in the country here but do not know whether it is come up or not. I have volunteers in my town garden that's come up from the seed of some that grew last year and is amazingly fine. It is in general upwards of six foot high. I have cut a few bunches at different times and the second growth is so quick that it started from ten to twelve inches in three days time. I wish to know if you have thought the seed I sent worth your attention at the Mosquitoes. I think it cannot fail.

I have acquainted Mr. Roupell with that paragraph concerning him. He mutters but I think he ought to be thankful, as I am certain the good Doctor is, for all your actual and intended services to him. His constituents or connections may also pray for Governor Grant. I do think upon my honor, that that settlement would have failed and that man been ruined under any other influence. If the main tracks that your Excellency has laid, and I hope nothing will disappoint it, the Doctor may stand firm. It is said here that he will make nigh twenty thousand bushels of corn, but if he comes up to your mark it is as much as I expect and a remittance in indigo will be no ways unwelcome at home.

I wish you would be so good as to send me a sample of indigo to brag with. I have seen some sent to Doctor Moultrie that is very fine. I hope our late dropping season which still continues has extended itself southward. If so your crops may turn out well. I have been much afraid that periodical droughts and inundations were becoming the natural enemies of the province…

James Grant Papers

******

Governor James Grant to the Earl of Hillsborough
St. Augustine, September 1, 1770
In my letter no. 30 I had the honor to lay before your Lordship, an account of the helpless and distressed state of the Greek Settlement at Smyrnea, and took the liberty to observe to your Lordship the necessity there was of continuing His Majesty's most gracious Bounty for the support of those adventurers.

Last year's bounty has been laid out entirely for their subsistence, and has actually saved them from starving, for without that well timed help from Government, there must have been an end of that numerous promising settlement.

Doctor Turnbull is diligent and assiduous, he resides constantly with his Greek colonists, and does as much as a man do to repair the first fault of exceeding the number of people to be imported and of corse the funds which his constituents had agreed to advance. In place of six thousand which was the stipulated sum, they have actually my Lord, paid £24,000, and are determined to go no farther.

The Greek settlers having been well fed last year have got into health and spirits. They work well, have cleared a great deal of ground, which the Doctor has put in very good order. The Greeks this year have raised a considerable quantity of provisions, such as Indian corn, pease, potatoes and greens of all kinds, and if supported they will soon get into a comfortable state, and be able to supply themselves with every necessary of life. Produce, and 'tis to be hoped useful produce to Great Britain, will of course follow.

But at present they are destitute of every convenience, they are ill clothed, many of them almost naked, and are obliged to live in small hutts put up in a hurry to shelter them from the weather upon their first arrival. Doctor Turnbull has neither money nor credit to supply them with clothes, and has not the necessary tools and materials to build houses for them. In that distressed situation he can only look up to His Majesty for His most gracious support by ordering the Royal Bounty to be continued to enable him to carry an extensive and usefull undertaking into execution with success. He presses me to lay his case before your Lordship, and to transmit for your Lordship's consideration an indent of such things as are absolutely necessary for the existence of the settlement.

The indent amounts to £1000 if the bounty is continued, and your Lordship so pleased to order Mr. Nixon, the Doctor's agent, to receive that money at the Treasury, he will be very carefull in the purchase and package of the assortment, which may be sent to Charles Town if no vessel offers for this port. The remaining thousand if your Lordship approves of the method, I shall continue to draw for upon the Treasury for the support of the settlement in the same manner as I drew for the Bounty of last year.

Indent of clothing, tools, etc., wanted for the distressed Greek Settlement under the direction of Andrew Turnbull Esquire at Smyrnéa, East Florida.

Best blue plains 3000 yards at 1/4 per yard £200
Best white plains 500 yards at 1/4 per yard 33.6.8
Checkt Linnens 3000 yards at 1/4 per yard 150
Stript Linnens 2000 yards at 1/? per yard 100
Stript Cottons 500 yards at 1/3 per yard 31.5
Scots Osnaburggs 4000 yards at 6 per yard 100
Negro Blankets 600 at 5/ each 150
Mens shoes of different sizes 600 pr 3/4 a pair 100
Indigo Sickles 60 Doz. At 8/6 pr. Doz. 25.10
Broad Hoes, Crowley's of a middling size
60 doz at 20/ per dozen 60
Building Nails the greatest part sixpenny 100
Total   £1050.1.8

Colonial Office Papers

CORRESPONDENCE

John Gordon to Governor James Grant
Charlestown, October 5, 1770

I did myself the honor to write your Excellency a few times by the post on Tuesday last and this morning have received a packet with your favor of the 1st of last month and the letters contained therein shall go by the Swallow packet. In one of my former letters I think I requested a sample of the North River indigo, which I shall be glad to have. Here we have had a black frost, by report within these fine days and the weather is still cold enough to sit by a fire in the middle of the day. By this opportunity you will receive two pipes of essence from on board of Captain Dundass who I presume will write to your Excellency.

I am sorry on Mr. Drayton's account to advise that his creditors here either stimulated by resentment of his politics or resentment, did last Saturday take out attachments against his estate and as I had information from one of the gentleman of the law that there attachments were to a very considerable amount. I judged it prudent to take the benefit of the term not from any suspicion of the ability of his security, but if Mr. Bull has nit been provident enough to take a counter security, Mr. Drayton will certainly thank me for taking care of his friend. If I had been a creditor of Mr. Drayton myself, I would not have taken the step, but in an affair of trust I do not think myself at liberty to disguise anything.

This affair was first agitated by Mr. Charles Pinckney Senior. Mrs. Drayton herself alarmed the rest of the creditors as soon as she knew his resolution and they afterwards came to an agreement and got Mr. Linckney to join them in it, not to move the matter any farther, but a Miss St. Julien who had about £1500 currency of her fortune in his hands became inexorable and all the rest followed her example. Should any of the creditors move the court for an order to sell, it may be necessary for your bond to be on the spot with a full power of attorney to act for principle as well as interest.

As I found some flour and rice of an inferior quality and under market price I have added ten barrels of such to the quantity you commissioned and as soon as I receive an account of the corn to be shipped I shall furnish your Excellency with a state of the whole agreeable to your directions. I judge that this vessel load will exceed the money in my hands by some trifle. There is no pork in the province at this season. I could only ship six hogsheads of home spun rum at 10 per hogshead and some that I have ordered to be taken out in case there should not be room enough for that and the corn too. I have charged it to the bounty account, but if any is landed in this province that account shall have credit for it.

Captain Tucker has been returned from the mosquitoes long ago. If your Excellency has an opportunity I request you will be pleased to direct Doctor Turnbull to order a good look out for this schooner that is bound to Mosquittoes. I hope she will sail in all next week…

James Grant Papers

******

Andrew Turnbull to Governor James Grant
Smyrnéa, October 22, 1770

In a letter of the 29th of June from Sir William Duncan, he says that the bounty of this year is entirely owing to Mr. Bradshaw, and that it is to remind him of the permission he gave to governor Grant to draw for it, which has engaged him to stay another winter in London. No doubt Sir William means that paragraph of Mr. Bradshaw's letter, which cannot be called a permission warranted in an official way. It seems like a private opinion, but if Mr. Bradshaw means it as a permission so much the better, the indent will be completed. I do not wish to have the money laid out in any other way than that which your Excellency proposed and has already forwarded.

Mr. Ross came here last night much alarmed by a piece of news which his overseer brought from town. He says that one Foster who lived among the Indians was ordered from among them as they had declared war and had already killed two traders. I laughed at Ross for his fears, alleging that if such a thing was suspected you would find means of averting it, or at worst an express would be sent so as to advise us to be on our guard. If there are any such apprehensions I flatter myself your Excellency will send a reinforcement to this port, and if arms can be borrowed from the troops or king's stores I should be glad of them that I may militia a hundred of our youngest men as a kind of a guard for the rest.

I am in distress for want of flour, having only one barrel left of two I borrowed from Mr. Penman and not one grain of rice. When that barrel is done, I shall be very badly off for my ailing people and lying in women. I have nothing else but corn and peas. As I dare not trust to Payne in such an emergency I beg your Excellency will please to order him to form some conveyance by water to send me a few barrels. There is no thinking of having anything by land. The horses which come from town here even without loads are so fatigued that they cannot recover till after a long time; they even die, of three bought for me in town lately one is dying having been bogged in the Matanzas, another is lame, and the third is still in a weakly state. Two months ago I also lost two of five I sent to Smarts for oznaburggs, the others were recovered with difficulty though they carried it to the Timoka only. I am sorry to be so troublesome to your Excellency, but cannot tell how to be relieved but by you.

We make better indigo every day. I have made about three hundred and fifty vats. We shall go on as long as the weather permits. I shall think myself high if I can get to five hundred vats. Mrs. Turnbull desires her best respects to your Excellency.

I had almost forgot to mention that Mr. Oswald has been with Sir. William Duncan to persuade him to abandon indigo and plant sugar… Oswald advises me to it also, on a foolish plan of the poor Danish settlers of Santa Cruz. I am resolved not to involve myself in any new scheme. When indigo have paid the expenses we have been at and also brought such sums as will enable us to undertake another scheme, it may be tried. I think sugars will do in this province but I am not persuaded that it will be a more profitable culture than indigo…

James Grant Papers

******

Andrew Turnbull to Sir William Duncan
Smyrnéa, October 27, 1770
… I am glad to see by your letter that the bounty is to be given this year. Governor Grant, not thinking himself sufficiently authorized to draw for it, desired me to give him a list of what we wanted from London, and desired that application might be made to Mr. Bradshaw for the money to execute that commission. The rest of the Money is intended to be laid out in Provisions from Charlestown.

I observe, Sir William, what you say about locating the last 15,000 acres to the west of St. John's River. As soon as the warrants for these tracts came to my hands, I sent the deputy surveyor Funk to locate them on the west side of that River, tho' not nigh its banks, where the lands are poor, but on the high lands, rather towards St. Marys and Nassau River. I hurried the locating of them as the best of the lands will be soon taken up. He is not yet returned with the surveys. Sir Richard Temple's tract is southwest from this place, on the east side of St. Johns. The back line of that land, and the back line of this I am now on, are about eight or nine miles distance from one another. I have Governor Grant's leave to take up the vacant land between them, if good, but it is mostly pine barren. I have not been at the expence of surveying any of it yet, nor will it probably be worth our while for anybody to be at that expence. I intend, however, to secure it by taking up some of it, if it is found to be tolerably good. As Sir Richard Temple's tract gives us a front on St. Johns it will insure us the convenience of shipping our goods from the inner parts of our tracts, either by that river or by this. The best tracts to the west of St. Johns will produce Rice and annual Indigo, but they will not be so valuable as the lands here where Indigo stands the winter. If two or three five thousand acre tracts more could be obtained I would endeavour to locate them to the south of this, perhaps nigh Cape Canaveral, where the lands and climate are very proper for the culture of

Indigo and Sugar, I will endeavour to get them, however, on family right to be thrown into the Mass.

You desire, Sir William, to know what care I have taken of my Family and you in case of any accident to me, and what agreement I have made with our people, and where I have deposited these contracts. As to my family, my will was made many years ago. I have not yet altered it, waiting till our affairs got on to a point of division of produce, which is now very nigh.

As to the care of the settlement in case anything happens to me, I endeavored to provide for that before I left Mahon. I wrote from thence for a Son of my Brother. I had seen him and fixed on him in my mind, as a person whose relationship to me and partly a dependance would attach to my interests. He came to me here above two years ago. He was not of much service to me the first six months, being chiefly employed in learning the languages of the People here, which he easily and soon attained. After that he was my storekeeper for about five months more, in which time I had frequent opportunities to observe him. His care and abilities were to my Mind.

I then put him on the command of our People next to myself, and I can justly say that he is a very fit person to have the care of this settlement He had the management of it twice last summer in my absence. I being then obliged to go to St. Augustine. I did not find any thing to find fault with on my return, on the contrary, I saw that he was equal to anything of that nature, being resolute, steady, and judicious, with all the care and foresight of age and experience, tho' he is not yet twenty three years of age. I think him in every respect the most proper person to manage your affairs here. However as a further security and satisfaction to you, I think that Governor Grant, William Drayton, Esq., and Captain Robert Bisset might be desired to take the general direction, subject this Andrew Turnbull, my nephew, to their orders. These three gentlemen will not refuse me this favour. They are not only men of the strictest probity, but also the most intelligent in agriculture of any in this country. Mr. Drayton is Chief Justice of this Province. Col. Faucett will inform you what you may want to know of Captain Bisset, his advice has often been of use to me here. As for my part, I should be glad to have my share entirely in the management of these gentlemen, but if any other you think of, are more to your mind, I will very willingly agree to it.

As I have mentioned my nephew, I think is proper to acquaint you on what terms we have him. I agreed to give him twenty pounds a year for the first two years, which was not much considering that his passages by the way of Liverpool, Virginia and Georgia, cost him above fifty pounds, besides he lost six months on this round. I must in conscience have given him forty or fifty pounds this year, but was sorry to add to our Expences. Luckily the governor hearing a very satisfactory account of his conduct and abilities, and being acquainted with the small salary I gave him, contrived to give him the salary of Schoolmaster which is twenty five pounds a year. I added five pounds more to the twenty I gave him before, which makes fifty. He is contented with it because the proposal comes from me, but he is worth four times that money to us. Even the most sorry overseers have forty and fifty pounds a year in this province. We have no school here, otherwise my nephew could not have that salary. His occupations are as many as most men could go through.

As to the agreements with our People, we are to be at the expence of bringing them into the province, but every other expence of settling, & etc., is to be paid from the produce of their labour. That debt liquidated, the profits of the lands on which they are settled are to be divided between proprietor and the farmer the first year after the debts are paid, which equal division of profits is to continue for ten years more after that first dividend is made. They, the Farmers, being as much subject to the Proprietor or his agent as a servant to a master, and this both in regard to what is to be cultivated, as to what they are to cultivate, and also in what mode or manner the Proprietor pleases. This agreement is a very advantageous one to us, and makes every Expence of the settlement fall on the labourers, which is one reason why I wish to establish many things before the debts are liquidated, which our funds do not admit of. When the Farmers are free of their debts, we must bear half the expense of every thing. But our immense expences already hinder me from doing some things which the People themselves desire me to do, alleging as an argument, that I ought to do it, as it is their desire and as they are to pay for everything, which is certain now they will soon do. They wish rather to be a year or two longer in debt than be punished in any thing. The longer we have them before the 11 years partnership comes on the better for us. One year's time from hence is better than three at present. When I send you the plan & etc. I will explain to you further the advantages of this agreement, and how it may be more so, and useful for the people at the same time. As to the contracts with these settlers I have them in my custody, but I think I should have registered them in the Registers' office. This, I own, did not occur to me, but it shall be done the first time I go to St. Augustine.

If the Disposition I mentioned above is to your mind, please to order an able Lawyer to draw it out, and send me two copies of it here. I will deposit one in the Registers' office, and send the other back to you after signing them. I wish this to be done as soon as possible, for tho' I have now recovered my health so perfectly, that it is equal to me whether I am out in the midday heats, or midnight damps, yet I think my life is a bad one. I am more exposed to the causes of sickness and accidents than any man on the settlement.

Mr. Delaire is just come in from measuring our cultivated lands, which has employed him for some days. He found it nine hundred and seventy acres.

I shall add some hundreds to it next spring. He is now taking a plan of our Houses here. As soon as these plans are done I will forward them to you. I can justly add that our land is in as high order as the Roots of Trees and such like embarrassments admit of. This Estate may be carried to a very high point of Emolument to the Proprietors, and that without extraordinary abilities in the manager, if the plan now begun is carried on.

I forgot to mention in the above that single men, I mean unmarried men, are engaged to us for seven years at five pounds sterling wages a year, one half to be paid to them in necessary clothing, and the other half at the Expiration of that term of seven years. My best Tradesmen are engaged at the same price. Thirty pounds a year are given for English tradesmen in this province, I would not give two of our five pound ones for three of them. Ours are sober and more under command.

Dundee City Archives

＊＊＊＊＊＊

Andrew Turnbull to Sir William Duncan
Smyrnea, October 29, 1770

If I could leave I would engage to bring many of them (Turks) away. Better for this settlement if I stayed here for some years. I want to stay until stability is assured. Another way would be to appoint an agent at Port Mahon to receive all Greeks who come, giving them four pence a day, and when the number of colonists fills the ship, bring them to Florida. A stock of provisions, enough to last for one year, should be in storage prior to their arrival.

Theodore Alexiano, a Greek at Mahon, to whom all the Greeks come for assistance, would be a proper agent. He has a copy of the agreement which I have with the Greeks here. Turnbull said his name could be used among the Greeks, and that it would be wise to ask the Governor of Minorca to provide protection.

Dundee City Archives

＊＊＊＊＊＊

Andrew Turnbull to Sir William Duncan
Smyrnéa, October 30, 1770

I'm heartily sorry that Governor Grants intends to leave us. He says he leaves for two years, but I doubt his ever coming back, as the family estate is now fallen to him. Two years at least of a lieutenant governor, who may trouble us here. New settlements need the support of the governor of the province. It was Turnbull's belief that governors could do favors and assist his settlement, and gave as an example Governor Grant's use of the provincial sloop to transport goods to and from New Smyrna without charge. Grant had always been frugal of public money, to a fault Turnbull said, although never when New Smyrna was concerned. Instead, he treated Smyrnéa as if it had been his private property. He could not have been more attentive to it.

Dundee City Archives

******

Andrew Turnbull to Governor James Grant
Smyrnéa, November 4, 1770

I return you thanks for your congratulations on Mrs. Turnbull's being brought to bed of a son. That piece of news was so old to me that when I wrote to your Excellency on the 22nd of last month I had quite forgot it. I in return congratulate you, Sir, most heartily, on the family estate falling into your hands. I think that you will have enough to do to defend yourself against matrimony now. I require also that you have obtained his Majesty's leave to go to England. My joy, however, is only because it is for your convenience and advantage. My wishes are rather that your stay among us was to be longer than you mention. I am apprehensive that when you are on the other side of the Atlantic the effects of pride and jealousy, which are at present only inconveniences to the owners, will then be felt by others.

I am sorry, Sir, that you troubled yourself when you favored me with the paragraph of Mr. Bradshaw's letters. I saw that the only thing to be done was what you planned and forwarded. We are much obliged to you for intending to solicit another years bounty. If obtained, it will be more than ever we could flatter ourselves of. I will apprise Sir William of your intentions, that he may give all the help he can.

The weather here was so cold the week before last that our weed did not steep, nor could we get above a third of the quantity of weed we generally had before. Besides the indigo was of an inferior quality to any we had made. The weather came round the fifth day, and now we make some floras and purples as before. We have made nigh four hundred vats, and I am afraid from the weather which set in today that we still should be able to make much more. The advice of a vessel for us was very agreeable. I sent the pilot to the bar yesterday to look out for him, but I am apprehensive that this gale of wind will make him keep in the offing.

I never thought the Indian affair a serious one and am glad to find by your letter that it is less so than I imagined. The coming of the East Florida to take away our produce will be doing us a great service as I intend to ensure, I should be glad to know if she is to carry it straight to Carolina or only to St. Augustine. If her destination is determined I beg your pardon, Sir, for troubling you with this question, but you see it is on account of the insurance. Mrs. Turnbull presents her best congratulations to your Excellency and wishes you joy of your estate…

James Grant Papers

******

Andrew Turnbull to Governor James Grant
Smyrnéa, November 10, 1770

This goes by Mr. Fraser who I imagine takes this jaunt to settle a correspondent to furnish him with provisions. He came here with very little. I supplied him as long as I had any, but he is not well pleased now, I believe because I do not give him what I have not. He thought it hard that I did not let him have fifty pounds of flour a week when I had only one barrel left. I gave him ten which with one third hominy as I make my bread at present, I thought enough for his family a week. I give him as much corn meal and peas as he wants. He has not said anything to me, but when he gets his grog aboard he has murmured a little. I have never taken notice of this nor shall not, as you may easily imagine, Sir. I wish him well, and shall always assist him with anything I can spare. I thought proper, however, to acquaint your Excellency with it that if he should say anything in town about my not furnishing him with what he wanted, you might be apprised of the reasons.

We make indigo still, three and four vats a day, but the weather does not let us get into the colors we had six months ago. I keep a sharp lookout for the vessel. Bisset has another bad fever on him. He is clearing in his swamp and wet himself very much. It threw a gout into his head with a fever of no good kind. This is the second time he has been marked with these disorders lately. He would fain be young.

James Grant Papers

******

Andrew Turnbull to Sir William Duncan
Smyrnéa, November 12, 1770

My last letter acquainted you that Mr. Delaire was measuring our cultivated land, that I might send you plans of that and of our buildings. Two copies of these accompany this, they are in a box with some pieces of our Indigo. You see by the ground plan, that we have nine hundred and seventy acres cleared and cultivated. It appears from the manner it is laid down in, to be but a slip, being the front of one of the narrowest sides of our land, because of its being on a navigable River. I intend to carry on the clearing and cultivation in the same breadth, which is nigh seven miles, except when a bad piece of land comes in my way. I am sorry I have not a large plan of the two tracts to send you, but if you cast your eye on the small plan of them, which I left with you in London, you will see that the ground plan I now send you is of a part, or rather of a large half of the front of these two tracts on Hillsborough River. It is called in that plan Hummock Land, & is divided in some places by Savannahs and meadows running in the same paralel with the River. The whole of that front of Hummock, including its' Savannahs, makes about sixteen hundred acres of which we now have in cultivation the nine hundred acres and seventy I mentioned above.

I have cut a canal thro' the Ridge on the river side, you see it in the ground plan almost a mile from this Town. This is to drain the meadows, and the lowest part of the Hummock. My intentions are to put this front of sixteen hundred acres into a state of plowing as soon as possible, that I may then remove half of our People to the east side of the Swamp, about a mile and a half to the west southerly from this hummock. You will see by the plan of the tracts, in your hands, that the large Swamp I speak of runs in the same direction with this River, which will be a great conveniency, as the Farmers on this side of it will not only be contiguous to the Settlements here, but be also in the same line with them, and divided by a pine barren with many savannahs, which will afford good pasture for the cattle of both settlements. When that line of Farms is compleated, another may be begun on the west side of the Swamp, which will be more convenient to them in one, for it is so wide that it will admit of two very well.

The Drain in the Swamp, which must be wide enough for boats of ten ton's burden, will cut it lengthways, and be a boundary between the two lines of Farms. The other great Swamp two miles behind that, and westward from it, may be settled with Farms on the same plan. This seems to me to be the best disposition for these two Tracts. Perhaps no part of America admits of a more regular laying out, and convenient settling than this we are upon. Every new Range of Farms will be within the Reach of aid and support of another. The high lands of all of them will answer well for Indigos, the lower for Sugars, and the lowest for Rice, but as Sugars promise to be a more profitable culture than Rice, the making the drain a little deeper than for Rice will fit the lowest Lands for Sugar. I have taken much pains lately in examining the swamps nearest us, and find it a most promising soil, when I can get a traverse survey of it taken, I shall be better able to tell you what proportion the high lands must bear to the lower. It seems to me that about half of it will be fit for Indigo, the other half may be made fit for Sugars.

These, Sir William, are the plans of cultivation I intend to pursue, if approved of. It may be expected that I should say something of the best and most expeditious method of carrying on these cultures. The People we have will in time settle the whole of what I mention, but it will be a long time. If you wish to have it done in fewer years, we must put more people on it, which might be begun in the autumn of the year 1772, by setting aside for this purpose, a fourth, fifth, or sixth of the amount of the yearly produce of this Settlement, this to be funded in London, and drawn for as wanted by an agent in Mahon, who would easily find a sufficient number of young People there to load a small vessel every autumn, he having orders to ship young People only, except when the young part of the family makes it advantageous to accept the aged also. These would probably be mostly Greeks and Foreigners. I mean not, however, that this having of more settlers supplied them from London direct, than purchasing what they want in America as I am obliged to do now, tho I know that I pay from thirty to fifty percent profit for many things I purchase for them, even more than that, for the greatest part of the goods sent to America are bought in England at one year's credit, which to American merchant is at least ten per cent more.

I think it would be better that they were supplied by us at thirty per cent profit which would not only be a gain to us, to whom of right it belongs, but would do our People a service at the same time. They would be twenty percent at least in pocket by it, if we purchased for ready money. By this means we shall have sixty five percent of their labor for many years. One half of the produce of this labour or fifty in a hundred, is ours by agreement, which with fifteen on their fifty, the other half will make sixty five in the hundred. This seems not only to be worth our while attending to, but I think we ought to do them this service, that they may be supplied better and cheaper than they can be otherwise. If a third years bounty is granted, it will be time enough to begin this in 1772, as that money will amply supply us with every common wear and necessaries until that time, and perhaps longer. But if a third years bounty is not given, it may be begun next winter, and if any extraordinary Expence is incurred by this, or by any other charge which I cannot immediately answer, I shall be glad to pay eight percent, the interest of this country, til I can reimburse it... But I would not be understood that I am impatient or pressing for more People. I am contented with these we have, and should not have proposed this, if you had not been particular in desiring me to acquaint you with my plan of cultivation. I have added a view of the advantages which might more speedily arise from an Increase of strength thrown into these tracts, which at present would be much more to our Interests, than settling others: one thousands pounds thrown into this, in the way I mentioned above, would render us more profit, than double that sum on a new settlement. I do not object, however, to the securing more Land in the Province...

Delaire measured our cultivated land. Two copies of his survey are enclosed in a box with pieces of indigo. You can see that we have 970 acres cleared and cultivated

Dundee City Archives

******

Andrew Turnbull to Sir William Duncan
Smyrnéa, November 12, 1770
That of our landing here in the sickly season of the year was the principal cause of all our Desarters. Our long passages by sea would not have been much felt by us, if the consuming our provisions and the bringing on of a scorbutic Habit among our people had been the only consequence of these delays, but our misfortune was that we were thrown back in time, and obliged to land in the most sickly season which had been known in the province, so that we were attacked by those disorders of the season before we had recovered from the languor and low spiritedness of a scorbutic habit. This caused the great loss we had. Our better acquaintance in the seasons and climate will enable us to shun these inconveniences in future.

If this proposal of bringing in of more people is approved of, I would be understood that it should not be begun 'till the autumn of the year 1772, when the profits arising from this settlement will be more ascertained than at present, and the Expences of feeding a few more people will not be so much felt by us as now. I think that one thousand pounds laid out yearly in bringing people here is not only enough to begin with, but also to continue it for some time…

Dundee City Archives

******

Andrew Turnbull to Sir William Duncan
Smyrnéa, December 3, 1770
When Mr. Delaire is at leisure another plan of the farmhouses and plantations, and of building timbers and other trees, which are intend for the River front of this land will be sent to Duncan.

Land near the settlement that is fit for planting is filled with large trees, but none of it produces lumber appropriate for building, thus Turnbull uses timber that must be cut and brought by water from twenty miles away. Cutting the trees and transporting them to the creek is very hard labor, and clearing the creek so it is navigable by boats of ten tons to load the timber is more hard labor.

On the geometrical plan the only planting done was a row of orange trees on each side of the road, set out twenty-five feet distant from one another each

160

way. That way the trees have room for the branches to spread out so that breeze can pass through and also provide ornament and utility. The orange trees at all times provide a pleasing evergreen appearance, and have a cheerful and rich look when in flower and fruit. In time they will both shade the road and be conducive to good health for the settlers because the cooling juice of the fruit is not only a wholesome acid to be used with the fish our People eat, but also one of the best remedies we have for the bilious disorder to which this country, with other hot countries, is subject.

Since the plan was sent to you I planted some Magnolia trees on each side of the great street which goes to the westward from the large middle wharfe. Planted in two rows, each 25 foot from the houses, with 40 foot clear between the rows, and 30 foot asunder in the line. I have also made 2 large ranges more of these trees, from North to South, beginning at the sides of the large middle wharfe on the banks of the River, these extend a half mile either way, and are at 30 foot distance from one another. I have gone no farther with them than to where this Town will probably extend. I think of extending these River Ranges to the side lines of the Tract, but not in magnolias, rather in mulberry trees, with some clumps of cedars, pines and other useful trees…

Magnolia is used for ship building, pines and cedars for houses, mulberry is used for silk worms. Plantings the trees will also prove beneficial for the settlers and for the proprietors as Moments of leisure and as a profit, useful, also for laborers relaxation from daily labor.

Dundee City Archives

******

Andrew Turnbull to Governor James Grant
Smyrnéa, December 3, 1770
The schooner Active, John Hawkins, Master, arrived here on Saturday night after a passage of twenty days from Charlestown. He will be unloaded today. Mr. Gordon had sent him to Winyaw for corn but could not get any, therefore filled him up with a coarse Carolina flour, at 47 shillings currency a hundred, the best flour is at 80 shillings. It is fresh and good and will be of equal service with corn. He has also sent twenty seven barrels of rice instead of what you ordered all to fill up. He says this cargo nigh balances the account. I wrote for some west India rum, which is come by the Active. He sends me six hogsheads more of northward rum, which he did in consequence of your order, though he says you did not mention the quantity. This, however, is very apropos and is a two years stock with the five I ordered. I am now as easy as I can wish. I shall not want any of the articles he now sends for one year at least, if not more, and as for corn I think I have enough till another crop. We shall find

room, however, for the supply from the second bounty, for which I shall be very thankful especially to you Sir.

John Gordon desires me to forward the enclosed for you. He tells me that it contains a letter from Mr. Arthur Gordon. I guess the contents from one I have from him though I never saw him, nor know anything of him, he desires my interest for his being attorney general. God help him if he has no other interest than mine. I have none that I know of, besides if I had he certainly would not imagine that I would solicit for anything under your government without having your leave and knowing that it was for a person you wished to have. Indeed, I think I could not even ask this question for I do not think it a fair one. I have answered Mr. Gordon this morning by the way of Charlestown and have wrote to this purpose that he may not trust to such a broken reed as my interest. Bisset, Mack, and Ross talk of going to town next week. Fraser brings down news of a Spanish war, as I have no letters from England, I cannot tell what credit to give to this. Mrs. Turnbull desires her respects to your Excellency…

James Grant Papers

******

Andrew Turnbull to Governor James Grant
St. Augustine, December 1770

I desired Mr. Penman to acquaint you yesterday that some business in the city and a desire I had to see my son did not admit of my paying my respects to you before today when I hurried to your home on my return from the country, but did not find you at home. I was so desirous to see you that I desired the servant to acquaint you that I would call again tomorrow morning. I am the more solicitous to wait on you as I understand from Mr. Penman, that you think I am hurt by your recommendations of Mr. Moultrie. I beg, Sir, to assure you that I was hurt only by you having wrote that it was incompatible with the interest of the Smyrnea settlement, having had good reason to convince me soon after your leaving the province, that it would have been the reverse.

As to the affair of the sloop I was obliged to acquaint my partners in England with my reason for not sending the indigo to London as they desired in a pressing manner. I was also then in distress for provisions and other necessaries from St. Augustine and would have given any freight for a vessel to bring to me what was intended to be sent by Bachop if he had not been cast away. That accident obliged me to go to St. Augustine, where there was not then even a boat to hire. In these distressing circumstances, I applied for the sloop, but was answered that I could not have her then nor afterwards. I pretended to no right nor do pretend to any, but asked this service as the greatest favor that could be done to me. More pressing letters and threats of protested bills if I did not send home the indigo drew from me a justification of myself, by acquainting my partners with the efforts I had made. I also meant to let Sir William Duncan see that he ought to have exerted himself in favor of our settlement in regard to the lieutenant governorship, which however, I never pointed at till experience convinced me that it would have been of advantage to the settlement and that I should be exposed to many losses, expenses, and inconveniences from its having gone into other hands. I will do myself the honor, Sir, to wait on you tomorrow morning. I am with the greatest respect...

James Grant Papers

******

The Earl of Hillsborough to Governor James Grant
Whitehall, December 11, 1770

Your despatches No. 38 & 39 have been received and laid before the King & I am very glad to find you have so good hopes that the improvement of the important colony under your government will not be impeded by any real difficulty attending the navigation into its ports.

I am very sensible of the advantage which the public may derive from the success of Dr. Turnbull's Settlement at New Smyrnea, but as the £2000 which His Majesty was most graciously pleased to grant for that purpose upon a former application from you, was at the time declared to be in consideration of the then distress of that colony and by no means intended to encourage any expectation of a further bounty. I cannot take upon me to authorize any further expence to the public on that account. I will, however, transmit your letter to the Lords of the Treasury and shall be very glad if it shall have the effect to obtain some further bounty in support of so meritorious an undertaking...

Colonial Office Papers

******

Andrew Turnbull to Sir William Duncan
Smyrnéa, December 1770

I have been experimenting with steeping, beating, and liming, and now know the right way to make indigo dye. The lack of drying houses hurt us some.

I sent two samples of sugar along with the last letter. Rum here is as good as that made in Jamaica. Mr. Forbes, maker of rum says it is fine. I enclose his letter to you. He is back at Smyrnéa and is still enthused about prospects for sugar and rum in East Florida.

Dundee City Archives

******

CORRESPONDENCE

Lord Hillsborough to James Grant
Whitehall, February 11, 1771

I acquainted you in my letter of the 2nd of last month with my Intention to lay before the King your Recommendation of Mr. John Moultrie to be Lieutenant Governor of East Florida, and I have the now the Pleasure to inform you that His Majesty has been graciously pleased in consequence thereof to confer that office upon that Gentleman, and his Warrant will be made out with all possible Dispatch and delivered to such Person as Mr. Moultrie shall authorize to call for it,

Colonial Office Papers

******

Andrew Turnbull to Sir William Duncan
St. Augustine, February 15, 1771

I have given up my residence in Town, My family agreed to live at Smyrnéa with me as exiles from every convenience and amusement.

Dundee City Archives

******

Andrew Turnbull to Sir William Duncan
Smyrnéa, April 18, 1771

Inclosed I send you the number of our people with their ages. Our arrival here in the worst and wettest season ever seen in this country bore very heavy on us. But even this bad season would not probably have proved so mortal if a previous poor living in the countries where these people came from had not impoverished their blood. The long voyage added to that bad state, and reduced them so low that they could not stand the shock of such a great change, as that from a dry Mediterranean air to a moist one. The air of this country is generally dry and wholesome, but unluckily for us, it was quite the contrary for many months after our arrival.

Our loss, which is about half, fell most on the very young and the older people. I would have sent you a list of them long ago, but waited till the health of those behind was so much confirmed as to ensure an increase rather than a decrease in future. This is now the case, and I am very certain of making fine Estates even with these left.

Whenever debts are paid and every account balanced, it will be easy for me to increase our numbers without stirring from this place, and without such expences and risks as were incurred by our first tryal. I mean, that is if it is found expedient and for our interest, such a step may be taken. I shall not, however, do anything either in this, or in things of much less moment, without the full command and approbation of the gentlemen concerned with me in this settlement.

The ages and number of people belonging to the settlement of Smyrnéa in East Florida this 18th of March 1770

```
Under one year old ----------------------------12
From one year to four years old ----------------25
From 4 to 8 ---------------------------------- 47
From 8 to 12 --------------------------------- 63
From 12 to 16 -------------------------------- 133
From 16 to 30 -------------------------------- 361
From 30 to 40 -------------------------------- 47
From 40 to 50 and upwards ------------------ 14
In all ---------------------------------------702
Males ----------------------------------------406
Females --------------------------------------296
In all ---------------------------------------702
```

Andrew Turnbull

Dundee City Archives

******

Andrew Turnbull to Sir William Duncan
Smyrnéa, May 3, 1771

Our Hogg pen has supplied us this year with about 120 Sterling of pork. The intense heat of last summer, however, caused a palsy of the loins, that led to the death of a number of hogs, otherwise enough would have been produced to feed all of our people. This year, however, the entire hog supply was raised at Smyrnéa.

Dundee City Archives

******

Andrew Turnbull to Governor James Grant
Smyrnéa, May 9, 1771

On information from two Indians of a settlement of Spaniards and Yamisies on Cape Florida and a misrepresentation of the people here by another Indian, brought an upper Creek Chief, the Cowkeeper, the Long Warrior and another head man with seventy two warriors and young men into this part of the country. At first they were sulky, out of humor, and beat some of a boat's crew they found at my cow keepers, but on having provisions sent to them and on being invited to this place, the head men, with twenty warriors came here last Friday, dined, got drunk, and went away in better humour. Two days afterwards they broke up their camp at the cowpen, and divided into two parties, one went round the head of St. Johns to return home. The other with the chiefs went thro' this place on Sunday. I ordered Langley Bryant and black Sandy to accompany the last party 'till they saw them pass the Southern plantations on this river. But the Indians went no further than Captain Bissets', being then convinced that they had been imposed on as to the Yamisie Settlement. They returned here yesterday, eat and drank a good deal and went away very happy. A Chief of the upper Creeks commanded the whole and kept them in such order that, except the first scuffle, which happened at the cowpen about some provisions, they have not committed the least irregularity. This chief beat some of them very severely for offering to kill a calf which belonged to me.

I gave them Governor Grant's talk, and told them by his desire that he was going to see the great King, but would return soon, that in the mean time there was another Governor at St. Augustine, who would be glad to see this head man. Bryant accompanies him to St. Augustine. The upper Creek Chief is a sober manly Indian and seemed to be very watchful over the others for fear they should do anything wrong; he staid here 'till all of them went away, as he saw that they were drunk. The Long Warrior returned to this place today to beg a calf for his people. I gave him one, and would rather give two at any time, than they should take one without leave.

As the party here of the 31st Regiment consists of a sergeant and eight men only, should be glad of a reinforcement, not so much for the protection a small number can give us, as for the appearance of our being under the care of government which these Indians seemed at first to doubt.

James Grant Papers

✳✳✳✳✳✳

Andrew Turnbull to Governor James Grant
Smyrnéa, May 10, 1771

I easily made up every difference between the Indian party and my people. They made very proper answers to your talk and were so well pleased with my treatment of them that they desired me to send them of anybody should molest me, that they would come with all their warriors and drive my enemies from me. I added to the talk with them that you was then going to see the great King, but that you would return soon, that in the meantime, a lieutenant Governor was at St. Augustine to give them provisions and presents as before. I found in the course of the talk with them that John Stewart, my cowpen man, had told them that I was to be Governor. This assisted to soften them at first when they were in very bad humour, and I cannot help thinking, Sir, that it would have been of importance to this settlement, that the lieutenant Governors commission had been given to me. It would have given me such an influence over the Indians, and in the province on many accounts it would have ensured the getting on of this settlement. I was perfectly easy when you was here. Your character among the Indians, your abilities, and readiness to assist ensured every thing. I have not that confidence in any other person, and shall take my measures accordingly. I shall think myself neglected, and that this settlement is not look't on in the light it should be by government. Your recommending a gentleman you had given your word to, does you honour, and must be approved of. If it was possible for me to respect you more than I do, that would have added to it, but Sir William was under no engagement, therefore ought to have urged the merits of our undertaking, with which no other in this province can even be put in competition.

Black Sandy, by whom I send this, is obliged to go off to the Indians at the cowpen, which hinders me from writing you a more correct letter. Mrs. Turnbull's wishes and mine are for the reestablishment of your health, and that you may succeed in every thing to your wishes.

James Grant Papers

******

Andrew Turnbull to Sir William Duncan
Smyrnéa, May 20, 1771

My nephew kept the men together and pacified the Indians with assistance of a rumor that I was appointed governor. I had a long talk with the Chiefs when I arrived. They went away in good humor, but it discouraged our People. I find I have neither power nor means to protect them.

Dundee City Archives

******

Andrew Turnbull to Sir William Duncan
Smyrnéa, May 25, 1771

I have been advised by Mr. Nixon to dictate to an English clerk a few hours a week, but can not spare the time: I have sometime fallen off the logg I have been sitting on for chairs, we had none then, so oppressed I have been with fatigue and lack of sleep; six hours in twenty-four is the most rest I ever take. I would not undergo these times again for all the money it has cost, nor indeed could I go through it a second time, the first has been too severe a grinding. My health and spirits bore it. I flagg now in both, and if I am not put on a better footing in this province than I am at the moment, I must leave the management of this Affair to other hands.

Dundee City Archives

******

Andrew Turnbull to Governor James Grant
Smyrnea on Hillsborough River, May 27, 1771

I troubled you with a letter about the Indian affair in agitation when you left this province. I had not sufficient information when I wrote that letter to speak with certainty of the particulars of that affair. They are come to my knowledge since. I shall therefore mention that the manner these Indians seized some people belonging to this place was so alarming and their messages so threatening that my family with other women were obliged to fly from hence at midnight in an open boat. Most of the farmer's wives with their children hid themselves among the mangrove islands on this river. The men were hindered with difficulty from going away, and when the alarm was over, the women were look't for, found, and brought back. I have been using my utmost endeavors since to make them get over the dread of the scalping knives or a roasting on the fire, as is sometimes the treatment captives meet with among Indians, but I find that their dread still hangs over them for they now employ all their leisure time in cutting out canoes to carry their families out of the reach of Indians in case of an attack which may be apprehended for I have discovered on enquiring into the late affair, that the intentions of these Indians were hostile to us, which from their former intimations and threatening I found to proceed from their being displeased because you had not met the Chiefs of this nation for almost four years to give them presents, which they expect yearly, from your having told them, Sir, at the first congress, that you would meet them often to keep up a friendship with them; and to give them the presents which the Great King sends them.

The Creek Indians have been out of humour for some time past about this affair, which many of them have often spoke of. From these and other murmurings, I conjectured when I heard of that Indian party, that their intentions were not favorable to us, which proved to be so from their own declarations at my cowpenn. I seemed, however, to give credit to what they told me afterwards was the reason of that armament, it being intended as they pretended against a Spanish and Yamisae settlement on Cape Florida where no such settlement, nor any other, exists, nor did they go farther than this place to look for it. This was the excuse they made after I had found means to make them lay aside their first intentions which they before declared were against this settlement and that it was on the account that they were without horses, women, and children; as is their custom of marching when in war. Besides the Chiefs refused for some days the several invitations made them to come to this place nor would they have come at all in a friendly manner if John Stewart, a cattle hunter, had not told them that I was appointed to govern the province, and that I was on my way from St. Augustine to meet the chief to have friendly talk with them. This made them imagine that I would bring presents for them such as Governors generally give, which brought them to better temper, and they came to me here as soon as I arrived. They had then laid aside their war colours, and were in their gayest paintings. They stayed with me one day and went away pleased with my manner of treating them and with the few presents I made them. But that the disappointment of my not having such presents as are furnished by government to give them might not sit heavy on their minds. I told them that the Governor at St. Augustine had presents for them on which the Chief disbanded his warriors, and went to make a visit to the Lieutenant Governor. I recommended this Chief to his particular notice as it seemed to be owing to his prudence and care that his people were restrained from hurting this settlement to which I think that he was partly engaged by my family, having robbed themselves of some beads and other trinkets which they sent to him to carry to his wife and children.

This incident, Sir, besides other things which happen daily, convince me that it would be of importance for the protection and safety of this small colony who, being foreigners, are suspected by Indians not to be English. The worst of which I feel much at present. When you governed the province, Sir, I was sure of being speedily assisted on every emergency. I do not know another man in whom I have the same confidence and am now without any certainty of assistance if wanted, for I wrote last week both Lieutenant Governor to desire that the party of soldiers there might be reinforced with five men to make up a secure command of a corporal and twelve men, not for any great help such a small number could give us, but to convince the Indians that we are under the care of government, which they seem to doubt. I was answered that they could not be spared at present.

This, Sir, is sufficient to convince me that any requisition I make will not be readily granted, for this of five men only was made after the arrival of the post, which brought advice from Lord Hillsborough that our disputes with Spain were made up, so that an unexpected call for troops on that account could not be alleged as an excuse for this refusal.

This, Sir, is one instance of many I could give, that your preferring Major Moultrie to me has lessened my influence much and it has already smote a drawback on my endeavors to get on that it will go right to break my spirit of colonizing and threatens to break the back of this settlement. I was pointed out by the Secretary of State to succeed you, Sir, as Lieutenant Governor, a letter of good authority tells me as much, your having stained the setting aside of these intentions has raised a suspicion against me that I am not well with government at home. This hurts me in my own mind, hurts me in the minds of my people, and has hurt my character so much that it will probably oblige me to give up all the advantages I have been struggling for. It would have been the reverse of this, Sir, if I had succeeded you in the Government of the province as the direction of assistance, when wanted, would then have been greatly in my own hands which would have influenced the Indians to have had a due respect for this settlements from the high light they regard a Governor in and the respect they have for every person or possession belonging to him; his having presents also to be disposed of among them as he thinks proper gives him every advantage of this native for the most savage Indian reveres the hand which feeds and clothes him.

With these advantages, Sir, I would have trusted my family here which is the best argument I could have made use of to convince my people that they have nothing to fear. And as to myself, I could have easily done the business of government by being ten days or a fortnight in town every month in the summer, and by residing there in the winter, when business is generally done, which indeed is yet so little that an active man might easily go through it in two days of every month. And as to the leisure since a governor might have, he certainly will employ it better that in forwarding such settlements as this; the conducting and managing of which you think, sir, requires my continued attendance and constant residence here. That opinion you never mentioned to me, Sir, to remove my family from St. Augustine, it was not for that reason, but that I and my family might be out of the disagreeable rebound as you termed it, of some bills then expected back in protest, which, however, did not happen. It could not be imagined at that time that it was necessary for me to reside in this place as I had then managed the affairs here for one year, which was from August 1768 when the mutiny was raised here, till August 1769, tho' I was in St. Augustine the greatest part of these two last months to purchase provisions for the people here. This was the first year also when things were not brought to that family regularity they are in at present with the help I have now. My reason for mentioning this, Sir, is that when I saw you last you was so strong in this opinion that you could hardly bear to be contradicted. I therefore dropped the dispute but I am apprehensive that without my consent or a sufficient knowledge of my mode of conducting this settlement, it has been given as an opinion and has been the cause of my being set aside.

James Grant Papers

******

John Moultrie to Major Alexander Mackenzie
Commanding His Majesty's troops in East Florida
St. Augustine, June 6, 1771

Doctor Turnbull, this day represented to me in council that a considerable body of armed Indians had lately appeared at Smyrnea, his settlement on the

Musquito, and that a party of their young men had been irregular and beat some of his people and that they had very much alarmed and terrified the rest.

Altho' I have not the least apprehension of their intention to commit any act of hostility, but am clearly of opinion that their nation are on the best terms with us; I think it would be doing that valuable young settlement an essential service to strengthen the detachment of the 31st regiment now posted there. They would demand respect from any hunting or other parties of Indians passing that way and prevent irregularities which might otherwise happen, and would also tend to quiet the minds of the affrighted settlers and give them confidence.

With the advice of his majesty's council I must therefore request, that you would as soon as possible reinforce the present small detachment now at Smyrnea with twelve men, they will make up the smallest number I think that ought to be there.

James Grant Papers

******

Andrew Turnbull to Governor James Grant
St. Augustine, June 13, 1771

An information from two Indians of a Settlement of Spaniards and Yamasies on Cape Florida, and a misrepresentation of the People here by another Indian brought an Upper Creek Chief, the Cowkeeper, the long Warrior and another head man with seventy two Warriors and young men into this part of the Country. At first they were sulky, out of humor, and beat some of a boats crew they found at my Cowpen, but on being invited to this Place, the head man with twenty Warriors came here last Friday, dined, got drunk, and went away in better humor. Two days afterwards they broke up their Camp at the Cowpen and divided into two parties, one went round the head of St. Johns to return home. The other with the Chiefs went through this place on Sunday. I ordered Langley Bryant and black Sandy to accompany the last party 'till they saw them pass the Southern Plantations on this River, but the Indians went no further than Captain Bisset's, being then concerned that they had been imposed on as to the Yamasie Settlement, they returned here yesterday, ate and drank a good deal and went away very happy. A Chief of the upper Creeks kept them in such order that except for what happened at the Cowpenn about some provisions they have not committed the least Irregularity. This Chief beat some of them very severely for offering to kill a calf which belonged to me.

I gave them Governor Grant's talk and told them, by his desire, that he was going to see the great King, but would return soon. That in the mean time there was another Governor at St. Augustine, who would be glad to see this head man. Bryant accompanies him to St. Augustine. The Upper Creek Chief is a sober manly Indian, and seemed to be very watchful over the others for fear they should do any thing wrong, he staid here till all of them went away, as he saw that they were drunk. The Long Warrior returned to this place today to beg a Calf for his People. I gave him one, and would rather give two at any time, than they should take one without leave.

As the party here of the 31st Reg. consists of a Sergeant and eight men only, I should be glad of a reinforcement, not so much for the protection a small number can give us, as for the appearance of our being under the care of Government which these Indians seemed at first to doubt.

Colonial Office Papers

******

David Yeats to Governor James Grant
St. Augustine, August 31, 1771

Since my last of the 2nd of July, we have had an almost continual drought, which has hurt the indigo planters much and nearly destroyed the rice. Mr. Drayton from double the quantity of land planted won't make so much rice as last year. Grant's Villa has suffered very considerable by it. The first cutting was finished some time ago, and according to Mr. Skinner's computation amounts to between six and seven hundred weight, the second I am afraid from the appearance of the weed won't yield much more. I saw it two days ago when they were beginning the second cutting, which would have been finished by this time had the season been favorable, for they delayed cutting in hopes of rain, and now are obliged to go on as the season advances fast in expectation of a third. The pond in the North field which used to supply two vats a day for sometime past has hardly been hardly been sufficient for one, tho' deepened four feet, a proof of the remarkable dryness of the season. They average considerably more a vat than last year, by means of steeping a little longer and adding a large proportion of lime water. Doctor Turnbull was the first to fall into this way. They have all followed his example and find it answers.

The Doctor Turnbull in his letter to me of he 25Th July gives the following account of his settlement. 'My first cutting has given me three thousand weight of much better indigo on the whole than last year's assortment. I think I shall go to above three thousand Guineas with this crop, and almost all from the old weed. This year's planting was blasted in May, the drought has hindered me from establishing it as yet. Our appearances of provisions are of plenty and out of danger as the corn is almost all turned down. I have averaged ten pounds a vat the first cutting. I expect to do more the second and third.'

Since I received the above letter the Doctor has gone thro' his second cutting which has given him four thousand weight. He expected six, would have made it had it not been for the remarkable dry weather. He has tried how far lime water may be carried in indigo making and has found that by liming very high that twenty-five weight a vat may be made which is the utmost, but then the indigo is poor stuff.

James Grant Papers

******

Frederick George Mulcaster to Govenor James Grant
St. Augustine, October 2, 1771

Dr. Turnbull is in town. He has lost his third cutting by the worm, such havock I never saw by so insignificant a reptile, he has, however, in his store house eight thousand weight of indigo and as the rains have just now set in he hopes still to have another cutting. The North River will also benefit by it for rain and Grants Villa have been great strangers to each other for some time. I had wrote you a long letter of its situation when I last saw it, but the account was so dreary that I took Owen's advice and threw it into the fire.

James Grant Papers

******

Andrew Turnbull to Governor James Grant
Smyrnea, October 28, 1771

I have the honor of your letter of the 17th of July. I am glad that you had such a good passage. Your taking so much trouble, Sir, about the affairs of the settlement and mine is another instance added to many of your friendship, for which I heartily thank you. My last letter you will recall, was not in such civil terms. I acknowledge it and am sorry that the situation I was then in, and not yet out of, made me angry and uneasy. The seeing myself, family, and people in danger from Indians and every kind of assistance or protection denied, without the satisfaction of having the least notice taken of it by the lieutenant Governor, notwithstanding my repeated solicitations, was alarming and threatened the bad consequences which are like to arise from your having obtained the government of this province for Mr. Moultrie. These apprehensions are not yet removed.

The Indians become more indolent every day, he more indolent in that business. They kill, and drive off my cattle into their own country. One Ohitchie carried off twenty head lately, and had drove thirty more as far as St. Johns, when some hunters sent after him obliged him to deliver them up. Tho' the damage they have done to this settlement is already considerable, it is as nothing to the damp it has thrown on the spirits of the settlers here, who see the labors of their hands distributed to idle insolent savages. I have between twenty and thirty of them on me at present. They pretend the country is full of water, and that they cannot hunt. I have repeatedly represented all this to Mr. Moultrie, but as no regard is paid to any requisition I make, I shift on as well as I can, till I hear from Sir William Duncan to whom I have made my situation known. If his answers do not come soon, or if they are not satisfactory, I must continue to pursue my resolution of coming to England to beg a protection form the Minister for America. I can foresee that I risk all by delaying; a little more of Indian insolence and this settlement will break up of itself which however I will endeavor to prevent as long as I can.

I intended to have carried my family to St. Augustine this winter, if the party quarrels there had not detained me. Drayton has resigned his seat in council, and it is with difficulty that three or four of that body can be brought together to do the very little business that there is to be done. Three only of them carried the address to the lieutenant Governor on his receiving his commission. I was not in town to make a fourth. Whatever objections I may have to the man who governs, I shall be cautious not to act against government.

Mr. Yeats will have acquainted you that I intend to resign the office of secretary in his favor, of it can be done. But if it cannot be done for him, it may be deferred till I have the honor of seeing you, tho' I confess that I will not hold it any longer. It is not worth my while for a miserable fifty pounds a year to lay myself under an obligation to a lieutenant governor for his allowing me to act by Deputy.

Sir William Duncan's coming out (to East Florida) is rather premature, but I am glad of it and will give me an opportunity of coming to London, and staying there some time to solicit my business. Let him lose an eye as I have done by the glare of white sand. He has forgot that I acquainted him of Mr. Murray's affair and asked his advice about it in a letter from Gibraltar. He may have lost that letter, but I have not lost his answer to it in which he particularly advises me what to do in that business. The clamor about my accounts is ungenerous and which I will regret if we do not hit it off better than we are like to do. By the last article in our last contract they are obliged to send out a clerk to their mind and at their expense in case I am prevented in doing that work by business, sickness or any other impediment. Almost every letter tells them that the nature of the direction here prevents me from sitting down to keep books of accounts to which if I had attended properly I should now have been in London with these books to show that the money was gone and the people either starved or despaired for want of being prompted to raise provisions for themselves. If the man Cutter had not been maimed in the mutiny, everything of that nature would have been in counting house order. He was hired at 100 Sterling a year for that purpose. My accounts, however, are in good order, for I was always very careful of the receipts and as my accounts have always been open and with people of credit, everything may be easily cleared up.

I am glad our indigo sold so well. I see that yours bore the bell. That was as it should be. The large package hurt the sale of mine. I made 8000 weight this year before the latter end of August, and had plants in the field for four thousand more, when millions of caterpillars appeared and did not leave me a green leaf, with only a part of the stalk. The bark of the stumps being also ground, they appeared dead for nigh a month, then shot out and when about six inches high was once more devoured by a new hoard of that destructive worm. By dint of labor night and day I cut about 89 vats of that short weed before the worms got to it and shall have about 9000 Sterling in all. Doses of fire, smoking, killing, and many more other things were tried to destroy them, but all in vain. Some other plantations in this part have them now, yet had them not before. Mrs. Turnbull desires her respects to your Excellency.

James Grant Papers

******

Andrew Turnbull to Sir William Duncan
London, April 6, 1772

I intended to have continued to manage it until the net return, clear of every expense and deduction, got up to ten thousand guineas yearly. I then resolved giving it into the hands of the proprietors. That prospect now vanishes, for the drawbacks and expenses put on me by Governor Grant and the Lt. Governor will soon oblige me to leave management, which I am to carry on with such opposition and disagreeable circumstances staring me in the face as can be thrown in my way by People, who are now convinced that my success and reputation lowers theirs.

I am to expect nothing but through the governor or lieutenant governor. I am therefore resolved to leave the settlement at Smyrnéa, and to take the people belonging to me into another Province. I can see through the thin veil of his Duplicity, and am not the Dupe of it. You will say that I entered warmly into this affair, which it is my duty to do, as it is in endeavoring to save a settlement risked by his neglect in the conduct of his government. This isn't the only allegation I could bring against him, but I go no farther. The consequence of all this and of you not taking the trouble to talk to Hillsborough by which you would have saved a thousand a year to the settlement, and ensured the management of it, that it would have got on very fast, besides the advantages which would have accrued to me. This has made me resolve to hasten back to put everything in order for a separation (disolving of the partnership), which I'll come here to affect the latter part of next year.

Carrying my own people away will be done with as much regard for your interest as possible. I mean only to secure myself not to hurt you. Nothing can ever induce me to any meanness of that kind.

I intended to build a good dwelling house on the settlement but shall not now. I can make a shift with this. I am in for one year more therefore shall not make any preparation for one except it is at your particular desire, and at your expense and for your conveniency. I shall put a stop also to all other buildings which are not immediately necessary. After separation, every man may build on his own plan.

We have double the number of acres in cultivation of Indigo than last year. The amount of money spent in the culture of indigo in East Florida amounts to £120,000 and that last year's crop of dye was 20,000 weight or but little less, of which we had above 9,000 so that notwithstanding the disadvantages we labored under, our 30,000 has done as much as the 90,000 employed by other hands. Proof and display of superior economy and abilities in the management of our affairs. The Smyrnea settlement would have always kept this superiority at every point if I had been properly protected and supported by government.

April 8th addendum: I've been with Lord Hillsborough and think he is inclined to do you and the settlement a service. If you ask, he will appoint me the governor of the province if and when Grant gives it up. This will certainly encourage me to stay in the Province of East Florida because I then could protect our People and make the Settlement thrive in the manner I wish and which I cannot do otherwise.

Dundee City Archives

******

Andrew Turnbull to Sir William Duncan
London, April 10, 1772

I shall continue to exert myself in carrying on the Settlement, and shall conceal my intentions of leaving it until we have settled all our affairs, and finally agreed on the mode of separation.

A separation is made obligatory by many circumstances the chief of which are the being exposed to Expenses and even Insults from Indians, on account of Governor Grant's having neglected to cultivate their friendship so far for me and the settlement, that it would be difficult for an Enemy to stir them up against me. The settlement ought to be protected and assisted by government instead of endeavors from the governor of the Province to keep me back. Grant smooths me over as much as he can, but shuns a quarrel with a man who he sees is hurt by the injuries he has done to the Greek Settlement and who, he sees, has every inclination to resist it.

Lord Hillsborough, however, seems desirous of assisting all you are concerned in, but thinks it would be troublesome to decide between Grant and me. I decline giving too much trouble and therefore will not push the appointment further.

Dundee City Archives

******

Andrew Turnbull to Sir William Duncan
London, April 16, 1772

Mr. Ramsay delivered me your letter of the 20th of March yesterday. You mention a letter of last October by Mr. Neilson. I neither have received that letter nor was it possible for me to know that Mr. Neilson was sent out. As to the division of the lands and everything else, I have put it off till about this time two years, when I shall be in this place that the many writings necessary in such a complex business may be properly drawn up and executed.

You complain, Sir William, that I kept you ignorant of the state of the contracts I made with the people, I explained that affair more fully in a letter to you from Port Mahon, than it is explained even in the contracts, and I have explained it twice since in letters from Florida. I shall certainly lay the state of the settlement accounts before Mr. Ramsay, merely because you desire it, tho' this is never done to a person who has not an authority as an attorney. Such a power to Mr. Ramsay would have saved both him and me double labour, as what is done by him now can neither be use to you nor me.

I am obliged to you, Sir William, notwithstanding, for your choice of Mr. Ramsay I shall always be happy in doing business with him, for he seems to me to be a person of the greatest probity, and with a proper turn for such transactions. I have brought copies of the contracts with me, these and every paper which could be required are recorded in that office at St. Augustine.

I have letters from Smyrnéa of a fresh date. Everything goes on well there. Mr. Neilson arrived at St. Augustine the latter end of January. I can find from Lord Hillsborough, who I saw at this house this morning, that he is acquainted with some differences among the people of the council there. I am happy in not being of that number for since the Chief Justice is resigned there are many of the others who are not of a turn for business of that nature, nor is it an honour to be one of the number. I am often with Governor Grant tho we differ in every point as to the use of public money. He is resolved to dispose of it as he pleases, and I think a proportionable share of it should be laid out in publick works and expenses useful to our settlement. We shall never agree on these points. He sees that I was not supported by you, Sir William, and that it is against me by being connected with Lord Temple, and therefore thwarts me in my reasonable demands for the settlers. I am happy in exerting myself for the object, tho' I think without effect, it is a particular satisfaction to me, not to have neglected any thing in my power. I have insisted much on a thousand pounds due to us for the first five hundred people carried into the province. Governor Grant got the sum, funded for that purpose, thrown into other savings of public money, and obtained an order for applying it otherwise. This was done, Sir William, when you was in London. I have boldly demanded that money, but am apprehensive I shall not obtain it, as it is now to be applied by Governor Grant for other uses, I am to have another hearing however, before Mr. Pownall about it at the Board of Trade.

I have not been able to obtain anything to alleviate the expenses we are at for Indians, tho' a considerable of many is given yearly to the province for that purpose, all this ought to convince you, Sir William, that whatever happens to our settlement will not be my fault, but I do not apprehend much from Indians while I am in the province. I am pretty certain I can ward off every blow of that nature.

Your taking notes of every culture, Sir William, will be of consequence; the culture of silk, sugars, vines, barilla, and of all the different commercial productions of Spain may be of great use. The climate where you are at present is similar in many respects to ours. There is a very extensive field of improvement yet unattempted in America. I intended to have solicited a patent for making a vegetable cochineal and madder like indigo, which would be very considerable cultures, but must defer them now, as it would not be well to begin anything which could not be carried to perfection in the two years we are to be concerned together, nor shall I attempt then and in all probability afterwards, there is so little encouragement from government for anything of that nature, that it is not worthwhile of anybody to attempt them. I think that the culture of talents of importunity and attendance would have more merit here than now than more solid qualifications. I shall be glad to hear from you at your leisure, and I beg my respects to Lady Mary.

Dundee City Archives

******

Andrew Turnbull to Sir William Duncan
London, June 30, 1772

I have been economical in cloathing and maintaining our People in East Florida since they arrived, which doesn't come to more than three pence a day a head. (The expenses of other settlements) being above double that sum. It now appears from the account of provisions and cloathing that it wasn't possible either to subsist or cloath people for less than I have done.

The partnership meeting should be in April 1774 when Mr. Grenville's heirs will be of legal age and a final settlement can be possible. Everything on such a footing as may facilitate the advantage of the whole and ascertain the property of each. Until then I will to keep on our partnership until I raise the settlement to 10,000 Sterling a year clear when the partners will meet and settle affairs.

I will begin a house for you next year as a venture. There must be a good house at any rate for the person who looks after the settlement. As you are in a climate like that of East Florida I beg your attention to the cultivation of everything. Sugar and vines in particular, paying attention to the heat of the weather in winter and summer by the thermometer to enable us to judge whether sugars will succeed with us or not and whether the winter cold kills standing canes or not.

Dundee City Archives

******

Andrew Turnbull to George Ramsay
Smyrnéa, December 12, 1772

We made no indigo this year until August, and none last after July, having been deprived of maybe half our crop both years. In one by a droughty spring, in the other by swarms of destructive worms. He hoped for better success in the future, and had taken measures to that end by acquiring watering engines and other machinery, which I am going to try, we'll get one better of these inconveniences and drawbacks. In meantime, the workers are busy putting so much land in order that, even with accidents, I hope to have from 15,000 to 18,000 weight of indigo next summer, and much more if the season is favorable.

One season more of experience will render us very expert. Our People cleared more land last winter. I have now begun to clear a dry swamp about two miles to the west of the present settlement with better soil than we've cleared and surveyed. The dry swamp contained 3,080 acres of fine dry swamp land, plus about 1,000 acres more of marsh and other land fit for planting. About 100 acres would be cleared during the winter of 1772-1773, and even more in the following winter. I am happy to have a large body of such good land contiguous to the tract I have now in cultivation.

The settlers are in robust health and high spirits. Every thing was conducted in my absence with attention, prudence, and economy.

Dundee City Archives

******

The Reverend John Forbes to Governor James Grant
February 23, 1773

Doctor Turnbull seems to be in tolerable spirits. He schemes great things in the planting way, and as he is happy in what I am afraid may be called his delusions, it is a pity to rob him of them. His people are healthy and increasing. Mr. Neilson is daily expected here, what alterations his account of Smyrnea will make I know not. Greatly to my satisfaction the Doctor has drop't or at least to me is quite silent on what we call politics and the affair of our administration.

The Reverend Forbes closed the letter with news of a winter storm: We have had a violent snow storm, several vessels I am afraid have been lost. The snow fell for twelve hours two or three inches deep, the indigo is not much hurt as the snow saved it from the frost.

James Grant Papers

******

Andrew Turnbull to George Ramsay
Smyrnéa, May 27, 1773

Inclosed with this you will find a long answer and I'm afraid a tedious one to your letter of the 2 nd of March. I have not wrote much to Mr. Nixon by this opportunity on the disagreeable subject of bills, all I can say about them is in this letter to you. If you think prorper you may read the whole of it to him. I have troubled you also with proposals which I have begged the favour of your communicating to Lord Temple and to Sir William Duncan.

I wish to assure Sir William that I do not desire to be unconnected with him in this settlement, and on that account, wish rather that he accepts of the yearly rent proposed than the other by purchase. If I become his farmer he will probably take a turn to this part of the world, the lease of ten years shall be no objection to my entering into such improvements as he thinks proper. I beg to add that if Lord Temple accepts of either of the terms proposed, there will not be a necessity of waiting for Sir William's determination, as it makes a separate affair; besides I do not mean to refuse accepting of one share on purchase or as a farm tho' the other Proprietor does not agree to either. I leave all this to your management.

Since my last letter to Sir William Duncan I have received one from him, in which he tells me that it will be inconvenient for him to be in London next year. I beg, my dear Sir, your assuring him that I mean to consult his conveniency and not my own in everything; my coming to Europe shall be at a time most convenient to him, and therefore I shall not think of stirring from hence 'till he tells me when it is convenient for him to meet me in London. I beg my respects to Mrs. Ramsay. I shall be anxious to have your answer to this.

If my bills come back, I've resolved to put what indigo we have into an open boat and carry it to Charleston myself to answer these demands. I have the boat ready and must not lose a minute, tho' attended with some danger in an open boat, to reinstate my credit at Charleston and to engage a house there to supply this settlement.

Dundee City Archives

THE NEW SMYRNA COLONY OF FLORIDA

Andrew Turnbull to George Ramsay
Smyrnéa May 27, 1773

Your letter of the 2 nd of March came to hand the 19 th of this month. I am sorry that Mr. Nixon was under the necessity of giving you trouble about my bills, I did not intend that either Lord Temple or Sir William Duncan should have been desired to supply more money; The reason of the expences which drew these bills from me is, that I am obliged to supply this Settlement with such provisions as we cannot raise here, and of which we were in so much want when these supplies arrived, that we had not one barrel of pork here, nor one hundred weight of either rice or flour, the two last wanted daily for the sick, women nursing, and children.

I mention this to explain the necessity of these bills drawn on Mr. Nixon on consigning our Indigo to him, which is not a new practice in America business, for it is done every day, and as I thought that the Indigo sent home would have been sufficient to refund these sums, I did not imagine that I was much out of the road of that kind of business. The failure of Mr. Reynolds has indeed lessened our friends, which adds to the weight of these bills on Mr. Nixon, but if he had told me positively when I was with him last year, that he would not advance anything for us in the future, it would not have been difficut for me then to have found a House in London to do this business for us, on condition of having the consignment of our indigo to reimburse the advances made in cash, for which an interest of five percent is commonly paid; this with two and a half per cent on the purchases, and as much on the sales brings ten per cent for the capital in that Trade: considerable sums of money are employed in this way by the merchants trading to South Carolina, their correspondents or factors in Charlestown supply the planters at one year's credit to be paid by that year's crop, which for the most part cannot even be put into the ground...without the credit.

I mention this to justify myself as far as customs in such cases can justify me, I do not mean, however, that I was induced to draw by those customs or to avail myself of them, for I would not have drawn for one half penny of the amount of the Indigo tho' with Twenty thousand pounds, if absolute necessity...had not compelled me. If seen in this light it will seem more excusable, but however that is, I think myself much obliged to Mr. Nixon for having accepted the bills then presented; tho' at a longer time; The State of credit in Europe has no doubt involved him in some difficulties, and I am sorry that my bills should add to his distress, which my present circumstances cannot alleviate, on the contrary, I must continue at least for this once to add to them, for I must give a bill on him by the next post for £94:18:6 Sterling to balance my last account with Mr. Gordon's House in Charles Town, S.C., in which are included the costs of seventeen bushels of indigo seed, two hundred bushels of salt and the freight of the vessel sent here with the coppers (stills). I do not know of any other demands on me for some months at least, except the fifty or sixty pounds which I mentioned in another letter for the twelve draught oxen commissioned from Georgia. I did not think that our provisions of this year would have amounted to so much by four hundred pounds as they had done, which proceeds from that kind of provision being at a much higher price than usual, but as I could not subsist without them, they must be paid for.

I have therefore said that I must continue to draw to pay for them, but if one bill comes back it will most effectually put a stop to that and everything else here, until I find means to pay those returned. Bills with extraordinary expenses on them, which I must endeavour to do by a contract with some house in Charlestown to supply me, and which I flatter myself will not be difficult, as men of capital there know the capability of settlements in this country better than the London Merchants. Money may be lost by giving credit to men in trade, that given to planters can hardly be said to be in risk. On these grounds I found an opinion that I can get over the bills if returned, tho' such a stop of the credit of this settlement will certainly do much hurt in many respects. I am also sorry that it will entirely break the connection between Mr. Nixon and this settlement as to the business of it, as the supplies and sales must then be thro' the Charles Town channel in the mode adopted even by the most opulent of the Carolina land holders. It would be much more agreeable to me if this does not happen, as the business of this settlement would probably have recompensed him in future for the trouble he has had, besides I think him an honest and an industrious merchant, I may not be so happy as to have the same confidence in another.

In answer, my dear sir, to the paragraph of your letter about raising of stock. I tried that of Hogs, but the Wolves and Tygers destroyed them as fast as raised. I shifted to another place, where I thought they would be less liable to be destroyed but with as bad success as at the first place, not withstanding I have not given it up, as I find that the clearing of the lands rids us in part of these destructive animals. I have also fed hogs in pen, but found it more expensive than purchasing salt pork.

In regard to the salting of fish...as a part of our food, we could not have subsisted here without it. It is by fish that I have reduced our quantity of pork to less than eighty barrels a year, and to the allowance per week of one-half pound only for each person of a certain age. I endeavoured to save that expence also, but found from experience that vegetable food without some of the animal kind brought on a weak digestion, acids and flatulences of the bowels, with obstructed viscera, dropsies, and a risk of life. These could not be prevented without meat. I was therefore obliged to give the half pound of pork per week, rather as a remedy than as a part of food. I have a right to call it remedy, from the intention of it as well as the small quantity given. I repeat however, that without fish we could not subsist on so small an allowance of pork.

I frequently salt between three and four thousand weight of fish in a day, but it is only certain seasons, and in favourable fishing days that we catch many, tho' we save five hundred pounds a year at least by fish. I have troubled you with a long detail of this part of our savings and subsistence, that you may judge of it, which your acquaintance with affairs of this nature enables you to do and I am so far from taking amiss what you write to me about saving expences for provisions, that I am much obliged to you for it, and shall always be glad of any hint of that kind which may occur to you.

I observe what you say about the disappointment from last year's crop, it was greatly so to me, all that I can do is to endeavour as much as the climate and seasons admit to better it in future. The failure of last year has indeed made me apprehensive that such accidents will happen oftener than was at first imagined, which gives me the more anxiety as I am sensible it will be very discouraging to Lord Temple and Sir William Duncan, and the more so as an expensive, tho' necessary apparatus of Husbandry, added to the partial failures of the crop from lands, the nature of which we are not yet well acquainted, with many other hindrances, will keep us out of great profits for a certain time, but cannot prevent our succeeding and that in a large way.

I do not mean to raise other expectations than what seem to me well founded, nor did I intend to deceive as to what I said of our last year's crop. I was deceived by appearances. I may also be deceived this year, and do really apprehend it, notwithstanding I venture to offer the Lord Temple Eighteen thousand pounds sterling for his property in this settlement and lands in East Florida, and the same sum to Sir William Duncan: it must not be understood that I can lay down the money, I mean that I will engage to pay interest of five per cent on the 18,000 pounds till it is all paid off, which may be at thirds every four years, the interest to ease on each third as paid off. A mortgage on their own lands and on mine as well as my personal security is the only offer I have to make them for the making good of this Engagement; that, however, is more than they have at present, having only a right to their own four-tenths each and not to my one-fifth.

I do not flatter myself that the profits of this settlement will enable me to pay even half of that money in the time mentioned, but I think that the improvement of the lands will give me a means of either borrowing money on them, or leasing them out on fines to pay the thirds at the times proposed. If this offer is not accepted, I shall be glad to farm their shares, each at one thousand guineas a year, free of all expences whatsoever, and this to be by lease fourteen years, and if it is found right to continue it, I will engage, even now, to give two thousand guineas for each share the next ten years after the first ten are elapsed. If the first proposal is agreed to, the interest may commence on the exchange of the writings; if the second, the event of a thousand guineas a year may commence on the first of January next, and in either case the writings may be sent to the attorney general here, or to any other person, that I may sign them, and that they may be registered in the Register's office of the province, which ensures the validity of them and proves it, by which step no fraud can ever be committed to the detriment of these writings.

Tho' I am convinced that these conditions are not disadvantages to me, I declare, however, that profit does not induce me to make these proposals, my sole reason is that I am apprehensive that I shall not be able to reimburse the money laid out so soon as is expected, this gives me uneasiness, and will probably hurry me to making a present and temporary advantage of our lands, which may probably wear them out too fast, and consequently cramp such a foundation as this settlement ought to have. I therefore beg the favour, my dear sir, of your proposing these modes of purchase or rent, and if accepted the writings may be sent out without delay. It is understood that I am to take on me all the debts and wages due by the settlement, the sums proposed being to be clear of every deduction.

I don't mean that I will not purchase nor farm one share without the other. I will agree to the above proposals with either Temple or Duncan tho the other does not accept of the terms proposed. If neither is accepted our affairs will then stand as they are now.

Dundee City Archives

******

Andrew Turnbull to George Ramsay
Smyrnéa, June 29, 1773

I observe what you say about making copper indigo and cutting it into 1 and 1/4 inch pieces. I regulate myself by advice from London in regard to making indigo as bear the highest prices and most marketable. That is how I made indigo last year of strong and deep color which your broker told me would sell best in general. Now you say they want me to make copper. You say you sent samples and recommended making indigo of size and shape of these samples. I never received any except those I sent for when I wrote for some pieces of every kind of indigo then at market.

I'm looking at samples and find the high priced Spanish Flora, which was the finest of all samples was so far from being in shapes and pieces of 1 & 1/4 inches, not one piece so large as a hazelnut and all without shapes or make whatever. The sample is dated February 26, 1771, and the market price was nine shillings, six pence per pound. The best Carolina copper was then selling at only five shillings.

Judging from the authority of your samples, it seemed best to imitate the high price sample, hence I made indigo equal to it in look and color tho' it didn't sell for quite 9 shillings. Perhaps our weed cannot give so strong a dye as that from

Guatemala, but the price ours sold at justifies my following the Spanish example rather than producing copper color, which didn't sell better than our ordinary blues, made by our newest and worst manufacturers. As to your brokers telling you the coppers would have sold better, I suspect their motive to be the old stale excuse of these men rather than a reality, the same excuse, by shifting sides, would probably have been called in had I sent coppers. If blues or purples are not so much in demand as copper it was for them to say so.

I cannot see the propriety of permitting these people to run down the quality, which I am confident is something better on the whole than the indigo sold last year, in part the first and second floras, which are seemingly equal to the best Spanish flora at 9.6 in 1771. I have all the samples and as good a light as the brokers I have recourse also to comparison to the finest Guatemala, which is the way to find out the truth of the quality they want to conceal so we cannot find out. I insist on your keeping samples of the indigo now in your hands. I'll prove to you that you ought not trust broker's judgment.

I shall ever endeavor to regulate myself according to the qualities of indigo wanted at market when the advices are directed by judgment and influenced by probity, not inconsistent and almost contradictory as that of your Brokers. These men have in general two views of everything and always two friends to serve, one the seller and the other the buyer, but as they find it difficult to serve both, they generally make out affairs to the advantage of one and expense of the other. I would rather have advised you pick up among other merchants and dealers. If advice gets to me early in October I'll have time to throw some lands into another culture for next year. This would be of great use to me.

Mr. Ross received a letter from Mr. Elliott dated March writes Mr. Waugh has seen his indigo of last year and said it was worth six shillings a pound. He has the character of being very intelligent in the article and his advices have always been the best of any sent into this province: nothing of the broker in them. It is necessary to mention that Mr. Elliott's indigo for two years past was so much inferior to ours that it was always sold for 1 to 2 shillings a pound cheaper than ours. This according to the opinions of the best judges and manufacturers of indigo. How can I reconcile this with the opinion of the Jews, who tell you our indigo is bad. Either they impose or they are not competent.

Dundee City Archives

✶✶✶✶✶✶

The Reverend John Forbes to Governor James Grant
August 23, 1773

The Doctor has made by his first cutting of indigo weed 4,000 weight; he expects to make in all 14,000. His people, I hear, a little dis-satisfied. I have the same opinion of that settlement: there will I am afraid be a mutiny some day. It will not bear its own expenses and pay the interest of the money laid out. The Doctor sees things in the usual light; he has his golden dreams.

James Grant Papers

******

David Yeats to Governor James Grant
St. Augustine, May 24, 1774

Dr. Turnbull's prospects are not at all promising either on provisions or indigo. A vast deal has been planted but destroyed by the dry weather and planted over a second time. He trusted rather too much to his old hammock land which seems to be wore out for a time and wants rest, as it produces little except crab grass which is exceeding troublesome on an indigo plantation. He has good land in the back swamp which he is now hard at work upon, but only little of it in good order for planting. On he whole I'm afraid his crop will turn out very short; his provisions and indigo seed have fallen short, and his People become troublesome to him again so that he must have an uneasy time of it.

James Grant Papers

******

The Reverend John Forbes to Governor James Grant
St. Augustine, November 1, 1744

Dr. Turnbull's affairs seem near a crisis; he has made nothing, neither provisions nor above 1500 weight in indigo, yet still the same tales of next year, new rich swamp, and etc., and he has no doubt that his constituents will support the settlement, that they want him to enter into a new contract and that he means to go home next year for that purpose. The People are dissatisfied and I suppose will feel hunger.

James Grant Papers

******

Andrew Turnbull to George Ramsay
Charleston, South Carolina, January 21, 1774

As I have always desired Mr. Nixon to acquaint you with everything relating to the Smyrnea Settlement I have not therefore troubled you lately with any letters. He told you, no doubt, that the Spring drought hurt us much, and that the caterpillar was destructive to our weed in the autumn, which is the reason that our crop this year amounts to only 1026 & 1/2 only, but as most of it is fine indigo, and such as is wanted at present in London, I flatter myself that it will sell for more than eight shillings a pound. I was offered 7 shilling & 2 pence from one person and could have had nigh 8 from another, but as I was doubtful of the abilities of the last I was afraid to risk such a sum in his hands.

I have therefore thought it best to ship it on the London, Captain Curling, and have consigned it to the House of Graham, Johnston and Co, merchants in London. My reason for sending it to that House is, that Mr. Nixon having refused paying a bill of £104 it stops my giving any more on him, not being negotiable from that refusal. I was therefore obliged to apply to the House of John Simpson & Co. Here in partnership with Graham, Johnson & Co. to supply provisions as I want immediately for the Settlement, also for a credit in London to pay the £104 mentioned with three hundred more for osnaburg and linens for the Settlement. Mr. Nixon also added that my partners were resolved not to advance any more money for the settlement. This was not said to one but to others, and would have hurt me if the opinion everybody here has of the success of the settlement was not greatly in our favour. All that, however true, might as well have been kept in. I know all partners of the house of Graham, Johnston and of John Simpson and Company. I have a very high opinion of their abilities and integrity.

I have desired Mr. Graham to ensure our indigo at £3000 Sterling, tho' I was offered here more than 3500, but I think it will sell for more than four both from its quality and advantageous packages for sale to the manufacturers. I have given Mr. Graham such directions for selling it as I think will be an advantage: a public sale is condemned by everybody. As to Mr. Nixon's advance for the settlement I mean and wish it to be done away by reimbursing him as soon as possible, except the £800 due by Reynolds. I am sorry that Mr. Nixon obliges me to put the business of the Settlement into another person's hands, but it must go so for now till I meet with Lord Temple and Sir William Duncan in London this time twelve month or soon after. I am very sorry that our affairs here have met with so many drawbacks.

I have land now prepared for 20,000 weight of indigo at least, even allowing for moderate droughts, & etc., but of this & everything else of this nature, I would not be understood to speak with infallible certainty. I am founded, however, when I say that our Settlement will soon be a very considerable one, we have such a large bottom of extensive tracts of land with great and active strength that we must succeed if properly employed, which I shall continue to do. Some sugars made at Mr. Elliott's plantation flatter us much that that culture will turn to great account, and the more so, as the season for cutting canes comes on immediately after that of our indigo, which will give us the advantage of double crops.

Dundee City Archives

CORRESPONDENCE

Andrew Turnbull to George Ramsay
Charleston, South Carolina, January 25, 1774

The indigo dye was loaded on a ship to London, along with a cask of 28 & 3/4 gallons of our Smyrnea honey. I asked Mr. Graham to send one-half of the honey to Mr. Ramsay. Eating honey with bread and butter in morning will be good for you, to carry off the bilious complaint you had when I was in London. It is excellent for preventing many disorders of the breast and bilious disorders.

I have asked Mr. Graham to tell me what the honey would sell for in London, as the settlement will probably produce one thousand gallons this year. The honey and wax the people make will in the future almost supply them with the many little necessaries we are obliged to purchase for them at present. In order to encourage them to this easy and useful piece of husbandry, I have only reserved for the proprietors about one-tenth of this produce. It is wholesome and even necessary for the health of our People in this warm climate for most disorders, especially autumnal ones which are from a bilious cause or have a tendency that way.

Dundee City Archives

******

Andrew Turnbull to George Ramsay
Smyrnéa, March 30, 1774

Your letter of the 25 th of October came by the Britannia at the beginning of this month. I observe what you say about the proposals I desired you to make to Lord Temple and to Sir William Duncan. The present circumstances make no great difference as to what I thought might be given then as an annual rent, but the purchase value of the lands is, in my opinion, much higher than at that time. This rise in value is from the experiments made last year in making of sugars in this Neighbourhood. We find that an acre of land will give of sugar and rum to the value of twenty pounds. And as the cane does not ripen here until the middle of October, the making of sugar comes in well immediately after our indigo crop is over, consequently all hands may be employed in it for a couple of months at least every year, in which time much good work may be done.

On this account the lands in the south part of this province are of a much more value than before the culture of sugar cane was ascertained. It would not be well therefore for the proprietors of this settlement to sell out. I wish them to profit of every advantage which may arise from it, as they must be great, but being still at some distance, I am apprehensive that they will lose patience. The prospect of these advantages is clear and certain to a person on the spot as I am, and the more so, as we are now clearing lands, which are not so liable to be burned up with droughts as those we were obliged to clear at first to render the country airy and healthy. That labour, however, is so far from being lost, that I hope to have much Indigo from twelve hundred acres of it this year.

The new land being cleared for provisions, of which we now have eight hundred acres, seven hundred of it will be in indigo next year when more new land will be cleared for provisions. We shall increase in quantity of land every year in this manner, consequently we have reason to expect larger crops, and the more so, as the first cleared lands will soon admit of plowing, which means one man with a boy will do more labour than eight men with a hoe. We shall then get on in a large manner, and with less labour. It is by mere dint of hard work that we get crops from rough woody lands where almost every stroke of a hoe meets with a root.

As to what you mention about a return every year of the quantity of land cleared, produce Indigo & etc. I am now getting an accurate survey made of every acre and shall make a return this year, on one sheet of paper in different columns of everything regarding the Settlement, so that the state, strength, number of people, & etc. may be seen at once. Our affairs here go on now so regularly, that time can be spared for accuracies of this nature. I think myself much obliged to you for every hint of this kind, I wish to be distinct and correct in everything.

I do not write to Sir William Duncan by this opportunity, as I cannot speak with any kind of certainty of our crop this autumn, which must be after the months of April and May. The drought in these months may burn up all our Indigo, when that is the case, we are obliged to plant again in June, but this gives little in proportion to that which comes on early. Please to present my respects to Lord Temple, and acquaint him with everything, if it is not troublesome to His Lordship.

Dundee City Archives

******

Andrew Turnbull to George Ramsay
Smyrnéa, January 31, 1775

Your letter by last post confirms the melancholy news of Sir William Duncan's death. I shall hurry to London in the fall to lay before Lady Mary Duncan and Lord Temple a state of their affairs here, which, not withstanding all the drawbacks, will soon justify our plan; but it cannot get on except it is supported for this year's supplies, to the amount of between six hundred and seven hundred pounds.

Please do not let the bills go unpaid. I am willing to pay eight percent interest, the legal interest here, until I can repay sums borrowed from the crop this year. If the bills come back, he warned, a twenty-four percent interest is added, thus a great deal of expense can be spared if the bills are paid

I sent our last year's small crop by Captain Lofthouse. The badness of the weed from the drought made the getting of dye from that weed so difficult, that it was impossible to make it tolerably good, nor could we attend much to the shape, but as we have a prospect for fine weed for this crop, you may depend on my attention to the shapes and colours you recommend.

Dundee City Archives

******

Andrew Turnbull to George Ramsay
Smyrnéa, August 10, 1775

Your letter of 6 May arrived yesterday. The news of Captain Duncan's coming here is very agreeable and satisfactory to me. I shall wait for him until the beginning of February. I cannot well stay longer, as I must be here again in the month of June for the Indigo making. I hope that Captain Duncan will find it convenient and even necessary, to stay here, a round of the seasons at least, that he may see everything, as it goes on thro' the year, and I heartily wish, that his stay may be for years. If he is to have an Interest, or share, in this settlement, he cannot be more usefully employed; especially as another Director is much wanted here, for my nephew and I have rather more on our hands in this season than can be managed by two persons.

One of my chief reasons for coming to Europe in the Spring is, that the several grants of land belonging to this partnership, may be divided in lots, or otherwise. For as the lands granted for the settlement are in several names, and above half in my name, these circumstances might give rise to disputes hereafter if not properly settled now. As to the lands now in cultivation by this settlement, these may be left undivided, if the partnership is continued. I have some other business in England but what I mentioned is the most material, and I think it of consequence, for I have learned lately that some of these lands having been grants to me after the date of our agreements, my heirs might dispute the right of them; I do not wish to leave any grounds for suits or pretexts for suits after my death.

I thank you much, my Dear Sir, for the machine for cutting of Indigo into proper sizes and shapes, if it is better than one I contrived here, I shall use it when it comes to hand. I have not only preserved the Indigo we have made this season from breaking, I have also made it all good, and of a proper shape so far, and as we have made our beginning in this way, I hope to be able to continue it. I am endeavoring to get about 500 pounds worth dried to send by Lofthouse. I am apprehensive that I cannot send more, because it will not be cured sufficiently to put into casks at the time he goes away.

I did not make a fair beginning of making Indigo until the first of this month. And as it takes six weeks or two months in drying, I cannot ship much for it splits and falls to pieces if dried quickly. I hope to continue making until the end of November.

I am much obliged to you for speaking to Mr. Graham and engaging him to accept my bills for provisions. I do not know of any more demands on me at present, and hope that the disagreeable business of drawing is at an end. I rejoice that Lord Temple is in a fair way of recovering from his late Indisposition. I wish his Lordship to have the satisfaction of seeing the success of this undertaking, and that he may enjoy that pleasure for many and many years to come.

Dundee City Archives

✶✶✶✶✶✶

The Reverend John Forbes to Governor James Grant
St. Augustine, November 1, 1775

Doctor Turnbull keeps pretty close at home, has made plenty of provisions and some indigo. Captain Adam Duncan, heir to Sir William's East Florida estate, is expected here daily from England. The Doctor talks, whether he comes or not, of going to England next year.

James Grant Papers

✶✶✶✶✶✶

Lady Mary Duncan to Dear Adam (Captain Adam Duncan, Sir William Duncan's nephew)
Rome, January 6, 1776

At last post I had a letter from Mr. Ramsay, that the wild Turnbull is coming to England, when all America is in rebellion tho' the Floridas are not in it, surely he must be mad, to leave all those people at such a time. Tho I can't express how much I feel for the care and trouble Mr. Ramsay has taken, throughout this whole affair. Let Lord Temple do as he pleases. There is three points I put in my caveat against. First, I will not spend one shilling more upon the Estate in Florida till I or you go there. Secondly, I will have no accounts pass'd till I come to England or go to Florida, because in the last he brought us in creditor to him, & tho Mr. Ramsay had infinite merit in setling them, yet he must believe the articles that Turnbull brings on his side, now I will settle my part of the account, when I have seen the country. Thirdly, I will agree to no division of lands till the year 1778, and lastly, I will enter into no agreement of any sort or kind till the year 1778. So that all reasons that can be alledged will be of no weight with me, please to tell Turnbull that if God should spare my life, health & strength enough remains, I shall have the satisfaction with my own Eyes, and the help of proper people, to divide, or farm it then; but till that period of time, I am resolv'd not to sign my name to any agreement whatever. Be so good not to send me any; I shall only burn it.

By the second agreement as he could not advance the money equal to us, that Estate when divided, his share is but a fifth or two fifths as will be seen in the agreement, besides he obliges himself to continue the care of that Estate upon the same forms as long as one or both of the proprietors chuses. I will not relinquish on my part, either of those two articles, it is the only hold we have upon him to keep his accounts hanging over his head, & to oblige him to continue it, till you or I see at leisure what he has done.

I am very glad you don't go there at present, it would be running a risk, at this time. Besides going there for a few months, in a property of that sort, I fairly think, would not be of so much service, there would not be time enough to examine it thoroughly, so as to come to a division or agreement, I cannot help observing when we sent Mr. Neilson, he immediately made some pretense to leave him there and come to England, now he hears of your coming, he must play the same trick, this has not a very honest appearance on his side, a man of good character in such circumstances, would have put off his journey, to show openly his works & expences upon the spot, not to come and tell us what he pleases; He takes us for little children, to give credit to his words, he must be joking, when he writes thus. Please to tell him from me, that to be convinced of his uprightness you or I must see with our own Eyes, how those great sums are laid out, if justly, & whether the returns for that money is in proportion remitted as much as could be reasonably expected, when well, & honestly managed, to the proprietors, or in a fair way of being so, those are the proofs, words is only loss of time, & an unessary fatigue to the lungs.

Dundee City Archives

******

Andrew Turnbull to Patrick Tonyn
Smyrnéa, March 7, 1776

In answer to your Excellency's letter of the 27 th of last month, I have the honour to acquaint you, Sir, that there are two hundred males on this settlement, from the age of sixteen to fifty.

I do not pretend to be a judge of their military abilities, but I can safely vouch for their loyalty to His Majesty, for their diligent and honest endeavors to fulfil their contracts with me, and for their affectionate care in supplying their families with the daily necessaries of life. And I think it a duty incumbent on me to beg that your Excellency would please to grant such a protection for these industrious foreigners as may prevent their being disturbed from agriculture without which they with their Families must starve.

Colonial Office Papers

******

Andrew Turnbull to Governor Patrick Tonyn
St. Augustine, March 15, 1776 (enclosed in Tonyn to Lord Germaine, March 22, 1776)

I have the honor of your Excellency's letter of the 4 th of this March, in which I am desired to give information against myself on a subject which your Excellency seems to think culpable.

If I had done anything which had a tendency that way, it would not be prudent to inform against myself, nor could it be required of me. But as I am conscious of my own innocence and that what I did, on the occasion you mention was to assist a most worthy and respectable man under disagreeable circumstances. I will relate to you, Sir, how that affair happened.

The greatest part of the principal inhabitants of this province, being not at Mr. Woods Tavern on the 27 th of last March, to prepare a dutiful and loyal address to the majesty, I was desired to take the chair and to profess that address to which I had the satisfaction to see a sincere and hearty concurrence. That business being over, some at the meeting went away, and Mr. Drayton's suspicion being then a general and interesting subject of conversation I was asked by some of the gentlemen near me, if I had not seen the charge against him and his defiance. I replied that I had a copy of these papers in my pocket, which Mr. Drayton had given me for my own private satisfaction. I was desired to read them, which I did, and I remember that I turned to the gentleman on my right hand and said that, in my opinion, Mr. Drayton had justified himself. And I sincerely own, Sir, that I think it still, and it is a satisfaction to me that this cannot contradict any opinion of your Excellency for as far as I can understand from the charge and defense mentioned your Excellency brought the charge against Mr. Drayton, and, therefore from a just delicacy did not give an opinion or vote, but that as I have been told, Mr. Drayton was suspended by the advice of four of the gentlemen of the council, and that two others of that honorable board were against the suspension. If that was the case I only differ in opinion from four gentlemen of the council, they are men, Sir, and not infallible. The other two gentlemen of that board certainly thought so and consequently were against the suspicion and I can assure your Excellency that their opinion was of great weight with the publick, for it coincided with what they had always entertained of Mr. Drayton's abilities and integrity as a judge, and as a loyal subject. This,

Sir, is evident form an address to him on this occasion by almost all the men of property and character in this province.

Why then, Sir, am I singled out and called on for information about this business, in which so many are concerned? And why am I not permitted to give my opinion, in conversation, where that opinion is founded on conviction, and from a most intimate knowledge of Mr. Drayton in his publick and private capacities?

If it is to gratify the resentment which your Excellency threatened me and others with on the 28 th of last Month, when at your own request a committee of seven myself included, of the oldest and principal inhabitants of his province, waited on your Excellency in a most respectful manner to present to you, a copy of a dutiful and loyal address to his majesty, and to desire your approbation, it will not look well on your part, Sir, I therefore beg that, as you are the representative of an August and great King, that you would not descend from that dignity, to pursue a hasty and undeserved resentment against me. Reflect, Sir, that after that public threat all will appear to spring from that motive. Consider also, by destroying me you involve in my ruin hundreds of His Majesty's most loyal and industrious subjects, who look up to me, and depend on me for every necessary of life.

I beg leave also to remind your Excellency that I settled here under the auspices of his present majesty. I was even made happy by his most gracious wishes for any success in an undertaking never before attempted on as large a scale by any private person, and that the majesty was pleased to order his governor of this province to assist me as much as was in his power

Reflect, Sir, on all these circumstances, and let not the hasty anger of a moment counteract His Majesty's most gracious intention towards me, nor carry you out of the line of government to gratify a private resentment to the destruction of a man whose most active life has been employed for the benefit of mankind and in his duty to his sovereign. I have always endeavoured, Sir, to render myself useful to the community I live in, and particularly to this province, in which I have resided many years with honour, decency, credit and reputation. Weigh me, Sir, in the balance against the men who are your informers and I dare say Sir that you will find them men of little property, credit, or consequence, I cannot have any enemies but such as come under this description.

Shun I beg Sir, the insinuations of such men, whoever they are, they are enemies to you, Sir, to me, and to the tranquility and peace of this province.

I hope, Sir, you will please to excuse the freedom of this advising style. I would not have presumed to trouble your Excellency on such a subject, but in my own defense, and to desire you to beware of men who endeavour to set your Excellency at variance with me. The intentions of such men are easily discoverable, Sir, by that just and never failing criterion that all good men endeavour to conciliate differences, but bad men busy themselves in making and widening breaches in friendship and mutual confiderce.

Colonial Office Papers

******

Governor Patrick Tonyn to Andrew Turnbull
March 18, 1776

I received your letter in answer to mine of the 4 th Instant. There could be no impropriety in desiring to know from yourself how far a report concerning your conduct at a meeting of the inhabitants was true.

Without criticising every particular paragraph of your letter, I must beg leave to observe for your satisfaction, and from those that gave you such intelligence, that your information concerning the proceedings of the Council is not consistent with Truth and with Fact. And I am sorry to have occasion to say that a perversion of truth and facts hath been too much a fashion with some people here.

Colonial Office Papers

******

Robert Bisset to Governor Patrick Tonyn
Palmerina, September 1, 1776

I this minute received your letter to Andrew Turnbull. This information is very alarming especially with regard to Doctor Turnbull's people, a great many of whom would certainly join them. And the plantations have neither arms nor ammunition, either to defend themselves or to endeavor to prevent them landing at Smyrnea. They can only come in with boats as our Barr has not water enough for the draught of any private vessel which must be built sharp for sailing. So that I think our plantations not in great danger, as we can get our Negroes out of the way. If such an event should happen most probably those that joined them of the Smyrnea settlements, would endeavor to plunder our plantations. However, I have a great confidence in the badness of our bar, which I hope will deter them from attempting anything here. I shall set out immediately for Smyrnea & will make the best dispensation I can for the defence of the place by arming those we can trust & disarming the suspected, and I shall acquaint all the Plantations and put them on their Guard.

We are much obliged to your Excellency for this early information, which shows your attention to the good of the Province & the security of the property of the settlers.

Colonial Office Papers

CORRESPONDENCE

Governor Patrick Tonyn to Andrew Turnbull
St. Augustine, August 11, 1778

Since your return your conduct in several instances has been so exceptional that I cannot agree to your acting in person as Secretary of the Province, and Clerk of the Council.

Colonial Office Papers

******

John Moultrie to Governor James Grant
St. Augustine, May 6, 1780

We have had a Spanish Plunder at the Musquito, took away some of Mr. Turnbull's and Watson's negroes. This has broke up all the plantations except Oswald's and my own, we stand fast.

James Grant Papers

******

Henry Yonge to George Ramsay
St. Augustine, December 5, 1780

As a suit in Chancery has been commenced by the representatives of the late Mr. Grenville and Sir William Duncan against Dr. Turnbull and others for a discovery of the expenditures of the Monies advanced by them for the Smyrnea settlement, and to enforce a division of the Lands belonging to the settlement, and the suit proceeded in so far as to have auditors appointed to inspect the several accounts, who could not proceed upon that business for want of the different vouchers, I am to request the particular favor of you to deliver them if not already in Mr. Grenville's possession, so as also to throw such lights upon the transactions of arrangement made by you, as may enable the auditors to proceed upon the business.

Dundee City Archives

******

David Yeats to Governor James Grant
St. Augustine, December 16, 1780

The Doctor is still practicing physic for the benefit of his family, tho' anxious to get to Charlestown where he will have a larger field, but he is detained by the Chancery suit between him and his copartners, which is still undecided. Two of his daughters are married—one to Mr. Holmes, a merchant at Pensacola, and the other to Mr. Marshal, agent to Mr. Ashby in this province. He informed me lately that he had written home to his friends to desire them to resign the Secretaryship in his name as he was determined to leave this town, and desired me to apply if I wished to succeed him. But after what happened and his not mentioning it to Governor Tonyn, I really did not know how to understand him, however, I have informed the governor of it, and if you think there is any chance for success, I shall be highly obliged to you for your interest.

James Grant Papers

******

David Yeats to Governor James Grant
St. Augustine, January 5, 1783
This town and the country is at present full of Refugees and Negroes from Carolina and Georgia so that both provinces are now completely evacuated and the Rebels in full and quiet possession of them, what a change! Doctor Turnbull and Mr. Penman remain at Charles Town. Mr. Roupell and his family are at St. Johns River on their way to this place. Should this province remain a British colony which I pray yet it may, and St. Marys River, it must soon become a flourishing colony with the number of inhabitants that are now in it.

James Grant Papers

******

Andrew Turnbull to Thomas Grenville
Charleston, September 30, 1786
I have the Honour to trouble you with this to request your giving into the Hands of Mr. James Penman, who will wait on you without delay such grants of Lands as may fall to my share in the Division of the Smyrnéa Tracts, as stipulated in the Deeds of Partnership. It is proper, however, to mention that I executed Deeds of Division of Lands in East Florida according to an arbitrary arrangement ordered by Gov. Tonyn; but as I was then a prisoner and compelled to that act as a price of liberty, as is mentioned in the Discharge from Chancery, it will readily occur to you, Sir, that it is not valid. Besides it was not done by Lot according to the express words of the Deeds of Partnership, but by compulsion and under such circumstances of false imprisonment that I would then readily have given up the whole to be out of Tonyn's hands. I trust, therefore, Sir, as it cannot affect your claims, that in justice, you will bring about a division with your Brother and Lady Mary Duncan's attorney, Mr. Woodcock; they cannot have any objection to this equitable request founded on the only Deed which can be valid and without which no claim can be established on just grounds.

In regard to the deeds executed in St. Augustine, as Tonyn only would flatter himself that such a Piece of Injustice would be approved of by Men of Honour, I am the more solicitous, Sir, for Relief by a compensation for my losses on account of a Load of Debt arising from Governor Tonyn having taken every thing out of my Hands, and from his having given away or disposed of that property without satisfying the creditors of the Smyrnéa concern, or paying one half percent the wages due at that time. I cannot pay that Debt with the Labour of years, which now bears hard on me, being in my sixtieth and seventh year, consequently it must bear harder and harder on me till I sink under it, if I am not relieved by a compensation for my losses; though I never can be compensated, nor can I retrieve ten of the best years of my life, and more than once at the Risk of that Life, in carrying on that enterprise, for which I am now kept an Exile from my country, and an alien in this state, until I pay the debts contracted for that settlement. I beg leave, Sir, therefore, to repeat my request that you will please forward that division that I may make my claims before the time given elapses.

In the list of claims sent to me, I see, Sir, that yours is only for £9,000, and Lady Mary Duncans £13,000, which I think must proceed from a mistake, for the monies advanced for the shares of the Right Honorable George Grenville and Sir William Duncan amount to £25,027:18:2 of which each advanced one-half, for a confirmation of this you will please to look into the book of accounts made out by Mr. George Ramsay. I think it right also to mention Sir, that there was more than six hundred pounds worth of cut timber on and nigh the wharf at Smyrnéa, of which I have the measurement, when Governor Tonyn took these affairs out of my hands. There were also ten large coppers of 150 gallons each double-bottomed which cost with the freight £400, two large copper stills with the worms and everything necessary. I left also ten double setts of indigo works with much other valuable property which might have been removed and sold for a considerable sum, transports having been sent on purpose to carry off the Inhabitants with their Effects, though it should have been removed immediately: it is to be expected, Sir, that Tonyn and Moultrie have accounted to you for all that property.

I think it right also to mention that as Governor Tonyn sent above a thousand settlers to set down on the Smyrnéa lands, he has no doubt accounted with you, Sir, for the percent usually paid for such a liberty: ten percent was the accustomed price paid by the settler to the proprietor on provisions, tar, turpentine, indigo and other produce, and eight percent on cut timber, viz. Scantling and Boards Shingles or Staves; if all this is not accounted for he wrongs you. Some of your property was no doubt given away to his needy dependants to preserve his influence among them, otherwise they would have abandoned him, for all knew his character, and therefore made him pay for what was deficient that way, which was not a little.

I cannot conclude, Sir, without taking the liberty to beg the favour of you not giving too much of your faith to any of Governor Tonyn's assertions to the contrary of what I have said; you will most certainly find, at last, that the Truth is not in him, for though I accused and proved him guilty to his face of the basest falsehoods, I find not withstanding that, even now in England, he does not suffer Truth to stand in his way when he wishes to establish or gain a point. I own sir that I am anxious to return to England to pull off the Mask of Deceit from that worst of men I know who pretended to the character of a gentleman.

It is with the greatest Respect that I have the honour to be, Sir, Your most obedient and must humble servant.

P.S. Oct. 15 th.: Sir, I beg leave to add to the above that, considering the glaring illegality of the oppressive alternative proposed to me by Gov. Tonyn, which was to remain a prisoner or to sign such deeds of division as he should order, I cannot think myself bound by deeds executed under these circumstances, consequently I conceive that claims granted in my name or made over to me, cannot be supported by any other person chosen except a fair division by lot takes place as stipulated in the Deeds of Partnership, or in the name of the company as a partnership, which certainly exists even to this day, and it seems to me that this mode of claim would be most to the advantage of all concerned, as it might then be made to the losses on the whole, which amount to above £37,000 Sterling in cash disbursed and in monies received for the produce and laid out on the Settlement, as appears by the book of accounts in your hands: if this mode of a claim is not adopted, nor a civision of lands on a just ground, it will probably give rise to some confusion in the claims, as it might oblige me, however unwilling, to state that the division by Gov. Tonyn was illegal, highly oppressive, and unjust in regard to property extorted from me.

I do not think that it would appear to the honour of any gentleman to avail himself of such a division by which my share was to be two ten thousand acre tracts, that were not only uncultivated, but even without a tree cut down, or smallest Hut raised on them, instead of my fifth share of lands which with unremitting labour for ten years I had been clearing, cultivating, and forming into a settlement by building more than one hundred and fifty houses on one cleared field of more than seven miles long, and on another of three miles with Indigo works, drains, wharves, bridges, waggon roads, etc. The injustice of such a division must strike on the bare attention of the circumstances, and certainly could not be supported even before a Turkish Tribunal.

Dundee City Archives

******

Edward Penman to Governor James Grant
Charleston, South Carolina, July 14, 1792
You will probably before now have been informed of the Death of our invaluable friend, Doctor Turnbull, about four months ago; perhaps also, you may have learnt, that (unfortunate circumstances) of many years standing, has left his family in very embarrassed circumstances. He has, however, left with may a veneration for his memory which can only cease with their existence, of which gives them the most sincere desire to render eery service to his family.

They have just–and in the opinion of many–well-founded claims on the British Government; and those probably only require to be mentioned to have its generosity and humanity extended to them. Major Pinckney, the American

Embassador to your Court, from his regard to the late worthy Doctor, and with the benevolence which characterizes him, has nobly undertaken to bring them forward.

I have heard you, Sir, express your esteem pour l'amiable Grecienne ; your intimacy with Mr. Pitt now affords you an opportunity of evincing it, and your respect for the memory of the man, who had few equals here below.

I presume to solicit it, and trust I shall not do it in vain. Major Pinckney will have the goodness to transmit you this. I shall show you Mrs. Turnbull's memorial, with which he has kindly charged himself. Perhaps this may serve as an introduction to one who so justly deserves to be known, and may through your joint executions procure that aid which is truly merited by the family of Dr. Turnbull.

James Grant Papers

******

James Grant to Edward Penman
London, February 27, 1793
Now permit me to tell you that I was astonished upon receiving your letter of the 14 th of July 1792 in favour of Mrs. Turnbull, who I certainly have great respect for. How could you, good sir, imagine that it was possible or in any shape admissable for me to join and concur with Minister from the States of America in bringing forward a petition to the Lords Commissioners of His Majesty's Treasury. There never was so wild an idea surely, but I sent him an excuse with a civil answer. The worst of it is that I am convinced he has not the most distance chance of succeeding.

James Grant Papers

ENDNOTES

1. Lib. of Congress, British Transcripts, Box 41, Lansdowne Mss. 1219, fo. 34.
2. Treasury 77/7. Indenture of Mar. 9, 1781.
3. Treasury 77/7, First Indenture.
4. CO. 5/541. pp 199-201, Grant to Shelburne.
5. C.O. 5/541. pp 199-201.
6. Forbes, p. 19.
7. Charleston Gazette, Mar. 14. 1792.
8. CO. 5/555. PP 277-281.
9. C/O 5/545 p. 25.
10. Landsdowne Mss. Vol. 88, f. 139.
11. CO. 5/549 p. 262.
12. CO. 5/544 pp. 37-42.
13. Bartram's Travels, p. 142.
14. Lansdowne Ms. Vol. 88 f. 133.
15. CO. 5/223 Vol. lettered Board of Trade No. 1.
16. Treasury 77/7, Memorial of Thomas Grenville, Esq.
17. CO. 5/563 p. 226-228; Lords of Trade to Shelburne.
18. Lansdowne, Vol. 88 i. 133.
19. Landsdowne Mss. Vol. 88 f. 147.
20. Latisdowne Ms. Vol. 88 f. 147.
21. Lansdowne Ms. Vol. 88 f. 135.
22. Lansdowne Ms. Vol. 88 f. 135.
23. Schoepf, pp. 233-236.
24. CO. 5/548 pp. 363-365.
25. Unwritten History of St. Augustine, p. 222.
26. CO. 5/544 pp. 37-42, Grant to Hillsborough.
27. Encyclopedia Britannica, Vol. XVIII, p. 554.
28. Unwritten History of St. Augustine, p. 202.
29. CO. 5/548. p. 363-365, Land Grant to Turnbull.
30. Lansdowne Ms. Vol. 88, fo. 133.
31. CO. 5/549, p. 81, Hillsborough to Grant.
32. CO. 5/549, Hillsborough to Grant.
33. Minorcans.

34 CO. 5/S44, pp. 37-42, Grant to Hillsborough.

35 The vicinity of New Smyrna was known as the "Mosquitoes" because of Mosquito Inlet, the outlet of the North Indian River.

36 CO. 5/541, p. 427.

The names of the ships and number of colonists in each were as follows:

Charming Betsy 232
New Fortune 226
Henry and Carolina 142
Hope 150
Elizabeth 190
American Soldier 145
Friendship 198
Betsy 120

Men, women and children 1403

37 CO. 5/541, pp. 423-424 Grant to Hillsborough.

38 Lans. Ms. Vol. 88 £. 147.

39 Lans. Ms. Vol. 88, f. 147.

40 Lans. Ms. Vol. 88, f. 151.

41 Lans. Ms. Vol. 88, f. 145.

42 CO. 5/544, pp. 37-42, Grant to Hillsborough.

43 Schoepf, pp. 233-236.

44 CO. 5/549, p. 49, Grant to Hillsborough.

45 CO. 5/549, pp. 77-78.

46 CO. 5/544, pp. 37-42, Grant to Hillsborough.

47 CO. 5/544, pp. 37-42.
(This account is based upon Governor Grant's report to Hillsborough and the Lords of Trade of the occurrence).

48 CO. 5/544, Grant to Hillsborough, pp. 37-42.

49 CO. 5/544, pp. 37-42.

50 CO. 5/552, p. 97-99.

51 CO. 5/544, pp. 99-102, Grant to Hillsborough.

52 This is the difficulty in a nutshell—the same difficulty which caused the other British colonies to be taken from their companies by the Crown.

53 CO. 5/544, pp. 99-102, Grant to Hillsborough.

54 CO. 5/544, pp. 200-201, Grant to Hillsborough.

55 Lansdowne Ms. Vol. 88, f. 155.

56 CO. 5/544, pp. 200-201, Grant to Hillsborough.

57 CO. 5/544, pp. 213-214.

58 CO. S/545, pp. 33-34.

59 CO. S/S45, pp. 33-34.

60 A coarse kind of linen.

61 T. 77/7, Second Indenture.

62 Treasury 77/7. Statement of London merchant who credited the colony with this sum to barter.

63 CO. 5/544, pp. 95-96.

64 CO. 5/545, pp. 60-61.

65 CO. 5/545. DP. 60-61. Grant to Hillsborough

66 Obituary, Charleston City Gazette, Mar. 14, 1792.

67 Forbes, p. 22.

68 CO. 5/545, pp. 81-82.

69 CO. 5/545, pp. 289-290.

70 CO. 5/546, pp. 227-228, Tonyn's letter to Germain.

71 T. 77/7.

72 Forbes, p. 21.

73 Lecky, Vol. Ill, p. 361.

74 CO. 5/545, p. 289-290.

75 CO. 5/545, p. 289-290.

76 Lans. Ms. Vol. 88, f. 157.

77 Lans. Mss. Vol. 88, f. 157.

78 Enc. Britannica, Vol. IX. p. 27.

79 Lans. Mss. Vol. 88, f. 157.

80 CO. 5/552, pp. 28-29.

81 CO. 5/552, p. 91-94.

82 CO. 5/552, p. 105.

83 CO. 5/552, p. 123.

84 Lecky, V. Ill, p. 403.

85 CO. 5/555, pp. 53-60.

86 CO. 5/555, pp. 277-281.

87 CO. 5/555, p. 281.

88 CO. S/SS6, pp. 117-118.

89 CO. 5/556, pp. 117-118.

90 CO. 5/546, pp. 53-54.

91 CO. 5/556, p. 55.

92 CO. 5/555, pp. 277-281.

93 CO. 5/555, pp. 277-281.

94 CO. 5/555, pp. 53-60.

95 CO. 5/556, pp. 501-502.

96 CO. 5/155 British Transcript in Washington library, Box 241.

97 CO. 5/546, pp. 113-115 Defense of Turnbull before Lords of Trade to Charges by Tonyn.

98 CO. 5/546, pp. 113-115 Defense of Turnbull before Lords of Trade to Charges by Tonyn.

99 CO. 5/556, pp. 113-115.

100 CO. 5/556, p. 463, Tonyn to Turnbull.

101 CO. 5/556, pp. 73-77.

102 CO. 5/556, pp. 505-512. Extracts from Minutes of East Florida Council.

103 CO. 104 CO. 5/556, pp. 97-99. Turnbull's application for reinforcements against the Indians.

105 CO. 5/544, Grant said there should be a hundred soldiers there to protect the settlers from the Indians, and the planters from the new colonists.

106 CO. 5/155 British Transcript in Washington Library, Box 241.

107 CO. 5/556, p. 463, Tonyn to Turnbull.

108 CO. 5/556, pp. 89-93.

109 When the address was presented to Tonyn.

110 CO. 5/556, pp. 89-93, Turnbull to Tonyn.

111 CO. 5/556 pp. 97-100 Tonyn to Turnbull. Punctuation of the original letter is copied.

112 CO. 5/546, pp. 77-85. Turnbull before the Lords of Trade.

113 CO. 5/556, pp. 505-512. Extracts from Minutes of Council.

113 CO. 5/S46, pp. 77-85.

114 CO. 5/556, pp. 505-512.

115 CO. 5/546, pp. 77-85.

116 CO. 5/556, pp. 505-512, Extracts from Minutes of Council. This Mr. Jollie, it will be recalled, had been prominent enough to be proposed for Grant's successors as Governor by Lord Hillsborough.

117 CO. 5/556, Extracts from Minutes of Council.

118 CO. 5/546, pp. 78-85, Turnbull before Lords of Trade.

119 CO. 5/SS6, pp. 495-498.

120 CO. 5/556, pp. 495-498.

121 CO. 5/556, pp. 232-235, Germain to Tonyn.

122 CO. 5/SS6, pp. 232-235, Germain to Tonyn.

123 CO. 5/556, p. 245.

124 CO. 5/568, Tonyn to Germain, pp. 337-338.

125 CO. 5/155, British Transcripts in Congressional Library at Washington, D. C, 241.

126 CO. 5/155 British Transcripts, Congressional Library, Box 241.

127 CO. 5/556, p. 744, Tonyn to Germain.

128 CO. 5/557.

128 CO. 5/557 pp. 439-440.

129 CO. 5/S56, p. 767, Andrew Turnbull to Arthur Gordon, Esq.

130 CO. 5/556, pp. 771-772, Bisset to Tonyn.

131 CO. 5/556 p. 76S.

132 CO. 5/546, pp. 49-51.

133 CO. 5/546, pp. 53-54.

134 Lansdowne Mss. Vol. 66, pp. 725-727.

135 CO. 5/546, pp. 49-51.

136 CO. 5/546, pp. 49-51. Smyrna spelled "Smyrnia" in these documents.

137 CO. 5/546, pp. 53-54.

138 CO. 5/546, pp. 49-51, 4th Charge.

139 CO. 5/54, pp. 49-51, 5th Charge.

140 CO. 5/546, pp. 49-51, 6th Charge.

141 CO. 5/546, pp. 49-51, 6th Charge.

142 Lansdowne Mss. Vol. 88, ff 173-174.

143 CO. 5/546, p. 51, Conclusion of Memorial.

144 Turnbull to Germain British Transcripts, Box 41, Lansdowne Ms. Vol. 1219, fo. 40.

145 CO. S/5S6, pp. 695-697. Germain said to Tonyn that his actions were Conduct in a Governor that appears to be rather the effect of sudden passion than Moderation and sound Policy."

146 CO. 391/88, p. 200. Extract from Journal of Trade and Plantations.

147 CO. 5/546, pp. 77-85. Defense of Turnbull before Lords of Trade.

148 CO. 5/557, pp. 115-121.

149 CO. 5/557, pp. 420-422.

150 CO. 5/557, pp. 225-226.

151 CO. 5/557, pp. 479-480. All of these charges are to be found in CO. 5/551, and several page references being given here simply to locate a few specific charges.

152 CO. 5/557, pp. 115-121, Germain to Tonyn.

153 British Transcripts, Box 41, Cong. Library, Lansdowne Mss. 1219, fo. 34.

154 CO. 5/5S7, No. 42.

155 Sackville Mss. America, 1755-7, No. 100, also Lans. Mss. Vol. 66, pp. 725-727.

156 Lansdowne Mss. Vol. 66, pp. 725-727.

157 Sackville Mss. America, 1755-7, No. 100.

158 CO. 5/557, pp. 115-121.

159 Treasury, 77/7.

160 CO. 5/5S8, pp. 499-500. Letters from Tonyn to Purcell, May 27, 1778.

161 CO. 5/557, pp. 420-422.

162 CO. S/S57, pp. 420-422.

163 CO. 5/558, p. 487.

164 Lans. Mss. Vol. 88, f. 113.

165 Lans. Mss. Vol. 66, pp. 725-727.

166 CO. 5/558, p. 487.

167 CO. 5/558, p. 491.

168 Lans. Mss. Vol. 88, f. 173-4.

169 Lans. Mss. Vol. 88 f. 193.

170 Lans. Mss. Vol. 88 ff. 175-6.

171 Lans. Mss. Vol. 66, p. 714.

172 CO. 5/558, pp. 101 fo. 3-4.

173 CO. 5/558, pp. 101-103-104.

174 Historical Mss. Commission. Amer. Mss. in Royal Institution V. 11, pp. 127-8; Letter from Tonyn to Gen. S. Henry Clinton.

175 Lans. Mss. Vol. 88, ff. 173-174.

176 Forbes, p. 29.

177 CO. 5/569, p. 79.

178 Lansdowne Mss. V. 1219, fo. 34.

179 CO. 5/558, pp. 484-6, Tonyn to Wm. Knox.

180 British Transcripts, Box 41, folio 49, Lans. Mss. Library of Congress.

181 British Transcripts, Box 4, in Congressional Library at Washington. Lans. Mss. 1219, fo. 34.

182 Lansdowne, Vol. 1219, fo. 34, British Transcripts, Box 41, Congressional Library, Washington.

183 Lans. Mss. Vol. 88, fo. 189.

184 Lans. Mss. Vol. 66, pp. 725-727.

185 Lans. Mss. Vol. 88 f. 189.

186 T. 77/9 Indenture of Feb. 21, 1781.

187 Historical Mss. Commission, Amer. Mss. in Royal Institute, Vol. II, pp. 127-128.

188 CO. 5/158, pp. 465-468.

189 Probate Records, Charleston Co. S. C Book B, p. 636.

190 Lans. Mss. Vol. 88 f. 189.

191 Treasury 77/20 (4).

192 British Transcripts, Box 41, Lans. Mss. Vol. 1219, fo. 40.

193 CO. 5/158, pp. 465-468.

194 Treasury 77/7, Memo.—Schedule and Valuation of Lady Mary Duncan's estate.

195 Fairbanks' History of Florida, (3d Ed.), p. 176.

196 CO. 5/561, pp. 359-361.

197 CO. 5/561, pp. 359-361.

198 Fairbanks' Hist, of Florida, p. 240.

199 Address of M. Michel before Med. Soc. South Carolina, Pamphlets Q No. 18, Charleston library.

200 T. 77/7.

201 T. 77/7.

202 CO. S/S62. Reports of Commissioners for Florida claims.

203 Probate Records, Charleston Co., S. C. Book B, p. 636.

204 Charleston City Gazette, March 14, 1792.

Type of English ship that would have carried passengers to the New Smyrna colony.

Ship name	Passenger count
American Soldier	145
Betsey	120
Charming Betsey	32
Elisabeth	190
Friendship	198
Henry and Carolina	142
Hope	150
New Fortune	226
Total	1403

BIBLIOGRAPHY
ORIGINAL SOURCES

(Note: References such as CO. 5/544 mean Colonial Office, Class 5, Vol. 544; P. C, Privy Council; W.O., War Office; A.O., Audit Office; T., Treasury.)

CO. 5/548 pp. 363-366: 18 June, 1766—Order in Council at Court of St. James of first land grant to Turnbull.

Pp. 365-367: 18 June, 1766—Like order to Sir William Duncan.

Pp. 362-367: 15 Jan., 1767—Minutes of Council of East Fla. Turnbull appointed to Council.

Pp 362-367: 17 Jan., 1767—Warrants of survey for Turnbull's and Duncan's lands.

P. 368: 23 June, 1767—Warrant of survey for 1000 acres for Turnbull.

P. 394: 13 May, 1767—Orders in Council.

CO. 5/541 p. 215: April, 1767—Turnbull's petition for the East Florida bounty.

CO. 5/541 p. 272: Return of grants of land in East Florida between 20 June, 1765 and 22 June, 1767.

CO. 5/544 pp. 37-42: 29 Aug., 1767—Gov. Grant to Hillsborough, Turnbull's arrival in Florida.

British Transcripts, Box 252, Library of Congress, Washington, D. C.: Mar. 31, 1767—Shelburne to the Lords of Trade on advisability of Turnbull's colony.

CO. 5/563 pp. 226-228: Apr. 16, 1767—Endorsement and grant of bounty by Lords of Trade for Turnbull's colony.

Privy Council, Register, Vol. 112: May 13, 1767—Grant of 5000 acres to each of Turnbull's four children.

Privy Council, Register, Vol. 112: May 13, 1767—Order in Council appointing Turnbull to East Florida council.

CO. 5/548: May 14, 1767—Shelburne to Governor of Florida, granting bounty to Turnbull.

CO. 5/549 p. 49: Dec. 25, 1767—Grant to Hillsborough. He had four months' provisions awaiting settlers at New Smyrna.

CO. 5/549 p. 54: Feb. 23, 1768—Hillsborough to Grant. Thinks Turnbull's plan the best idea so far for development of Florida.

Kings Mss. 211, British Museum: 1768 Vol. II—Survey ad brief comment on New Smyrna by Wm. Gerard de Brahm.

CO. 5/549 p. 75: Mar. 10, 1768—Hillsborough to Grant. Turnbull sailing from Minorca.

CO. 5/549: Mar. 12, 1768—Grant to Hillsborough. Turnbull at Milo on Sept. 24, and now expected daily.

CO. 5/549 p.81: May 12, 1768—Hillsborough to Grant. Turnbull at Gibraltar with 1000 colonists.

CO. 5/541 pp. 423-424: July 2, 1768—Grant to Hillsborough, Turnbull's Colony the largest which ever came to America in one body.

CO. 5/541 p. 427: July 2, 1768—Names of the eight ships and number of colonists in each, 1403 people in all.

CO. 5/544 pp. 37-42: Aug. 29, 1768—Grant to Hillsborough. The mutiny at New Smyrna.

CO. 5/549 p. 262: Sept. 14, 1768—Hillsborough to Grant. The King wishes Turnbull success.

CO. 5/544 pp. 95-96: Oct. 20, 1768—Grant to Hillsborough. The leaders of the mutiny captured.

CO. 5/544 pp. 99-102: Dec. 1, 1768—Grant to Hillsborough. Great size of colony makes government aid necessary.

CO. 5/549 p. 339: Dec. 10, 1768—Hillsborough to Grant. The King concerned to hear of mutiny and approves Grant's action in lending aid to Turnbull.

CO. 5/544 p. 187: Jan. 3, 1769—Grant to Hillsborough. Thinks government aid would be needed for such extensive plan.

CO. 5/544 pp. 192-193: Jan. 14, 1769—Grant to Hillsborough. Order restored at New Smyrna after two ringleaders in mutiny executed.

CO. 5/544 pp. 200-201: Mar. 4, 1769—Grant to Hillsborough. Seven miles cleared but money needed at New Smyrna.

CO. 5/550 p. 67: Mar. 30, 1769—2000 pounds from British Board of Trade and Plantations for relief of New Smyrna.

CO. 5/550 pp. 72-73: April 3, 1769—Hillsborough to Grant. Approval of execution of two and pardon of rest of mutineers at New Smyrna.

CO. 5/550 p. 97: June 7, 1769—Hillsborough to Grant. The King approves of Grant's policy at New Smyrna, but warns him not to spend beyond Parliamentary grant.

CO. 5/544 p. 205: July 20, 1769—Grant to Hillsborough. Vines planted and Barilla tried by Turnbull. Indigo, cotton and rice shipped.

CO. 5/544 pp. 213-214: July 21, 1769—Grant to Hillsborough. Colony has cost proprietors 28,000 pounds. Too large for private undertaking.

CO. 5/544 pp. 221-222: Sept. 18, 1769—Grant to Hillsborough. Relief shall not exceed amount granted New Smyrna.

CO. 5/550 pp. 137-138: Nov. 4, 1769—Hillsborough to Grant. Approval of Grant's pardon of three mutineers.

CO. 5/545 pp. 33-34: Sept. 1, 1770—Grant to Hillsborough. Turnbull needs 1000 pounds for clothes and equipment. Indent included of articles needed.

CO. 5/545 p. 45: Oct. 2, 1770—Grant to Hillsborough. Mr. De Brahm refused to allow letters to be carried on his vessel, causing Grant some trouble with supplies at New Smyrna.

CO. 5/551 pp. 157-158: Dec. 11, 1770—Hillsborough to Grant. Government cannot grant any further bounty to New Smyrna.

CO. 5/545 p. 74: Dec. 14, 1770—Grant to Hillsborough. Road needed to plantations of Turnbull and others at Mosquitoes.

CO. 5/552 p. 38: February 15, 1771—Grant to Hillsborough. Last of bounty accounted for at New Smyrna.

CO. 5/552 p. 25: Mar. 8, 1771—Robinson to Pownall. Lords of Trade cannot grant further bounty to New Smyrna.

CO. 5/545 pp. 81-82: Mar. 20, 1771—Grant to Hillsborough. Bounty will not be granted unless Hillsborough urges measure before Lords of Trade.

CO. 5/545 p. 85: Mar. 20, 1771—Grant to Hillsborough. Turnbull could not be governor on account of his colony and will not interfere with Moultrie's appointment.

CO. 5/552 p. 30: April 1, 1771—Hillsborough to Grant. Regrets inability of government to grant further bounty at New Smyrna.

CO. 5/552 pp. 97-99: May 9, 1771—Turnbull to Grant or Moultrie. Indians frighten settlers at Mosquitoes.

CO. 5/552 pp. 85-88-89: May 23, 1771—Moultrie to Hillsborough. No cause for anxiety over Indians at New Smyrna.

CO. 5/552 pp. 101-102: June 6, 1771—Moultrie to McKenzie. Asks for detachment of troops to guard New Smyrna from Indians.

CO. 5/552 p. 105: June 6, 1771—McKenzie to Moultrie. Refuses troops.

CO. 5/552 pp. 91-94: June 13, 1771—Moultrie to Hillsborough. Complains of Turnbull's varying reports and McKenzie's refusal.

CO. 5/546 pp. 100-101: Sept. 25, 1771—Moultrie to Hillsborough. Fine road completed to New Smyrna.

CO. 5/545 p. 123-124: Oct. 20, 1771—Moultrie to Hillsborough. Turnbull's constant residence at his colony makes him rare attendant in Council.

CO. 5/552 p. 123: Dec. 4, 1771—Hillsborough to Moultrie. Glad alarm over Indians at Mosquitoes has subsided.

CO. 5/546 p. 136: Dec. 28, 1771—Moultrie to Hillsborough. Drayton and Turnbull resign from Council.

CO. 5/545 pp. 206-207: Aug. 20, 1772—Moultrie to Hillsborough. Mr. Forbes made visiting Minister to Mosquitoes.

CO. 5/545 pp. 289-290: Feb. 19, 1773—Moultrie to Dartmouth. Prosperity and good humor at New Smyrna.

CO. 5/555 p. 281: Nov. 23, 1774—Copy of Bryan's letter to Drayton on Indian lands dispute.

CO. 5/555 pp. 53-60: Dec. 30, 1774—Tonyn to Dartmouth. Condemns Drayton for part in Indian lands quarrel.

CO. 5/555 pp. 227-281: Drayton's complete account of Indian lands question presented to Tonyn.

CO. 5/556 pp. 117-118: Nov. 1, 1775—Tonyn to Dartmouth. Further complaints of Drayton, Turnbull and Penman for trying to run the province.

CO. 5/556 p. 55: Dec. 20, 1775—Address of praise by Grand Jury headed by Turnbull and directed to Drayton.

CO. 5/556 pp. 501-502: Feb. 15, 1776—Governor threatens Turnbull if he sides with Drayton.

CO. 5/556 pp. 113-115: Feb. 27, 1776—Address of loyalty to King headed by Turnbull.

CO. 5/556 p. 463: Mar. 4, 1776—Tonyn to Turnbull. Demands explanation for public defense of Drayton.

CO. 5/556 p. 105: Mar. 7, 1776—Turnbull to Tonyn. Two hundred men at New Smyrna of military age.

CO. 5/556 pp. 89-93: Mar. 15, 1776—Turnbull to Tonyn. Sarcastic reply to Tonyn's reprimand for siding with Drayton.

CO. 5/556 pp. 97-100: Mar. 18, 1776—Tonyn to Turnbull. Intends to charge him before Council.

CO. 5/556 pp. 73-77: Mar. 22, 1776—Tonyn to Germain. An opposition loyal address and complaints of Drayton's faction.

CO. 5/556 pp. 505-512: Mar. 30, 1776—Minutes of East Florida Council suspending Turnbull, with minority opposition.

CO. 5/556 pp. 495-498: Apr. 2, 1776—Tonyn to Germain. Accuses Turnbull and Drayton of disloyalty.

CO. 5/556 p. 109: May 10, 1776—Turnbull to Germain. Presents address and asks audience.

CO. 5/556 pp. 232-235: June 14, 1776—Germain to Tonyn. Reprimand, and full reinstatement of Drayton.

CO. 5/556 p. 245: July 1, 1776—Turnbull to Germain. Asks for extension of leave of absence.

CO. 5/568 pp. 337-338: July 19, 1776—Tonyn to Germain. Indian disorders at New Smyrna.

CO. 5/556 p. 744: Aug. 21, 1776—Tonyn to Germain. Can raise only one Company at New Smyrna.

CO. 5/556 p. 767: Sept. 1, 1776—Turnbull, Jr., to Gordon. Unrest at Mosquitoes caused by American invasion.

CO. 5/556 pp. 771-772: Sept. 10, 1776—Bisset to Tonyn. Fears disloyalty among Minorcans.

CO. 5/556 p. 765: Sept. 8, 1776—Tonyn to Germain. Has always doubted New Smyrna's advantages to province, and now finds it in state of unrest.

Lans. Vol. 1919 fo. 40: Mar. 16, 1780—Turnbull to Germain. Full arraignment of Tonyn and of Germain himself for tolerating him.

Historical Mss. Commission Amer. Mss. in Royal Institution Vol. II, pp. 127-128: May 27, 1780—Tonyn to Clinton. Tries to prejudice him against Drayton, Turnbull and Penman.

CO. 5/158 pp. 465-468: June 15, 1781—Turnbull to Germain. Will never return to Florida until Tonyn removed from office.

Treasury 77/20(4): May, 1780—Turnbull and Penman allowed to remain in Charleston as British subjects.

CO. 5/560 pp. 289-290: July 25, 1781—Tonyn to Germain. Evacuation of Florida progressing well except for Minorcans.

T. 77/9: Mar. 9 and Oct. 2, 1781—Various agreements between Turnbull and partners during life of the colony.

T. 77/7: Nov., 1783—Refugees hiding in many of the 100 unburnt buildings at New Smyrna.

T. 77/7: May 6, 1784—Schedule and valuation of Grenville, Duncan and Turnbull lands in Florida.

CO. 5/561 pp. 359-361 Apr. 4, 1785—Tonyn to Germain. Will be no more than 3 or 4 British left in Florida.

T. 77/17: May 2, 1786—Turnbull gives Penman power of attorney to try to obtain reimbursement from government for loss of land in cession of Florida.

T. 77/7: Dec. 30, 1786—Grenville and Duncan heirs file claim for similar reimbursements with full account of the business transactions of the colony.

CO. 5/546 pp. 49-51: Sept. 19, 1776—Turnbull before Lords of Trade, with charges against Tonyn.

CO. 5/556 pp. 695-697: Nov. 6, 1776—Germain to Tonyn. Reproof for treatment of Turnbull.

CO. 5/546 pp. 53-54: Dec. 6, 1776—Another list of charges against Tonyn by Turnbull.

CO. 391/83 p. 20: Dec. 10, 1776—Lords of Trade demand explanation from Tonyn.

CO. 5/155: Jan. 30, 1778—Turnbull to Germain. Asks reinstatement in office.

CO. 324/43 p. 413: July 11, 1776—King grants extended leave of absence from Florida to Turnbull.

CO. 5/546 pp. 77-85: Feb. 17, 1777—Defense of Turnbull to charges made by Tonyn. (No charges regarding Minorcans).

CO. 5/546 p. 75: Feb. 17, 1777—Turnbull asks Lords of Trade to reinstate him in office.

CO. 5/557 pp. 115-121: Apr. 14, 1777—Germain to Tonyn. Reinstatement of Turnbull and reproof for Tonyn.

CO. 5/557 pp. 225-226: May 8, 1777—Yonge to Tonyn. Minorcans file complaints against Turnbull.

CO. 5/557 pp. 479-480: May 8, 1777—Affidavits of Minorcans.

Treasury 77/7: List of buildings completed by 1777 at New Smyrna and their cost.

CO. 5/557 p. 420: May 8, 1777—Tonyn to Germain. Paying particular attention to New Smyrna.

Historical Mss. Commission Sackville Mss. Vol. II, p. 82: Dec. 8, 1777—Turnbull to Germain. Tonyn's illegal dealings ruining the settlement.

CO. 5/558 pp. 101-103-104: Dec. 29, 1777—Tonyn to Germain. Tries to prove New Smyrna could never have been profitable.

CO. 5/546 pp. 227-228: Jan. 19, 1778—Tonyn to Germain. An inaccurate resume of his quarrel with Drayton and Turnbull.

CO. 5/558 p. 8: Feb. 19, 1778—Germain to Tonyn. Condemns the encouragement of desertion of New Smyrna by settlers.

CO. 5/558 p. 495: May 4, 1778—Purcell to Tonyn. Complains that Turnbull accused him of falsehood.

CO. 5/558 pp. 499-500: May 27, 1778—Tonyn to Purcell. Pompous defense of Purcell.

CO. 5/558 p. 487: Aug. 7, 1778—Turnbull to Tonyn. Intends to live in St. Augustine and act as Secretary.

British Transcripts, Box 252, Library of Congress, C.O. 5/158 p. 469: Aug. 11, 1778—Tonyn to Turnbull. Refuses to allow him to act as Secretary.

Sackfille Mss. America, 1755-7, No. 100: Dec. 8, 1777—Turnbull to Germain. A full account of Tonyn's persecution of him and bribery among Minorcans.

CO. 5/569 p. 79: Aug. 20, 1778—Tonyn to Germain. 30 Negroes carried off from New Smyrna.

CO. 5/559 pp. 40-42: Aug. 27, 1778—Tonyn to Prevost. Desires troops to guard Mosquitoes.

CO. 5/558 pp. 484-6: Sept. 26, 1778—Tonyn to Knox. "Will be inexpressible satisfaction to be of service to the unfortunate partners of Turnbull."

Br. Transcripts, Box 41, folio 47, Vol. 1219, Lansdowne, Mss.: Feb. 17, 1780—Order placing Turnbull under arrest.

Lans. Mss. Vol. 1219, folio 49: Feb. 17, 1780—Demurrer of Turnbull to charges made against him.

Library of Congress, Br. Transcripts, Box 41, Lans. Mss. 1219, fo. 34: Mar. 14, 1780—Turnbull to Shelburne. Asks letter of introduction to Cornwallis and tells of his hopelessness over the situation.

Audit Office Declared Accts. Buncle 1261 Roll 154: Mar. 9, 1787—Account by Grant of 2000 pounds bounty spent at New Smyrna, 1769-70.

CO. 5/562: Mar. 14, 1788—Report of Commissioners for East Florida claims. Turnbull received £916. 13. 4.

City Gazette and Daily Advertiser, Charleston, S. C.: Mar. 14, 1792—Obituary of Turnbull. Mar. 17, 1792—Will of Turnbull.

Probate Records, Charleston, Co., S. C. Book B. p. 636: Address of M. Michel before Medical Society. Turnbull one of first members of Society.

LANSDOWNE MSS.

Vol. 88, f. 133: Sept. 1, 1766—A. Turnbull to E. of Shelburne, enclosing Dr. Turnbull's Narrative.

Vol. 52, pp. 294-288-289: Jan. 17 and 29, 1767—A. Turnbull to E. of Shelburne (abst.) with abstract of reply, May 14, 1767.

Vol. 52, f. 139: May 1, 1767—A. Turnbull to E. of Shelburne (abst.)

Vol. 52, f. 135: July 10, 1767—A. Turnbull to E. of Shelburne.

Vol. 52, f. 147: Feb. 27, 1768—A. Turnbull to E. of Shelburne. (Ext. and Abst.)

Vol. 52, f. 151: Mar. 28, 1768—A. Turnbull to E. of Shelburne. (Ext.)

Vol. 52, f. 145: Apr. 4, 1768—A. Turnbull to E. of Shelburne.

Vol. 52, f. 155: Sept. 24, 1769—A. Turnbull to E. of Shelburne. (Ext.)

Vol. 52, f. 157: Oct. 3, 1774—A. Turnbull to E. of Shelburne. (Ext.)

Vol. 52, f. 163: Nov. 10, 1777—A. Turnbull to E. of Shelburne. (Ext.)

Vol. 52, f. 173: Dec. 16, 1777—A. Turnbull to E. of Shelburne.

Vol. 52, f. 175: Dec. 23, 1777—A. Turnbull to E. of Shelburne. (Ext.)

General Patrick Tonyn
colonial governor of East Florida from 1775 to 1783

SECONDARY SOURCES

Avarette, Mrs. A.
The Unwritten History of St. Augustine.

Bartram, Wm.
Travels Through North and South Carolina, Georgia and East and West Florida. London, 1794.

Brinton, D. G.
Notes on the Floridian Peninsula. Philadelphia, 1859.
Florida and the South.

Dewhurst, Wm. W.
History of Saint Augustine, Florida. New York, 1885

Fairbanks, George R.
History of Florida. 1871.
History and Antiquities of St. Augustine, Florida.
New York, 1858.
Spaniards of Florida.

Forbes
Sketches, Historical and Topographical of the Floridas.
New York, 1821.

Lanier, Sidney
Florida, Its Scenery, Climate and History. Philadelphia, 1875.

Lecky, Wm. Edward
A History of England in the Eighteenth Century, Vol. III. New York,
1891.

Mease, James M.
Bulletin Bl de la Societe De Geographie, V. VII. Paris, 1827.

Romans, Capt. Bernard
A Concise History of East and West Florida. New York, 1876.

Schoepf, Johann David
Travels in the Confederation. (Trans, from German by A. J. Morrison). Philadelphia, 1911.

Sewell, R. K.
Sketches of St. Augustine. New York, 1848.

Stoddard, Major Amos.
Sketches, Historical and Descriptive, of Louisiana Philadelphia, 1812.

Vignoles, Charles
Observations upon the Floridas. New York, 1823.

Williams, J. L.
Territory of Florida. New York, 1837.

In addition to the works referenced in the preceding bibliography, information about Andrew Turnbull and New Smyrna is available from the New Smyrna Museum of History *www.nsbhistory.org,* the Southeast Volusia Historical Society, 120 Sams Avenue, New Smyrna Beach, Florida 32168, and the Turnbull Clan Association *www.turnbullclan.com.*